REVISE FRENCH

A COMPLETE REVISION COURSE FOR GCSE

Gloria Richards BA(Hons), LLCM, Dip Ed
Senior Tutor to the Sixth Form,
Brynteg Comprehensive School, Bridgend

Charles Letts & Co Ltd
London, Edinburgh & New York

First published 1982
by Charles Letts & Co Ltd
Diary House, Borough Road, London SE1 1DW

Revised 1983
Revised 1986
Revised 1987

Illustrations: Michael Renouf, Ian David Baker

British Library Cataloguing in Publication Data

Richards, Gloria
Revise French: a complete revision course
for GCSE.—4th ed.—(Letts study aids)
1. French language—Examinations, questions, etc.
I. Title
448 PC2112

ISBN 0-85097-781-9

Printed and bound in Great Britain by
Charles Letts (Scotland) Ltd

PREFACE

This book is designed as a revision aid for all candidates studying for the GCSE examination in French. It has been written after analysing the requirements of the new Examining Groups in England, Northern Ireland, Scotland and Wales. The emphasis is on thorough revision followed by plenty of practice in those skills which will be tested in the GCSE French examinations. All examining groups will have tests in speaking, reading, listening and writing. You will not have to take all the tests that are set but will take a combination of papers in order to gain the maximum number of marks at your particular level.

All the people involved in the preparation of this revision aid have many years' experience of teaching and examining. They have also been closely involved in the preparation and moderation of the new syllabuses for the GCSE examinations. Follow the advice given in this book carefully and work consistently in the months leading up to your examination. In this way, you will be well prepared to show the examiners what you *know, understand* and *can do.*

Gloria D. Richards 1987

Acknowledgements

I wish to express my thanks to the following people for their help in producing this book:

Joan Delin, Richard Lees and Keith Way, who acted as consultants; my husband, Vaughan Richards, and my father, Samuel Blythe Farnsworth, for the photographs; the staff of Letts for their guidance and professional help; and above all my husband and daughter for their continuing support and encouragement.

The author wishes to point out that the answers given to the specimen questions are not supplied by the Examining Group, but are her own suggestions.

The permission of the Northern Ireland Schools Examinations Council, and of the Scottish Examinations Board, to make use of specimen questions, and of HMSO for permission to reprint extracts from the National Criteria, is gratefully acknowledged. Acknowledgement is also due to the Théatre National de Paris, to FUAJ (the French Youth Hostel Association), and to Autoroutes du Sud de la France for permission to reprint extracts from their leaflets.

INTRODUCTION AND GUIDE TO USING THIS BOOK

The aim of this book is to help you to prepare as fully as possible for the GCSE French examination. Its main objective is to help you to revise and practise those skills which will be tested in the examination. The key to success in French examinations lies in the thorough preparation and practice of certain skills—speaking, listening, reading, writing. Check the analysis table of syllabuses to see which combination of tests you will have to do to achieve the grade for which you are aiming.

The Core Material in this book aims to cover the syllabus content of all GCSE examining groups. It includes Vocabulary Topics, Structures and Grammar, Notions and Functions as well as specimen questions. All examining groups will set tests in speaking, listening, reading and writing. The various combinations of tests for the different levels of each examining group follow the analysis table of syllabuses. Check your section carefully to make sure that you will be attempting those tests which you know you can do well in order to gain the maximum number of marks at your level.

Specimen answers are given at the back of the book to help you with many of the questions set in this book. Some of the tests in the writing section (those of a highly individual nature) do not have answers because almost all answers would be different. However, in order to practise this type of question, you could perhaps do them for 'extra homework' and ask your teacher to mark them for you.

If, when checking your answers at the back of the book, you find that you have made a lot of mistakes (e.g., grammatical, vocabulary, etc.) go back to the relevant core section and relearn that section. Always try the self-test units to make sure that you have really understood the section that you have been learning. Keep practising until you make very few mistakes.

Practice is a very important part of any revision programme. Too many candidates do not do justice to themselves because they lack practice in answering the various types of question. You should set aside a predetermined period of time each week, not only to revise your topics, but also to practise answers.

Remember . . .

REVISE THOROUGHLY.

PRACTISE CAREFULLY.

CONTENTS

GCSE FRENCH

One of the most significant innovations in the GCSE examinations is 'that candidates across the ability range are given opportunities to demonstrate their knowledge, abilities and achievements: that is, to show what they know, understand and can do.' In other words there is ONE examination for all candidates, but with differentiated papers. Candidates of different abilities will take different papers, but in some instances with a common element. You will need to check carefully the French syllabus for your own particular examining group to see which combination of tests you will need to take to achieve the maximum number of marks at your particular level. On pages vii and viii is a summary of GCSE differentiated papers and weightings.

Pupils being prepared for the GCSE examination in French will be trained 'to use French effectively for the purposes of practical communication.' The emphasis therefore is on acquiring certain skills to form a sound base for the present and future use of the language. The GCSE examination has certain common-core assessment objectives in the three skill areas of listening, reading and speaking. There are also additional assessment objectives which include basic writing and higher level objectives in speaking, listening, reading and also writing. The compulsory element of coursework will in most cases consist of an oral assessment. The maximum grade available to a candidate entered for only the common-core basic level tests is given in the table on page viii. Each additional test will increase your chances of gaining a higher grade but you must remember that a very high overall level of competence will be required to achieve the maximum available grade. Candidates aiming for the higher level grades will also have to perform well at the basic level. It is expected that candidates will attempt a wider range of tests than the minimum number required for any particular grade. Always consult the syllabus of your own examination board to check which tests you will have to do.

Differentiation

In the GCSE examination marks will be awarded for a candidate's *positive* achievements (i.e., for showing what he/she knows, understands and can do). Differentiation means that candidates across the ability range will be given opportunities to demonstrate their knowledge, abilities and achievements at different levels. GCE O-level/CSE examinations, for the most part, highlighted relative failure at tasks. By setting differentiated papers, the GCSE examining groups hope to reverse this situation by marking positively the candidate's achievement across a range of tests.

Analysis of examination weightings

Test	London/East Anglia	MEG	NEA	NI	Southern	WJEC	Scottish
Listening	25%	see syllabus for details	25%	25%	25%	25%	25%
Reading	25%	see syllabus for details	25%	25%	25%	25%	25%
Speaking	25%	see syllabus for details	25%	25%	25%	25%	50%
Writing	25%	see syllabus for details	25%	25%	25%	25%	Op at C endorsement

Key: C=credit level

Analysis of examination syllabuses: listening

Sources	London/East Anglia	MEG	NEA	NI	Southern	WJEC	Scottish
Messages	B/H	B/H	B/H	B/H	G/EX	B/H	F/G/C
Conversations	B/H	B/H	B/H	B/H	G/EX	B/H	F/G/C
Public announcements	B/H	B/H	B/H	B/H	G/EX	B/H	F/G/C
Directions/instructions	B/H	B/H	B/H	B/H	G/EX	B/H	F/G/C
TV/radio	B/H	B/H	H	B/H	G/EX	B/H	F/G/C
Interviews	B/H	B/H	H	H	EX	B/H	F/G/C

Key: F=foundation level G=general level B=basic level C=credit level EX=extended level H=higher level

Analysis of examination syllabuses: speaking

Task	London/East Anglia	MEG	NEA	NI	Southern	WJEC	Scottish
Role-play	B/H	B/H	B/H	B/H	G/EX	B/H	F/G/C
Conversation	B/H	B/H	B/H	B/H	G/EX	B/H	F/G/C
Questions based on written/visual stimuli	—	—	—	—	G/EX	—	—
Teacher examiner	●	●	●	●	●	●	●
External moderation	●	●	●	●	●	●	●
Internal moderation	—	—	—	—	—	—	●

Key: F=foundation level G=general level B=basic level C=credit level EX=extended level H=higher level

Analysis of examination syllabuses: reading

Type of test	London/East Anglia	MEG	NEA	NI	Southern	WJEC	Scottish
Adverts	B/H	B/H	B/H	B/H	G/EX	B/H	F/G/C
Brochures/leaflets	B/H	B/H	B/H	B/H	G/EX	B/H	F/G/C
Correspondence	B/H	B/H	B/H	B/H	G/EX	B/H	F/G/C
Labels/menus	B/H	B/H	B/H	B/H	G/EX	B/H	F/G/C
Magazines/newspapers	H	H	H	H	G/EX	H	F/G/C
Time-tables	B/H	B/H	B/H	B/H	G/EX	B/H	F/G/C
Public notices/signs	B/H	B/H	B/H	B/H	G/EX	B/H	F/G/C
Book extracts	—	—	—	—	G/EX	—	F/G/C

Key: F=foundation level G=general level B=basic level C=credit level E=extended level H=higher level

Analysis of examination syllabuses: writing

Task	London/East Anglia	MEG	NEA	NI	Southern	WJEC	Scottish
Cards/notes/messages	B/H	B	B	B	G/EX	B	—
Letter(s)	B/H	B/H	B/H	B/H	G/EX	B/H	—
Accounts/reports based on pictures	H	H	H	H	EX	H	—
Form-filling	B/H	—	—	—	—	—	—
Prepared assignments	—	—	—	—	—	—	Op
Dictionaries allowed	—	—	—	—	—	—	●

Key: F=foundation level G=general level B=basic level C=credit level EX=extended level H=higher level Op=optional

Grade combinations/general outline

Board	Grade G	F	E	D	C	B	A
London/East Anglia	BL+BR+BS	BL+BR+BS	BL+BR+BS	BL+BR+BS+1 other	BL+BR+BS+ BW+1 other	BL+BR+BS+ BW+HW+1 other	BL+BR+BS+BW+ HW+2 or 3 others
MEG	BL+BR+BS	BL+BR+BS	BL+BR+BS	BL+BR+BS+1 other	BL+BR+BS+ BW+1 other	BL+BR+BS+ BW+HW+1 other	BL+BR+BS+BW+ HW+2 others
NEA	BL+BR+BS	BL+BR+BS	BL+BR+BS	BL+BR+BS+1 other	BL+BR+BS+ BW+1 other	BL+BR+BS+ BW+HW+1 other	BL+BR+BS+BW+ HW+2 others
NI	BL+BR+BS	BL+BR+BS	BL+BR+BS	BL+BR+BS+1 other	BL+BR+BS+ BW+1 other	BL+BR+BS+ BW+HW+1 other	BL+BR+BS+BW+ HW+2 others
WJEC	BL+BR+BS	BL+BR+BS	BL+BR+BS	BL+BR+BS+1 other	BL+BR+BS+ BW+1 other	BL+BR+BS+ BW+HW+1 other	BL+BR+BS+BW+ HW+2 others
Southern	GL+GR+GS	GL+GR+GS	GL+GR+GS	GL+GR+GS+1 other	GL+GR+GS+GW+ 1 other	NS (but will include tests as Extended)	NS (but will include tests as Extended)
Scottish*	**7** Foundation	**6** Foundation	**5** Foundation/general	**4** General	**3** General	**2** General/credit	**1** Credit

Key BL=basic listening BR=basic reading BS=basic speaking BW=basic writing HL=higher listening HR=higher reading HS=higher speaking HW=higher writing EXL=extended listening EXR=extended reading EXS=extended speaking EXW=extended writing GL=general listening GR=general reading GS=general speaking GW=general writing NS=not specified

*Check all SEB syllabuses for detailed descriptions.

Examination Boards: Addresses

NORTHERN EXAMINATION ASSOCIATION

JMB	Joint Matriculation Board Devas Street, Manchester M15 6EU
ALSEB	Associated Lancashire Schools Examining Board 12 Harter Street, Manchester M1 6HL
NREB	North Regional Examinations Board Wheatfield Road, Westerhope, Newcastle upon Tyne NE5 5JZ
NWREB	North-West Regional Examinations Board Orbit House, Albert Street, Eccles, Manchester M30 0WL
YHREB	Yorkshire and Humberside Regional Examinations Board Harrogate Office—31-33 Springfield Avenue, Harrogate HG1 2HW Sheffield Office—Scarsdale House, 136 Derbyshire Lane, Sheffield S8 8SE

MIDLANDS EXAMINING GROUP

Cambridge	University of Cambridge Local Examinations Syndicate Syndicate Buildings, 1 Hills Road, Cambridge CB1 2EU
O & C	Oxford and Cambridge Schools Examinations Board 10 Trumpington Street, Cambridge and Elsfield Way, Oxford
SUJB	Southern Universities' Joint Board for School Examinations Cotham Road, Bristol BS6 6DD
WMEB	West Midlands Examinations Board Norfolk House, Smallbrook Queensway, Birmingham B5 4NJ
EMREB	East Midlands Regional Examinations Board Robins Wood House, Robins Wood Road, Aspley, Nottingham NG8 3NH

LONDON AND EAST ANGLIAN GROUP

London	University of London Schools Examinations Board Stewart House, 32 Russell Square, London WC1B 5DN
LREB	London Regional Examinations Board Lyon House, 104 Wandsworth High Street, London SW18 4LF
EAEB	East Anglian Examinations Board The Lindens, Lexden Road, Colchester, Essex CO3 3RL

SOUTHERN EXAMINING GROUP

AEB	The Associated Examining Board Stag Hill House, Guildford, Surrey, GU2 5XJ
Oxford	Oxford Delegacy of Local Examinations Ewert Place, Summertown, Oxford OX2 7BZ
SREB	Southern Regional Examinations Board Avondale House, 33 Carlton Crescent, Southampton, SO9 4YL
SEREB	South-East Regional Examinations Board Beloe House, 2-10 Mount Ephraim Road, Tunbridge TN1 1EU
SWEB	South-Western Examinations Board 23-29 Marsh Street, Bristol, BS1 4BP

WALES

WJEC	Welsh Joint Education Committee 245 Western Avenue, Cardiff CF5 2YX

NORTHERN IRELAND

NISEC	Northern Ireland Schools Examinations Council Beechill House, 42 Beechill Road, Belfast BT8 4RS

SCOTLAND

SEB	Scottish Examinations Board Ironmills Road, Dalkeith, Midlothian EH22 1BR

1 STRUCTURES AND GRAMMAR REVISION

Here is an extract from the National Criteria/French for GCSE.

AIMS

- to develop the ability to use French effectively for purposes of practical communication,
- to form a sound base of the skills, language and attitudes required for further study, work and leisure,
- to develop an awareness of the nature of language and language learning,
- to promote learning skills of a more general application (e.g. analysis, memorizing, drawing of inferences) . . .

In order to achieve these aims, students need to learn and revise thoroughly all that they have been taught in preparation for the GCSE examination.

The ability to use the structures and grammar of the language is essential in order to communicate effectively. However extensive your range of vocabulary may be, you will not be able to understand or to be understood with any degree of accuracy unless you have a good working knowledge of the basic sentence structures and grammatical features of the language. Thorough revision and practice of these features will increase your confidence and provide you with a sound base for the examination.

Begin your revision programme in plenty of time so that you will be able to cover all the grammar revision sections which you know that you will need, and then do the grammar tests. These short tests are designed to find out if you have grasped the grammatical points. If at the end of any test you are still unsure of the points tested, revise the section again and then re-do the test.

1 ARTICLES

Remember these points:

(a) The definite articles (**le**, **la**, **l'**, **les**=the) are used more frequently in French than they are in English. Remember to use them in such expressions as:
Children like ice cream. **Les** enfants aiment **les** glaces.
Poor Mary has forgotten her book. **La** pauvre Marie a oublié son livre.
He prefers red wine to white wine. Il préfère **le** vin rouge **au** vin blanc.

(b) When preceded by the preposition **à**, the forms of the definite article are:
au, **à la**, **à l'**, **aux**.

When preceded by the preposition **de**, the forms are:
du, **de la**, **de l'**, **des**.

(c) The indefinite articles (**un**, **une**, **des**=a, some) are omitted when giving people's occupations:
My father is an engineer. Mon père est ingénieur.
Her brothers are students. Ses frères sont étudiants.

(d) The partitive articles (**du, de la, de l', des**=some) are contracted to **de** or **d'** in the following instances:

(i) After a negative:
J'ai des pommes. Je n'ai pas **de** pommes.
Il a de l'argent. Il n'a pas **d'**argent.
N.B. also: J'ai une voiture. Je n'ai pas **de** voiture.

(ii) When an adjective precedes the noun:
des livres; **de** gros livres
des robes; **de** jolies robes

2 NOUNS

Making nouns plural

As in English, the plurals of nouns in French are normally formed by adding 's' to the singular noun, e.g. un garçon, des garçons.

However, there are several important exceptions to this rule which you will be expected to know. Check carefully the following plural forms which do not follow the normal rule:

l'animal (m)	les animaux	*animal(s)*
le bijou	les bijoux	*jewel(s)*
le bois	les bois	*wood(s)*
le cadeau	les cadeaux	*present(s)*
le caillou	les cailloux	*pebble(s)*
le chapeau	les chapeaux	*hat(s)*
le château	les châteaux	*castle(s)*
le cheval	les chevaux	*horse(s)*
le chou	les choux	*cabbage(s)*
le ciel	les cieux	*sky/heaven skies/heavens*
l'eau (f)	les eaux	*water(s)*
le feu	les feux	*fire(s)* (pl. also=*traffic-lights*)
le fils	les fils	*son(s)*
le gâteau	les gâteaux	*cake(s)*
le genou	les genoux	*knee(s)*
le hibou	les hiboux	*owl(s)*
le jeu	les jeux	*game(s)*
le journal	les journaux	*newspaper(s)*
le mal	les maux	*evil(s)/harm(s)/hurt(s)*
le nez	les nez	*nose(s)*
l'œil (m)	les yeux	*eye(s)*
l'oiseau (m)	les oiseaux	*bird(s)*
l'os (m)	les os	*bone(s)*
le prix	les prix	*price(s)/prize(s)*
le tableau	les tableaux	*picture(s)*
le temps	les temps	*time(s)/weather(s)*
le timbre-poste	les timbres-poste	*postage stamp(s)*
le travail	les travaux	*works*

N.B. also: madame **mes**dames
mademoiselle **mes**demoiselles
monsieur **mes**sieurs

Family names do *not* change in French when they are used in the plural:
We are going to the Gavarins. Nous allons chez les Gavarin.

3 ADJECTIVES

(a) When you are writing in French, you must pay special attention to the endings of words. Adjectives in English have the same form in the singular and the pluraL.

e.g. *singular:* the little boy
plural: the little boys

In French, you must check the endings of *all* words, especially adjectives.
e.g. *singular:* le petit garçon
plural: les petit**s** garçons

(b) Another important difference between English and French is the position of adjectives. In English, adjectives precede the noun:
the white house; the intelligent girl

In French, all but a few common adjectives are placed *after* the noun:
la maison **blanche**; la fille **intelligente**

These are the adjectives which **do** precede the noun in French; try to memorise them:
beau bon excellent gentil grand gros jeune joli long mauvais même (=*same*) meilleur nouveau petit vieux vilain

Some adjectives change their meaning according to their position:

un **cher** ami	*a dear friend*
un vin **cher**	*an expensive wine*
un **ancien** élève	*a former pupil*
un bâtiment **ancien**	*an old building*
mes **propres** mains	*my own hands*
mes mains **propres**	*my clean hands*

(c) The spelling of adjectives in French changes according to the gender of the noun they are describing, as well as according to whether the noun is singular or plural:
le **vieux** livre
la **vieille** maison

An adjective is normally made feminine by the addition of 'e'.
e.g. joli/jolie

When a word already ends in 'e' it does not change.
e.g. jeune (m *and* f)

There are also a number of adjectives which have irregular feminine forms. These must be learnt:

Masculine singular	*Feminine singular*		*Masculine singular*	*Feminine singular*	
ancien	ancienne	*old*	gentil	gentille	*nice*
bas	basse	*low*	gras	grasse	*fat*
beau	belle	*beautiful*	gros	grosse	*big*
blanc	blanche	*white*	jaloux	jalouse	*jealous*
bon	bonne	*good*	long	longue	*long*
bref	brève	*brief*	neuf	neuve	*brand new*
cher	chère	*dear*	nouveau	nouvelle	*new*
doux	douce	*sweet*	premier	première	*first*
épais	épaisse	*thick*	public	publique	*public*
entier	entière	*entire/whole*	roux	rousse	*auburn, russet*
faux	fausse	*false*	sec	sèche	*dry*
favori	favorite	*favourite*	secret	secrète	*secret*
fou	folle	*mad*	vieux	vieille	*old*
frais	fraîche	*fresh*	vif	vive	*lively*

Note also the forms **bel**, **nouvel**, **vieil**. These are used before masculine singular words beginning with a vowel or 'h'.
e.g. un **bel** homme
un **nouvel** élève
un **vieil** autobus

4 INDEFINITE ADJECTIVES

(a) Autre(s), other
Les autres élèves sont sages. *The other pupils are good.*
J'ai une autre robe rouge. *I have another red dress.*

(b) Chaque, each
chaque, élève, *each pupil*
chaque maison, *each house*

(c) Même(s), same
Nous avons vu le même film. *We saw the same film.*
Ils ont les mêmes disques. *They have the same records.*

(d) Plusieurs, several
J'ai acheté plusieurs livres. *I have bought several books.*

(e) Quelque(s), some
pendant quelque temps, *for some time*
Quelques élèves sont arrivés. *Some pupils have arrived.*

(f) Tel, **telle**, **tels**, **telles**, such
Pay special attention to the position of this word.
un tel homme, *such a man*
une telle femme, *such a woman*
de tels hommes, *such men*
de telles femmes, *such women*

(g) Tout, toute, toutes, all (+article)
tout le fromage, *all the cheese*
toute la famille, *all the family*
tous les garçons, *all the boys*
toutes les jeunes filles, *all the girls*

5 COMPARATIVE AND SUPERLATIVE OF ADJECTIVES

(a) The comparative and superlative forms of adjectives are quite simple when the adjective precedes the noun:

more, **plus** the most, **le (la, les) plus**	less, **moins** the least, **le (la, les) moins**	as, **aussi**
stronger, plus fort *the strongest*, le plus fort la plus forte les plus fort(e)s	*less strong*, moins fort *the least strong*, le moins fort la moins forte les moins fort(e)s	*as strong*, aussi fort

In all three cases **que** is used to complete the comparison. It can mean *as* or *than*.
Pierre est plus fort que Jean. *Peter is stronger* than *John*.
Les lions sont aussi forts que les tigres. *Lions are as strong* as *tigers*.

Be particularly careful with:
better, **meilleur** un meilleur élève, *a better pupil*
best, **le meilleur** le meilleur élève, *the best pupil*

(b) When an adjective follows the noun, it keeps the same position when it is made comparative or superlative:
une histoire plus amusante, *a more interesting story*
In the superlative, the definite article must be repeated after the noun:
l'histoire **la** plus amusante, *the most interesting story*

(c) 'In' with a superlative is translated by **de**:
L'élève le plus intelligent **de** la classe. *The most intelligent pupil in the class.*

6 DEMONSTRATIVE ADJECTIVES

masculine	*feminine*	*plural*
ce	cette	ces

There is a special masculine singular form which is used before a vowel or 'h': **cet**.

These adjectives correspond to the English *this, that/these, those.*

ce livre *this book, that book*
cet homme *this man, that man*
cette maison *this house, that house*
ces élèves *these pupils, those pupils*

-ci and **-là** may be added for extra emphasis:

ce livre-ci, *this book (here)*
ce livre-là, *that book (there)*, etc.

7 POSSESSIVE ADJECTIVES

	masculine	*feminine*	*plural*
my	mon	ma	mes
your	ton	ta	tes
his/her	son	sa	ses
our	notre	notre	nos
your	votre	votre	vos
their	leur	leur	leurs

(a) Before a singular feminine noun beginning with a vowel or 'h', use **mon, ton, son**:
son amie, *his(her) girlfriend*
ton histoire, *your story*
mon auto, *my car*

(b) son=his *or* her
sa =his *or* her

The difference in usage depends on the gender of the possession and *not* on the gender of the owner:
sa maman, *his mother* or *her mother*
son stylo, *his pen* or *her pen*

8 ADVERBS

(a) Adverbs of manner are normally formed by adding **-ment** to the feminine form of the adjective:
heureuse (f), *happy* → **heureusement**, *happily*
douce (f), *sweet, gentle* → **doucement,** *sweetly, gently*

As usual, there are exceptions to this rule. Here are some of the more common ones:

constamment *constantly*
énormément *enormously*
évidemment *evidently*
gentiment *nicely*
mal *badly*
précisément *precisely*
profondément *deeply*
vraiment *truly, really*

Note the irregular form **mal**.

Of all the adverbs which candidates misspell, the word **vite** (*quickly*) is the word which is most frequently misspelt. **Vite** is now the only spelling of this word. It does *not* have the same ending as the other adverbs above.

(b) One of the most important things to remember about adverbs in French is their position in relation to the verb. In English, we often place the adverb before the verb. In French, the adverb *never* comes between the subject and the verb of a sentence. The normal position for the adverb in French is *after* the verb.
e.g. Je vais **souvent** à Paris. *I often go to Paris.*

When using the perfect tense, however, the adverb is nearly always placed between the auxiliary and the past participle.
e.g. J'ai **trop** mangé. *I've eaten too much.*

Occasionally, the adverb in French is placed at the beginning of a sentence, but there are hidden dangers here, especially with such words as **aussi** and **ainsi** (*thus*). It is better, therefore, to keep to the general rule of placing the adverb after the verb.

(c) Adverbial **tout**
Tout=all, altogether, quite. When used before an adjective, **tout** does not agree with the adjective unless the adjective is feminine and begins with a consonant:

Elle est toute seule. *She is all alone.*
Elles étaient tout émues. *They (f) were quite moved.*

9 COMPARATIVE AND SUPERLATIVE OF ADVERBS

These are formed in a similar way to the comparatives and superlatives of adjectives, except that, because they are adverbs, they are invariable. There are no feminine or plural forms of the article.

e.g. Marie chante **le plus fort**. *Mary sings the loudest.*

Note also: best, **mieux**, the best, **le lieux**
e.g. Elle chante le mieux. *She sings the best.*

10 PERSONAL PRONOUNS

(a) Subject pronouns

singular	*plural*
1 je	nous
2 tu	vous
3 il/elle/on	ils/elles

Remember that **on** is a third person singular pronoun, so the verb must agree with it:
On **va** en ville,
even though in translation we might use another personal form:
They/we are going to town.

(b) Object pronouns

The normal positions are:

1	2	3	4	5	
me					
te	le				
(se)	la	lui			
nous	les	leur	y	en	verb
vous					
(se)					

Je te le donne. *I give it to you.*
Il m'en a parlé. *He talked to me about it.*
Nous les y enverrons. *We'll send them there.*

The object pronouns always keep to this order, except in *affirmative commands.*
In affirmative commands:
(i) The object pronouns follow the verb and are joined to the verb by hyphens.
(ii) Columns 1 and 2 change place.
(iii) Me becomes **moi**, and **te** becomes **toi**, except before **en** when they become **m'en** and **t'en**.

Examples:
Affirmative statement: *I have given some to him.* Je **lui en** ai donné.
Negative statement: *I have not given any to him.* Je ne **lui en** ai pas donné.
Affirmative command: *Give some to him.* Donnez-**lui-en**.
Negative command: *Don't give any to him.* Ne **lui en** donnez pas.
Affirmative command: *Give them to me.* Donnez-**les-moi**.
Affirmative command: *Give me some.* Donnez-**m'en**.

11 POSSESSIVE PRONOUNS

These correspond to the English 'mine', 'yours', 'his', etc.

	singular		*plural*	
	masculine	*feminine*	*masculine*	*feminine*
mine	le mien	la mienne	les miens	les miennes
yours	le tien	la tienne	les tiens	les tiennes
his/hers	le sien	la sienne	les siens	les siennes
ours	le nôtre	la nôtre	les nôtres	les nôtres
yours	le vôtre	la vôtre	les vôtres	les vôtres
theirs	le leur	la leur	les leurs	les leurs

Usage
Où est ton billet? Voici **le mien**. *Where is your ticket? Here is mine.*
Je n'ai pas de voiture. Pouvons-nous y aller dans **la vôtre**?
I haven't a car. Can we go there in yours?

In this last sentence 'yours'=your car. Since 'car' is feminine in French (**la voiture**), the feminine possessive pronoun must be used irrespective of the gender of the possessor.

Possession may also be expressed in the following way:
A qui est ce stylo? Il est **à** moi. *Whose pen is this? It's mine.*

12 DEMONSTRATIVE PRONOUNS

These pronouns are used to say '*this one/that one*', and in the plural, '*these ones/those ones*'.

singular		*plural*	
masculine	*feminine*	*masculine*	*feminine*
celui	celle	ceux	celles

If you wish to stress 'this/these' or 'that/those', then the endings **-ci** or **-là** respectively may be added:

Voici deux livres. Celui-ci est à moi. Celui-là est à Natalie.
Here are two books. This one (here) is mine. That one (there) is Natalie's.
Ces chaussures sont à 200F, mais celles-là sont à 150F.
These shoes cost 200F, but those cost 150F.

Always check carefully the gender of the pronouns you are using.

Ceci/cela (this/that)
Ecoutez ceci. *Listen to this.*
Qui a dit cela? *Who said that?*

Cela is often shortened to **ça**:
Qui a dit ça? *Who said that?*
Ça, c'est vrai. *That's true.*

13 DISJUNCTIVE PRONOUNS

These pronouns are also sometimes called 'emphatic' or 'stressed' pronouns.

moi	*me/I*	nous	*us/we*
toi	*you*	vous	*you*
lui	*him/he*	eux	*them (m)/they*
elle	*her/she*	elles	*them (f)/they*

The word **-même** may be added to the above words to translate **-self**:

moi-même *myself*, toi-même *yourself, etc.*

Note also **soi-même**, *oneself.* Use this when you are using **on**.
On peut le faire soi-même. *One can do it oneself.*

Disjunctive pronouns should be used:

(a) After prepositions:
devant moi, *in front of me*
sans eux, *without them*
chez elle, *at her house*

(b) To emphasize a pronoun at the beginning of a sentence:
Moi, je l'ai fait. I *did it.*
Lui, il est venu. He *came.*

(c) When a pronoun stands alone:
Qui l'a fait?–Moi. *Who did it?–I did.*

(d) In comparisons:
Vous êtes plus intelligent que moi. *You are more intelligent than I.*
Il est aussi grand que toi. *He is as tall as you.*

(e) With **c'est** and **ce sont**:
C'est vous. *It's you.*
Ce sont elles. *It's them (f).*
Ce sont is used only with the third person plural.

14 RELATIVE PRONOUNS

(a) **qui** who, which (*subject*)
que whom, that (*object*)
dont whose, of whom, of which
Voici les enfants qui sont sages. *Here are the children who are good.*
Voici les enfants que vous n'aimez pas. *Here are the children whom you don't like.*
Voici le livre dont vous avez besoin. *Here is the book which you need.*

(b) **ce qui** that which (*subject*)/what
ce que that which (*object*)/what
ce dont that of which/what
Dites-moi ce qui est arrivé. *Tell me what has happened.*
Dites-moi ce que vous avez fait. *Tell me what you did.*
Dites-moi ce dont vous avez besoin. *Tell me what you need.*

(c) m. **lequel** (the . . .) which
f. **laquelle** (the . . .) which
m.pl. **lesquels** (the . . .) which
f.pl. **lesquelles** (the . . .) which

These relative pronouns are used with prepositions:
Voilà la table sur laquelle vous trouverez vos livres.
There is the table on which you will find your books.
Regardez cette maison devant laquelle il y a un agent de police.

Look at that house in front of which there is a policeman.
The above relative pronouns combine with **à** and **de** to become:

m.	**auquel**	**duquel**
f.	**à laquelle**	**de laquelle**
m.pl.	**auxquels**	**desquels**
f.pl.	**auxquelles**	**desquelles**

Nous irons au jardin public au milieu duquel se trouve un petit lac.
We shall go to the park in the middle of which there is a little lake.
Ce sont des choses auxquelles je ne pense pas.
They are things I don't think about. (penser **à**=to think about)

Lequel etc. may be used on their own as questions:
J'ai rapporté un de vos livres.–Lequel?
I've brought back one of your books.–Which one?
Puis-je emprunter une de tes cravates?–Laquelle?
May I borrow one of your ties?–Which one?

15 INDEFINITE PRONOUNS

autre, other
J'ai vendu quelques livres mais je garderai **les autres.**
I have sold some books but I shall keep the others.

chacun(e), each one
Regardez ces voitures. **Chacune** est d'occasion.
Look at those cars. Each one is second-hand.

N'importe is a very useful indefinite pronoun:
n'importe qui, anybody
N'importe qui peut le faire. *Anybody can do it.*
n'importe quoi, anything
Rapportez n'importe quoi. *Bring back anything.*
n'importe quel(le)(s), any
Vous le trouverez dans n'importe quelle épicerie. *You will find it at any grocer's.*

plusieurs, several
As-tu des disques? Oui, j'en ai plusieurs. *Have you any records? Yes, I have several.*

quelqu'un, someone
Attendez-vous quelqu'un? *Are you waiting for someone?*
quelques-un(e)(s), some, a few
Quelques-uns de vos élèves sont paresseux. *Some of your pupils are lazy.*

tout, everything
Il connaît tout. *He knows everything.*

tout le monde, everybody
Tout le monde est arrivé. *Everybody has arrived.*

16 CONJUNCTIONS

car, for (because)
Do not confuse this with the preposition **pour**. If you wish to use the word 'for' meaning 'because', remember to use **car**.

Il a dû rentrer à la maison à pied **car** il avait perdu la clé de sa voiture.
He had to walk home for he had lost his car key.
Car is an alternative to **parce que** (because).

comme, as
Faites **comme** vous voulez. *Do as you like.*

depuis que, since (*time*)
Il a commencé à neiger **depuis que** je suis sorti.
It has begun to snow since I went out.

donc, so (*reason*)
Do not use this word at the beginning of a sentence, but it may introduce a clause.
Il est malade, *donc* il est resté à la maison.
He is ill, so he stayed at home.

lorsque, **quand**, when
Be very careful when using these conjunctions. The future tense is frequently needed in French after these two conjunctions where in English we use the present tense:
Je te téléphonerai quand je serai à Paris.
I shall telephone you when I am in Paris. (i.e. *when I shall be in Paris*)
Similarly, the future perfect is used where in English we use the perfect tense:
Je viendrai quand **j'aurai fini** mon travail.
I shall come when I have finished my work. (i.e. *when I shall have finished my work*)

NB **Dès que** and **aussitôt que** (as soon as) follow the same rule.
Dès qu'il sera à la maison, je te téléphonerai.
As soon as he is at home, I shall telephone you.

parce que, because
Il n'a pas réussi parce qu'il n'a pas travaillé.
He didn't succeed because he didn't work.
NB there is *no* hyphen between these two words.

puisque, since (*reason*)
Il travaille dur puisqu'il désire réussir.
He is working hard since he wants to succeed.

pendant que, during, while
Pendant qu'il lisait son journal, on a sonné à la porte.
While he was reading his newspaper, someone rang the door-bell.

tandis que, while, whilst (*contrast*)
Christophe a bien travaillé tandis que Pierre n'a rien fait.
Christopher has worked well while Peter has done nothing.

17 PREPOSITIONS

One of the most important things to remember as far as prepositions are concerned is that frequently there is no one single word in French which will translate a particular word in English. Pupils in the early stages of learning French often ask such questions as 'How do you translate "in"?' There are of course several ways of translating 'in', e.g. **dans**, **en**, **à**, etc. Usually only one of these will be appropriate in the particular circumstances. Below are some guidelines for the use of some everyday prepositions.

About

à peu près, approximately
J'ai à peu près cinquante livres. *I have about fifty books.*

à propos de, concerning
Je voudrais vous parler à propos de votre visite. *I should like to speak to you about your visit.*

au sujet de, on the subject of (similar to **à propos de**)
Il parlait au sujet des vacances. *He was speaking about the holidays.*

de quoi, of what
De quoi parles-tu? *What are you speaking about?*

environ
J'arriverai à dix heures environ. *I shall arrive about ten o'clock.*

vers (similar to **environ**)
Nous partirons vers deux heures. *We shall leave about two o'clock.*

Along

le long de
Il marchait le long du quai. *He was walking along the platform.*

avancer, to move along
Avancez, messieurs, s'il vous plaît. *Move along, gentlemen, please.*

dans
Il marchait dans la rue. *He was walking along the street.*

sur
La voiture roulait vite sur la route. *The car was going quickly along the road.*

NB for *along with* use **avec**:
Marie est allée au supermarché avec Suzanne. *Mary went to the supermarket along with Susan.*

Among(st)

parmi
Il a caché le trésor parmi les rochers. *He hid the treasure among the rocks.*

entre
Nous étions entre amis. *We were among friends.*

Before

avant
Venez avant midi. *Come before noon.*

déjà (already)
Je l'ai déjà vu. *I've seen it before.*

devant (place)
Tenez-vous devant la classe. *Stand before the class.*

By

à
Je viendrai à vélo. *I'll come by bike.*

de
La vieille dame descendait la rue, suivie d'un voleur. *The old lady went down the street, followed by a thief.*

en
J'y suis allé en auto. *I went there by car.*

par
Les enfants ont été punis par leur mère. *The children have been punished by their mother.*

près de (=near)
Asseyez-vous près du feu. *Sit by the fire.*

For

depuis

Depuis is used with the *present* tense to express 'has/have been . . .' in a time clause:
J'apprends le français depuis cinq ans. *I have been learning French for five years.*
Il est ici depuis trois jours. *He has been here for three days.*

Similarly the *imperfect* tense is used to express 'had been . . .':
Il habitait Paris depuis deux ans. *He had been living in Paris for two years.*
Nous l'attendions depuis deux heures. *We had been waiting for him for two hours.*

pendant (=during)
Nous avons travaillé pendant trois heures. *We have worked for three hours.*

pour
For future or pre-arranged time:
Nous serons là pour trois semaines. *We shall be there for three weeks.*

In

à
Les enfants sont à l'école. *The children are in school.*

Other useful expressions:
à l'intérieur, *inside*
à Londres, *in London*
à la mode, *in fashion*
au lit, *in bed*
au soleil, *in the sun*
à voix haute, *in a loud voice*

dans
Ils sont dans la salle à manger. *They are in the dining-room.*

de
Elle s'habille de noir. *She dresses in black.*

en
J'habite en France. *I live in France.*
Vous y arriverez en quatre heures. *You will get there in four hours.*
Elle s'habille en pantalon. *She dresses in trousers.*

sous
J'aime marcher sous la pluie. *I like walking in the rain.*

sur
Un sur vingt a un magnétoscope. *One in twenty has a video tape-recorder.*

On

à
à droite, *on the right*
à gauche, *on the left*
à pied, *on foot*
Nous allons à l'école à pied. *We go to school on foot.*
à son retour, *on his/her return*
A son retour, il est allé la voir. *On his return he went to see her.*

dans
Je l'ai recontré dans l'autobus. *I met him on the bus.*

de
d'un côté, *on one side*
de l'autre côté, *on the other side*

en
en vacances, *on holiday*
en vente, *on sale*

par
par une belle journée d'été, *on a fine summer's day*

sur
sur la table, *on the table*
This is the most obvious translation of 'on'; but, as is shown above, there are other words which must be used in certain circumstances.
Remember that with dates, 'on' is *not* translated:
Elle est venue lundi. *She came on Monday.*

Out

dans
Il a pris une lettre dans le tiroir. *He took a letter out of the drawer.*

Dans is used here because we think of what the object was *in* just before it was taken out.

hors
hors de danger, *out of danger*
hors d'haleine, *out of breath*
hors de la maison, *out of the house*
hors de vue, *out of sight*

par
Elle regardait par la fenêtre. *She was looking out of the window.*

sur
See also 'in'.
neuf sur dix, *nine out of ten.*

Over

au-dessus
Il a tiré au-dessus de ma tête. *He fired over my head.*

par-dessus
J'ai sauté par-dessus le mur. *I jumped over the wall.*

d'en face, over the way (i.e. opposite)
Elle habite la maison d'en face. *She lives in the house over the way.*

plus de (more than)
J'ai plus de mille francs. *I have over a thousand francs.*

sur
Mettez la couverture sur le lit. *Put the blanket over the bed.*

Since

depuis
See also 'for'.
Il n'a rien fait depuis son arrivée. *He has done nothing since he arrived.*

Until

jusqu'à
Nous y resterons jusqu'à minuit. *We shall stay there until midnight.*

If you wish to use a clause following 'until', remember that you must then use **jusqu'à ce que**+subjunctive.
Je resterai ici jusqu'à ce qu'il vienne. *I shall stay here until he comes.*
à demain , until tomorrow

Translation of 'up, down, in, out' with a verb of motion

In sentences such as:
He ran into the house,
She ran down the street,

it is better to change the preposition into a verb:
Il **est entré** dans la maison en courant.
Elle **a descendu** la rue en courant.

You will notice that the verb in the original sentence has now become a present participle+**en**. Remember that **descendre** (which is normally conjugated with *être* in the perfect tense) is here conjugated with **avoir** as the verb has a direct object, 'la rue'.

As you can see from the above examples, there is no simple way of translating one French word with a single corresponding word in English. You must have a sure knowledge of individual French phrases and of the different ways of expressing even simple words like 'in' and 'on' if you are to achieve 'Frenchness' in both oral and written work. Careful reading of French passages will help you to become more aware of French expressions. Try to read a few lines of good French each day and make a note of, *and learn*, as many useful phrases as possible.

18 VERBS

The most important part of any sentence is the verb. In almost all examinations, the incorrect use of verbs is heavily penalized. You must make sure, therefore, that you revise the sections on verbs carefully. The main tenses which you must be able to use are: *present, future, imperfect, conditional, perfect* and *pluperfect*. These are the main tenses that you will be expected to speak and write accurately.

There are also other tenses which you will be required to know at the Higher level, but mainly for recognition purposes. These are the past historic, the future and conditional perfect, and, occasionally, the simpler forms of the present subjunctive. You must check to see which tenses are specified by your Examining Group for active use and which will be for recognition purposes only.

French verbs are more difficult to learn than English verbs because each verb has several different forms. English verbs usually have no more than two or three different forms in each tense, e.g.:

I go,	you go,	he goes,	she goes,	we go,	you go,	they go
1	1	2	2	1	1	1

French verbs, however, can have as many as six different forms, e.g.:

je vais,	tu vas,	il va,	elle va,	nous allons,	vous allez,	ils vont,	elles vont
1	2	3	3	4	5	6	6

You must set time aside each week to revise verbs carefully. You must learn all the forms of each verb, paying particular attention to spelling.

The other main difficulty with French verbs is that there are many common irregular verbs which have to be learnt separately as they do not fit into the normal verb patterns. This, too, takes time to check thoroughly.

The sections that follow cover the main types of regular verb and the main irregular verbs in the tenses which you will be expected to know. Always remember that the correct spelling (including the correct use of accents) is *very* important.

Many verbs are regular and conform to the patterns given below for the various tenses.
There are three main types of regular verb, usually referred to by the last two letters of the present infinitive.
Type 1: **-er** verbs, e.g. donn**er** (to give)
Type 2: **-ir** verbs, e.g. fin**ir** (to finish)
Type 3: **-re** verbs, e.g. vend**re** (to sell)

Remember that each type has different endings. Check these endings carefully.

19 THE PRESENT TENSE

Type 1: regular -er verbs

The majority of **-er** verbs in French follow this pattern:

donner—to give

je donn**e**	I give
tu donn**es**	you (*singular*) give
il donn**e**	he gives
elle donn**e**	she gives
nous donn**ons**	we give
vous donn**ez**	you (*plural or polite singular form*) give
ils donn**ent**	they give (*masculine form*)
elles donn**ent**	they give (*feminine form*)

You will see that the endings for type 1 regular verbs are:
-e, **-es**, **-e**, **-e**, **-ons**, **-ez**, **-ent**, **-ent**.

These are added to the stem of the verb, i.e. the infinitive **donner** minus the **-er** ending. Other regular verbs follow the same pattern:

regarder→je regard**e**
arriver →j'arriv**e***
parler →je parl**e**

Irregular -er verbs

The most common irregular **-er** verbs which may occur are listed below. Check each one carefully. Not every verb has the same degree of irregularity.

For example, the verb **manger** (to eat) has only one irregularity in the present tense, which is the addition of 'e' in the **nous** form, i.e. nous man**ge**ons. The 'e' is added to keep the 'g' sound soft.

Similarly the verb **commencer** requires a cedilla (¸) in the **nous** form, to keep the 'c' sound soft: nous commen**ç**ons.

The pattern of the following verbs is more irregular:

jeter—to throw	**appeler**—to call
je je**tt**e	j'appe**ll**e
tu je**tt**es	tu appe**ll**es
il je**tt**e	il appe**ll**e
elle je**tt**e	elle appe**ll**e
nous jetons	nous appelons
vous jetez	vous appelez
ils je**tt**ent	ils appe**ll**ent
elles je**tt**ent	elles appe**ll**ent

You will see that the actual endings of the present tense of **jeter** and **appeler** are the same as those for the regular **-er** verbs. The irregularity occurs in the doubling of the consonant.

Some other **-er** verbs are irregular because of the addition or changes of accents, e.g. **espérer**, **répéter**, **acheter**, **lever**, **mener**. The irregularities in all these verbs occur in the singular and the third person plural forms. Try to be as accurate in your use of accents as you would be with spelling.

espérer—to hope	**répéter**—to repeat	**acheter**—to buy
j'esp**è**re	je rép**è**te	j'ach**è**te
tu esp**è**res	tu rép**è**tes	tu ach**è**tes
il esp**è**re	il rép**è**te	il ach**è**te
elle esp**è**re	elle rép**è**te	elle ach**è**te
nous espérons	nous répétons	nous achetons
vous espérez	vous répétez	vous achetez
ils esp**è**rent	ils rép**è**tent	ils ach**è**tent
elles esp**è**rent	elles rép**è**tent	elles ach**è**tent

lever—to lift	**mener**—to lead
je l**è**ve	je m**è**ne
tu l**è**ves	tu m**è**nes
il l**è**ve	il m**è**ne
elle l**è**ve	elle m**è**ne
nous levons	nous menons
vous levez	vous menez
ils l**è**vent	ils m**è**nent
elles l**è**vent	elles m**è**nent

* When speaking and writing French remember to omit the 'e' of **je** when it is followed by a vowel or 'h'. NB especially **j'habite**.

-er verbs whose infinitives end in **-oyer** or **-uyer** change the 'y' to 'i' in the singular and the third person plural forms:

envoyer—to send	**ennuyer**—to annoy
j'envoie	j'ennuie
tu envoies	tu ennuies
il envoie	il ennuie
elle envoie	elle ennuie
nous envoyons	nous ennuyons
vous envoyez	vous ennuyez
ils envoient	ils ennuient
elles envoient	elles ennuient

Type 2: regular -ir verbs

The endings for the present tense of these verbs are:
-is, -is, -it, it, -issons, issez, -issent, -issent

These are added to the stem of the verb, i.e. the present infinitive minus the **-ir**.

finir—to finish

je finis	nous finissons
tu finis	vous finissez
il finit	ils finissent
elle finit	elles finissent

Irregular -ir verbs

There are several important irregular **-ir** verbs which do not follow the above pattern, e.g.:

courir—to run	**dormir**—to sleep	**fuir**—to flee
je cours	je dors	je fuis
tu cours	tu dors	tu fuis
il court	il dort	il fuit
elle court	elle dort	elle fuit
nous courons	nous dormons	nous fuyons
vous courez	vous dormez	vous fuyez
ils courent	ils dorment	ils fuient
elles courent	elles dorment	elles fuient

ouvrir[1]—to open	**partir**[2]—to leave	**venir**[3]—to come
j'ouvre	je pars	je viens
tu ouvres	tu pars	tu viens
il ouvre	il part	il vient
elle ouvre	elle part	elle vient
nous ouvrons	nous partons	nous venons
vous ouvrez	vous partez	vous venez
ils ouvrent	ils partent	ils viennent
elles ouvrent	elles partent	elles viennent

Type 3: regular -re verbs

Regular **-re** verbs have the following endings added to the stem:
-s, -s, -, -, -ons, -ez, -ent, ent.

vendre—to sell

je vends	nous vendons
tu vends	vous vendez
il vend	ils vendent
elle vend	elles vendent

Irregular -re verbs

The verb **être** is the most irregular of **-re** verbs:

être—to be

je suis	nous sommes
tu es	vous êtes
il est	ils sont
elle est	elles sont

[1] Although **ouvrir** is an **-ir** verb, it acts like an **-er** verb in the present tense. Other verbs which are like **ouvrir** include: **couvrir** (to cover), **cueillir** (to pick), **découvrir** (to discover), **offrir** (to offer).
[2] The verb **sortir** has the same pattern as **partir**: je sors, il sort, vous sortez, etc.
[3] The verbs **devenir** (to become), **tenir** (to hold), and **retenir** (to hold back) have the same pattern as **venir**: je deviens, il retient, nous tenons, etc.

Listed below are some of the more common irregular **-re** verbs.

battre—to beat
je bats
tu bats
il bat
elle bat
nous battons
vous battez
ils battent
elles battent

croire—to believe
je crois
tu crois
il croit
elle croit
nous croyons
vous croyez
ils croient
elles croient

mettre—to put
je mets
tu mets
il met
elle met
nous mettons
vous mettez
ils mettent
elles mettent

boire—to drink
je bois
tu bois
il boit
elle boit
nous buvons
vous buvez
ils boivent
elles boivent

dire—to say
je dis
tu dis
il dit
elle dit
nous disons
vous dites
ils disent
elles disent

prendre—to take
je prends
tu prends
il prend
elle prend
nous prenons
vous prenez
ils prennent
elles prennent

conduire—to drive
je conduis
tu conduis
il conduit
elle conduit
nous conduisons
vous conduisez
ils conduisent
elles conduisent

écrire—to write
j'écris
tu écris
il écrit
elle écrit
nous écrivons
vous écrivez
ils écrivent
elles écrivent

rire—to laugh
je ris
tu ris
il rit
elle rit
nous rions
vous riez
ils rient
elles rient

connaître—to know
je connais
tu connais
il connaît
elle connaît
nous connaissons
vous connaissez
ils connaissent
elles connaissent

faire—to do, make
je fais
tu fais
il fait
elle fait
nous faisons
vous faites
ils font
elles font

suivre—to follow
je suis[1]
tu suis
il suit
elle suit
nous suivons
vous suivez
ils suivent
elles suivent

craindre—to fear
je crains
tu crains
il craint
elle craint
nous craignons
vous craignez
ils craignent
elles craignent

lire—to read
je lis
tu lis
il lit
elle lit
nous lisons
vous lisez
ils lisent
elles lisent

vivre—to live
je vis[2]
tu vis[2]
il vit[2]
elle vit[2]
nous vivons
vous vivez
ils vivent
elles vivent

Verbs ending in -oir

In addition to the three main types of verb, there is a fourth group, the infinitives of which end in **-oir**. All of these verbs are irregular. The more common ones are listed below.

avoir—to have
j'ai
tu as
il a
elle a
nous avons
vous avez
ils ont
elles ont

s'asseoir—to sit down
je m'assieds
tu t'assieds
il s'assied
elle s'assied
nous nous asseyons
vous vous asseyez
ils s'asseyent
elles s'asseyent

devoir—to owe
je dois
tu dois
il doit
elle doit
nous devons
vous devez
il doivent
elles doivent

falloir—to be necessary
3rd person singular only:
il faut—it is necessary

pleuvoir—to rain
3rd person singular only:
il pleut—it is raining

[1] Although this part of the verb has the same spelling as the first person singular, present tense of the verb **être** (to be), the sense of the rest of the sentence will indicate which verb is being used.

[2] These forms have the same spelling as the past historic tense of the verb **voir** (to see). Once again, the sense of the sentence will indicate which verb and tense are being used.

pouvoir–to be able
je peux
tu peux
il peut
elle peut
nous pouvons
vous pouvez
ils peuvent
elles peuvent

savoir–to know
je sais
tu sais
il sait
elle sait
nous savons
vous savez
ils savent
elles savent

vouloir–to want
je veux
tu veux
il veut
elle veut
nous voulons
vous voulez
ils veulent
elles veulent

recevoir–to receive
je reçois
tu reçois
il reçoit
elle reçoit
nous recevons
vous recevez
ils reçoivent
elles reçoivent

voir–to see
je vois
tu vois
il voit
elle voit
nous voyons
vous voyez
ils voient
elles voient

Reflexive verbs

In addition to the above verbs, you will need to revise the present tense of reflexive verbs. The present tense endings of these follow the patterns already given. The difference is that an extra pronoun, called a reflexive pronoun, precedes the verb.

se coucher–to go to bed

je **me** couche	nous **nous** couchons
tu **te** couches	vous **vous** couchez
il **se** couche	ils **se** couchent
elle **se** couche	elles **se** couchent

20 THE FUTURE TENSE

When you are talking about something which is going to happen in the future, you can often avoid using the future tense by using the present tense of **aller** plus an infinitive:

Je **vais acheter** des chaussures samedi prochain. *I will (am going to) buy some shoes next Saturday.*
Using the verb **aller** plus an infinitive instead of the future tense will often add a touch of 'Frenchness' to your speech. However, you must still be able to recognize and use the correct forms of the future tense.
All verbs have the same endings in the future tense in French. They are:
-ai, **-as**, **-a**, **-a**, **-ons**, **-ez**, **-ont**, **-ont**.

Type 1: -er verbs

The future endings are added to the whole of the infinitive:

donner

je donnerai–*I shall give*	nous donnerons
tu donneras	vous donnerez
il donnera	ils donneront
elle donnera	elles donneront

Type 2: -ir verbs

The future endings are added to the whole of the infinitive:
finir

je finirai–*I shall finish*	nous finirons
tu finiras	vous finirez
il finira	ils finiront
elle finira	elles finiront

Type 3: -re verbs

The final 'e' of the infinitive is omitted, before adding the appropriate endings:
vendre

je vendrai–*I shall sell*	nous vendrons
tu vendras	vous vendrez
il vendra	ils vendront
elle vendra	elles vendront

The future tense of irregular verbs

Listed below are the future tenses of the common irregular verbs, which you will be expected to know. The endings are the same as for all other verbs in the future tense, but you must check carefully the spellings of these irregular verbs.

acheter	j'achèterai	*I shall buy*	faire	je ferai	*I shall do*
aller	j'irai	*I shall go*	falloir	il faudra	*it will be necessary*
apercevoir	j'apercevrai	*I shall perceive, notice*	jeter	je jetterai	*I shall throw*
			mourir	je mourrai	*I shall die*
appeler	j'appellerai	*I shall call*	pleuvoir	il pleuvra	*it will rain*
s'asseoir	je m'assiérai	*I shall sit down*	pouvoir	je pourrai	*I shall be able*
avoir	j'aurai	*I shall have*	recevoir	je recevrai	*I shall receive*
courir	je courrai	*I shall run*	répéter	je répéterai	*I shall repeat*
cueillir	je cueillerai	*I shall pick*	savoir	je saurai	*I shall know*
devoir	je devrai	*I shall owe, I shall have to*	tenir	je tiendrai	*I shall hold*
			venir	je viendrai	*I shall come*
envoyer	j'enverrai	*I shall send*	voir	je verrai	*I shall see*
être	je serai	*I shall be*	vouloir	je voudrai	*I shall want*

21 THE IMPERFECT TENSE

This tense is *one* of the past tenses in French. You must remember that it is not the only past tense. As its name suggests, it is an 'unfinished' tense and should not be used for completed actions.

The imperfect endings are:

-ais, -ais, -ait, -ait, -ions, -iez, -aient, -aient.

Except for the verb **être**, the imperfect tense is always formed from the stem of the first person plural of the present tense.

e.g. nous **donn**ons → je donnais *I was giving*
nous **finiss**ons → je finissais *I was finishing*
nous **vend**ons → je vendais *I was selling*
nous **all**ons → j'allais *I was going*

Examples of verbs in the imperfect tense:

finir	**aller**
je finissais—*I was finishing*	j'allais—*I was going*
tu finissais	tu allais
il finissait	il allait
elle finissait	elle allait
nous finissions	nous allions
vous finissiez	vous alliez
ils finissaient	ils allaient
elles finissaient	elles allaient

The verb **être** is the only verb whose imperfect tense is *not* formed in the above way. The imperfect tense of **être** is as follows:

être

j'étais—*I was*	nous étions
tu étais	vous étiez
il était	ils étaient
elle était	elles étaient

You must be very careful in your use of the imperfect tense. The following English expressions can all be translated by the imperfect tense:

I went
I was going
I used to go
I would go
} **j'allais**

(a) *I went* to town every Saturday. **J'allais** en ville tous les samedis
Here 'went' signifies a repeated action in the past which should be translated by the imperfect tense.

(b) *I was going* to telephone you later. **J'allais** te téléphoner plus tard.

(c) *I used to go* to their house every day. **J'allais** chez eux chaque jour.
Here the action is a repeated action in the past as in **(a)**. The imperfect tense is therefore required.

(d) *I would go* (= used to go) to town on Fridays. **J'allais** en ville le vendredi.
Even the word 'would' may need to be translated by the imperfect tense if it means 'used to'. Remember that 'would' is translated by the conditional tense (see below) when you wish to suggest a condition.

22 THE CONDITIONAL TENSE

For most candidates, this tense will be for recognition purposes only. Candidates may wish, however, to include this tense in their oral exam or in the free composition section. The formation of this tense is really an amalgamation of the stem of the future tense and the endings of the imperfect tense.

Future		**Conditional**	
je serai	*I shall be*	je ser**ais**	*I should be*
j'aurai	*I shall have*	j'aur**ais**	*I should have*
je finirai	*I shall finish*	je finir**ais**	*I should finish*
je voudrai	*I shall want*	je voudr**ais**	*I should like (want)*

Je voudrais is one of the most useful examples of the conditional tense in French. It is used constantly, especially when shopping or asking for something (e.g. booking a hotel room or campsite, asking the way, etc.). For further examples see the role-play section.

Here is an example of a verb in the conditional tense:

vouloir

je voudrais–*I should like (want, wish)*	nous voudrions
tu voudrais	vous voudriez
il voudrait	ils voudraient
elle voudrait	elles voudraient

There are no exceptions in the formation of the conditional tense. All verbs follow the above rule.

The conditional implies that something *would* happen if something else did. It is often used after or before a clause beginning with **si** (if), which is in the imperfect tense:

S'il faisait beau, j'irais à la piscine.
If the weather were fine, I would go to the swimming pool.
Elle viendrait avec nous, si elle avait assez d'argent.
She would come with us if she had enough money.

23 THE PERFECT TENSE

Candidates will need to use this tense in almost all sections of the examination. All Examining Groups include a knowledge of the perfect tense in their syllabuses. You should therefore pay special attention to this tense when revising. More marks are lost through the incorrect use of this tense than for any other single reason.

In French the perfect tense has two main forms:

1 Those verbs which are conjugated with **être.**
2 Those verbs which are conjugated with **avoir** (this is by far the largest group).

1 Verbs conjugated with 'être'

(a) The verbs in the following list are all conjugated with **être**. It is not difficult to learn this list as there are only sixteen verbs.

aller	*to go*	partir	*to leave*
arriver	*to arrive*	rentrer	*to go back*
descendre	*to go down*	rester	*to stay*
devenir	*to become*	retourner	*to return*
entrer	*to enter*	revenir	*to come back*
monter	*to go up*	sortir	*to go out*
mourir	*to die*	tomber	*to fall*
naître	*to be born*	venir	*to come*

Because the above verbs are conjugated with **être**, the past participles will agree with the subject of the verb.

arriver

je suis arrivé(e)–*I have arrived, I arrived*	nous sommes arrivé(e)s
tu es arrivé(e)	vous êtes arrivé(e)(s)
il est arrivé	ils sont arrivés
elle est arrivée	elles sont arrivées

The past participles of all the **-er** verbs in the list above will also end in **-é**:

aller	je suis allé(e)	*I went*
entrer	je suis entré(e)	*I entered*
monter	je suis monté(e)	*I went up*
rentrer	je suis rentré(e)	*I went back*
rester	je suis resté(e)	*I stayed*
retourner	je suis retourné(e)	*I returned*
tomber	je suis tombé(e)	*I fell*

The past participle endings for the other verbs in the list are as follows:

descendre	je suis descendu(e)	*I went down*
devenir	je suis devenu(e)	*I became*
revenir	je suis revenu(e)	*I came back*
venir	je suis venu(e)	*I came*
partir	je suis parti(e)	*I left*
sortir	je suis sorti(e)	*I went out*
mourir	il est mort, elle est morte	*he died, she died*
naître	je suis né(e)	*I was born*

(b) *Reflexive verbs*

All reflexive verbs are conjugated with **être**. For example:

se laver

je me suis lavé(e)—*I washed myself*	nous nous sommes lavé(e)s
tu t'es lavé(e)	vous vous êtes lavé(e)(s)
il s'est lavé	ils se sont lavés
elle s'est lavée	elles se sont lavées

Note the use of **t'** and **s'** before the vowel in the **tu** and **il/elle** forms.

Other reflexive verbs follow this pattern. The only variation will be in the past participle when the verb is not an **-er** verb. For example:

s'asseoir	je me suis assis(e)	*I sat down*
se souvenir	je me suis souvenu(e)	*I remembered*
se taire	je me suis tu(e)	*I became silent*

Special note

In certain cases the ending of the past participle does *not* agree with the reflexive pronoun. This happens when the verb is followed by a direct object. For example:
Elle s'est lavée. *She washed herself.*

Here the past participle agrees with the reflexive pronoun. But:
Elle s'est lavé les mains. *She washed her hands*

Here the verb is followed by a direct object and the past participle does *not* agree.

2 Verbs conjugated with 'avoir'

Except for the categories given in **1(a)** and **1(b)** above, all other verbs in French are conjugated with **avoir** in the perfect tense. Remember that the past participles of these verbs do *not* agree with the subject of the verb.

donner	**finir**
j'ai donné—*I have given, I gave*	j'ai fini—*I have finished, I finished*
tu as donné	tu as fini
il a donné	il a fini
elle a donné	elle a fini
nous avons donné	nous avons fini
vous avez donné	vous avez fini
ils ont donné	ils ont fini
elles ont donné	elles ont fini

3 -re verbs

Vendre

j'ai vendu—*I have sold, I sold*	nous avons vendu
tu as vendu	vous avez vendu
il a vendu	ils ont vendu
elle a vendu	elles ont vendu

In addition to the three main types of verb listed above, there are many irregular verbs which have irregular past participles. These irregular verbs are still conjugated in the normal way with **'avoir'**, but it is very important that you know the exact form of the irregular past participle.

Given below are some of the more common irregular verbs, in the perfect tense, which you will be expected to know.

avoir	j'ai eu	*I had, I have had*
boire	j'ai bu	*I drank, I have drunk*
conduire	j'ai conduit	*I drove, I have driven*
connaître	j'ai connu	*I knew, I have known*
courir	j'ai couru	*I ran, I have run*
craindre	j'ai craint	*I feared, I have feared*
croire	j'ai cru	*I believed, I have believed*
devoir	j'ai dû	*I had to (owed), I have had to (have owed)*

dire	j'ai dit	*I said, I have said*
écrire	j'ai écrit	*I wrote, I have written*
être	j'ai été	*I have been, I was*
faire	j'ai fait	*I made, I did, etc.*
falloir	il a fallu	*It has been necessary, it was necessary*
lire	j'ai lu	*I read, I have read*
mettre	j'ai mis	*I put, I have put*
ouvrir	j'ai ouvert	*I opened, I have opened*
pleuvoir	il a plu	*It rained, it has rained*
pouvoir	j'ai pu	*I have been able, I was able*
prendre	j'ai pris	*I took, I have taken*
recevoir	j'ai reçu	*I received, I have received*
rire	j'ai ri	*I laughed, I have laughed*
savoir	j'ai su	*I knew, I have known*
suivre	j'ai suivi	*I followed, I have followed*
tenir	j'ai tenu	*I held, I have held*
vivre	j'ai vécu	*I lived, I have lived*
voir	j'ai vu	*I saw, I have seen*
vouloir	j'ai voulu	*I wanted, I have wanted*

Special note

In certain circumstances, the verbs in **1(a)** which are normally conjugated with **être** may be conjugated with **avoir**. This change occurs when the verb has a direct object. For example:
Il a descendu l'escalier. *He went down the stairs.*
Elle a sorti un billet de 100 francs. *She took out a 100 franc note.*

Preceding direct object agreements

Although verbs conjugated with **avoir** in the perfect tense never agree with the subject of the verb, there are occasions when the past participle does agree with the *direct object* when this direct object *precedes* the verb. For example:

1(a) J'ai vu **la maison**.
Here the direct object follows the verb. Therefore, no agreement is made.

1(b) Voici **la maison** que j'ai achetée.
Here the direct object precedes the verb. Therefore, an agreement is made by adding 'e' (since **maison** is feminine) to the past participle.

2(a) J'ai acheté **ces livres**.
No agreement is made as the direct object follows the verb.

2(b) J'ai vu ces livres. Je **les** ai achetés.
The agreement is made here since the direct object **les** precedes the verb.

24 THE PLUPERFECT, FUTURE PERFECT AND CONDITIONAL PERFECT TENSES

When listening to spoken French, or reading French you will need to recognize the following tenses:

(a) the pluperfect tense
(b) the future perfect tense
(c) the conditional perfect tense.

These tenses are formed from the imperfect, future and conditional tenses of **avoir** and **être** plus the past participle of the required verb. If a verb is conjugated with **avoir** in the perfect tense, then it will be conjugated with **avoir** in the tenses given above. Similarly, those verbs which are conjugated with **être** in the perfect tense will still be conjugated with **être** in the above tenses. For example:

Perfect:	j'**ai** fini	*I (have) finished*
Pluperfect:	j'**avais** fini	*I had finished*
Future perfect:	j'**aurai** fini	*I shall have finished*
Conditional perfect:	j'**aurais** fini	*I should have finished*
Perfect:	je **suis** allé(e)	*I went, I have gone*
Pluperfect:	j'**étais** allé(e)	*I had gone*
Future perfect:	je **serai** allé(e)	*I shall have gone*
Conditional perfect:	je **serais** allé(e)	*I should have gone*
Perfect:	je me **suis** lavé(e)	*I (have) washed myself*
Pluperfect:	je m'**étais** lavé(e)	*I had washed myself*
Future perfect:	je me **serai** lavé(e)	*I shall have washed myself*
Conditional perfect:	je me **serais** lavé(e)	*I should have washed myself*

Given below are complete examples of:

The pluperfect tense	**The future perfect tense**	**The conditional perfect tense**
aller	**finir**	**se laver**
j'étais allé(e)	j'aurai fini	je me serais lavé(e)
—I had gone	*—I shall have finished*	*—I should have washed myself*
tu étais allé(e)	tu auras fini	tu te serais lavé(e)
il était allé	il aura fini	il se serait lavé
elle était allée	elle aura fini	elle se serait lavée
nous étions allé(e)s	nous aurons fini	nous nous serions lavé(e)s
vous étiez allé(e)(s)	vous aurez fini	vous vous seriez lavé(e)(s)
ils étaient allés	ils auront fini	ils se seraient lavés
elles étaient allées	elles auront fini	elles se seraient lavées

25 THE PAST HISTORIC TENSE

The past historic tense is sometimes used in written French instead of the perfect tense. The past historic tense will only be required for recognition purposes, if at all. Some forms of the past historic tense are very different from the form of the infinitive and may cause you difficulty if you have not revised this tense carefully. Check the syllabus of your Examining Group to see if this tense is required.

Type 1: -er verbs

The past historic endings added to the stem of the verb are:
-ai, -as, -a, -a, -âmes, -âtes, -èrent, -èrent.

donner

je donnai—*I gave*	nous donnâmes
tu donnas	vous donnâtes
il donna	ils donnèrent
ella donna	elles donnèrent

Type 2: -ir verbs

The past historic endings added to the stem of the verb are:
-is, -is, -it, -it, -îmes, -îtes, -irent, irent.

finir

je finis—*I finished*	nous finîmes
tu finis	vous finîtes
il finit	ils finirent
elle finit	elles finirent

You will notice that the singular form of the past historic tense of **-ir** verbs resembles the present tense of the verb. However, by looking carefully at the passage of French with which you are dealing, you will know which tense is being used. The meaning of the passage or the tense of the other verbs used will help you to decide.

Type 3: -re verbs

Type 3 verbs have the same endings in the past historic tense as Type 2 verbs.

vendre

je vendis—*I sold*	nous vendîmes
tu vendis	vous vendîtes
il vendit	ils vendirent
elle vendit	eles vendirent

The past historic of irregular verbs

(a) The following verbs have the same endings as Type 2 and Type 3 verbs above, but the stems of the verbs in the past historic are irregular.

s'asseoir	je m'assis	*I sat down*
conduire	je conduisis	*I drove*
craindre	je craignis	*I feared*
dire	je dis	*I said*
écrire	j'écrivis	*I wrote*
faire	je fis	*I made*
joindre	je joignis	*I joined*
mettre	je mis	*I put*
plaindre	je plaignis	*I pitied*
prendre	je pris	*I took*
produire	je produisis	*I produced*
rire	je ris	*I laughed*
voir	je vis	*I saw*

(b) In the past historic tense certain irregular verbs have the following endings:
-us, -us,-ut, -ut, -ûmes, -ûtes, -urent, -urent.

apercevoir	j'aperçus	*I noticed*
avoir	j'eus	*I had*
boire	je bus	*I drank*
connaître	je connus	*I knew*
courir	je courus	*I ran*
croire	je crus	*I Believed*
devoir	je dus	*I had to*
être	je fus	*I was*
falloir	il fallut	*it was necessary*
lire	je lus	*I read*
mourir	il mourut	*he died*
paraître	je parus	*I appeared*
plaire	je plus	*I pleased*
pleuvoir	il plut	*it rained*
pouvoir	je pus	*I was* able*
recevoir	je reçus	*I received*
savoir	je sus	*I knew*
se taire	je me tus	*I became silent*
vivre	je vécus	*I lived*
vouloir	je voulus	*I wanted*

Here is an example of a verb in the past historic tense with the above endings:

avoir

j'eus–*I had*	nous eûmes
tu eus	vous eûtes
il eut	ils eurent
elle eut	elles eurent

The verbs **tenir** and **venir** and their compounds (e.g. **revenir**, **retenir**) have special past historic forms which must be learned separately.

tenir	**venir**
je tins–*I held*	je vins–*I came*
tu tins	tu vins
il tint	il vint
elle tint	elle vint
nous tînmes	nous vînmes
vous tîntes	vous vîntes
ils tinrent	ils vinrent
elles tinrent	elles vinrent

The past historic tense is translated into English in the same way as the perfect tense. The difference between them is that the perfect tense is used when speaking or writing a letter about what has happened in the past, and the past historic tense is used for a literary, narrative account of events in the past.

26 THE SUBJUNCTIVE

The subjunctive will rarely be required at GCSE level. However, an easy subjunctive may occur in a passage of French for comprehension purposes and Higher-level candidates may wish to use the subjunctive in their writing test, if appropriate.

The present subjunctive is formed from the third person plural, present indicative:

donner ils donnent → **je donne**
finir ils finissent → **je finisse**
vendre ils vendent → **je vende**

The endings for the present subjunctive are:
-e, -es, -e, -e, ions, -iez, -ent, -ent.

finir

je finisse	nous finissions
tu finisses	vous finissiez
il finisse	ils finissent
elle finisse	elles finissent

There are also several irregular verbs whose subjunctive you may need to recognize:

aller → j'aille, nous allions, ils aillent
avoir → j'aie, il ait, nous ayons, ils aient
être → je sois, nous soyons, ils soient
faire → je fasse, etc.

* Care must be taken to differentiate between this and the continuous past tense: the imperfect.

pouvoir → je puisse, etc.
savoir → je sache, etc.
vouloir → je veuille, nous voulions, ils veuillent

Given below are some of the constructions which require the use of the subjunctive:

(a) il faut que . . . *it is necessary that . . .*
Il faut que vous travailliez. *You must work.*

(b) bien que . . . *although . . .*
quoique . . . *although . . .*
afin que . . . *in order that . . .*
avant que . . . *before . . .*
jusqu'à ce que . . . *until . . .*
Je veux vous parler avant que vous sortiez.
I want to speak to you before you go out.

Bien que le temps fasse mauvais, nous allons sortir.
Although the weather is bad we are going to go out

(c) vouloir que . . . *to wish that . . .* (*to want*)
préférer que . . . *to prefer that . . .*
regretter que . . . *to regret that . . .*(*to be sorry that . . .*)
Je veux que vous restiez. *I want you to stay.*
Je regrette que vous soyez malade. *I am sorry that you are ill.*

(d) il est possible (impossible) que . . . *it is possible (impossible) that . . .*
douter que . . . *to doubt that . . .*
Il est impossible qu'il réussisse. *It is impossible for him to succeed.*

There are other tenses of the subjunctive mood and other occasions when the subjunctive is required, but they are not required at this level.

27 THE PASSIVE

The passive in French is formed as in English, using a suitable tense of 'to be' (**être**) plus the past participle of the verb required:
Il **a été mordu** par un chien. *He has been bitten by a dog*

However, most French people prefer to avoid using the passive by making the verb active in some way. There are a number of ways of doing this:

(a) The agent of a passive sentence can become the subject of an active sentence:
Un chien l'a mordu. *A dog bit him.*

(b) Where the agent is not mentioned, **on** can be used as the subject:
On a vendu cette maison. *This house has been sold.*

(c) Sometimes a reflexive verb can be used:
Les cigarettes se vendent ici. *Cigarettes are sold here.*

Caution

In writing, it is very tempting for candidates to use the passive in French to try to translate their thoughts which are often in the passive in English (e.g. she is called, I am bored, they were saved, etc.). It is always very easy for an examiner to recognize those candidates who have thought out their sentences in English and then tried to translate them into French in the writing section. Their compositions will be littered with passive-type English sentences clumsily translated word for word into French. The result is a very poor non-French composition. Always try to use a known French construction in your answers and avoid the passive in French where possible.

Beware of English sentences which contain a passive, such as 'He is called Peter' which should be translated with a reflexive verb:
Il **s'appelle** Pierre.

28 THE IMPERATIVE

(a) Commands in French are formed from the **tu**, **nous**, and **vous** forms of the present tense of verbs, omitting the pronouns. For example:
finis! *finish!* (singular)
finissons! *let us finish!*
finissez! *finish!* (plural)

(b) **-er** verbs omit the **'s'** in the second person singular imperative:
tu portes → **porte** *carry*
tu vas → **va** *go*
NB the second person singular imperative of **aller** retains the **'s'** when followed by **'y'**:
Vas-y *Go on/go there.*

(c) The following verbs have irregular imperatives:
avoir → aie, ayons, ayez
être → sois, soyons, soyez
savoir → sache, sachons, sachez
vouloir → veuille, veuillons, veuillez

(d) The reflexive pronoun is retained in the imperative of reflexive verbs and follows the rules for object pronouns, i.e. in the affirmative, the pronoun follows the verb and is joined to the verb by a hyphen; the pronoun **te** becomes **toi**.
Dépêche-toi! *Hurry up!*

But in a negative command, the pronoun keeps its original position and spelling:
Ne te dépêche pas! *Don't hurry!*

Here are examples of all three imperatives in the affirmative and in the negative:

se lever—to get up
Lève-toi. Ne te lève pas.
Levons-nous. Ne nous levons pas.
Levez-vous. Ne vous levez pas.

29 THE PRESENT PARTICIPLE

The present participle (e.g. going, looking, selling) is normally formed by adding **-ant** to the stem of the first person plural of the present tense:

aller	nous allons	→ **allant**	*going*
regarder	nous regardons	→ **regardant**	*looking*
finir	nous finissons	→ **finissant**	*finishing*
vendre	nous vendons	→ **vendant**	*selling*
dire	nous disons	→ **disant**	*saying*

The following irregular verbs do *not* form the present participle from the stem of the first person plural of the present tense:

avoir	**ayant**	*having*
être	**étant**	*being*
savoir	**sachant**	*knowing*

Do not, however, try to use the present participle in such expressions as 'I am going', 'they are eating', etc. Expressions such as these should be translated by the present tense—**je vais**, **ils mangent**, etc.

A present participle is not finite (i.e. not complete in itself). It should be used in such expressions as:
He went home singing. Il est rentré **en chantant.**
Seeing that she was ill, he telephoned the doctor.
Voyant qu'elle était malade, il a téléphoné au médecin.

The use of **en** + present participle, as in the first example above, is one that you are very likely to need. It is a frequent testing point in prose composition and you should also be able to incorporate it into free composition.

En + present participle can also mean 'by/on/when doing . . .':
En rentrant à la maison il a trouvé ses clés. *On returning home he found his keys.*
En travaillant dur, ils ont réussi. *By working hard, they succeeded.*

Check carefully the following examples where a present participle is used in English but *not* in French:

(a) He left *without saying* goodbye.
Il est parti **sans dire** au revoir.

(b) I shall have breakfast *before leaving.*
Je prendrai le petit déjeuner **avant de partir.**

(c) *Instead of working,* he went to play football.
Au lieu de travailler, il est allé jouer au football.

Note the use of the infinitive in the above three sentences. Do not be misled by the English present participle.

(d) *After getting up* late, we missed the bus.
Après nous être levés en retard, nous avons manqué l'autobus.

Note the use of the perfect infinitive after **après**. This construction needs special care because of the reflexive verb. The subject of the main part of the sentence (**nous**) dictates which reflexive pronoun must be used before **être.**

(e) I saw some boys *fishing* in the river.
J'ai vu des garçons **qui pêchaient** dans la rivière.

You must check very carefully before using a present participle in French to see if, in fact, you need to use a present participle construction, or if, as in the cases above, you need to use a different construction.

30 VERBS FOLLOWED BY PREPOSITIONS

Some verbs in French can be directly followed by an infinitive:
Je sais nager. *I can swim*
Tu veux venir? *Do you want to come?*

Many, however, require the addition of a preposition before the following infinitive. Try to learn as many of the following as possible:

aider à *to help to . . .*
apprendre à *to learn to . . .*
s'attendre à *to expect to . . .*
commencer à *to begin to . . .*
consentir à *to agree to . . .*
continuer à *to continue to . . .*
se décider à *to make up one's mind to . . .*
forcer à *to compel to . . .*
hésiter à *to hesitate to . . .*
inviter à *to invite to . . .*
se mettre à *to begin to . . .*
obliger à *to oblige to . . .*
ressembler à *to look like . . .*
réussir à *to succeed in . . .*
s'arrêter de *to stop (doing)*
avoir l'intention de *to intend to . . .*
avoir peur de *to be afraid of (doing)*
avoir besoin de *to need to . . .*
cesser de *to stop (doing)*
décider de *to decide to . . .*
défendre de *to forbid to . . .*
demander de *to ask to . . .*
dire de *to tell to . . .*
empêcher de *to prevent from . . .*
essayer de *to try to . . .*
faire semblant de *to pretend to . . .*
finir de *to finish (doing)*
menacer de *to threaten . . .*
offrir de *to offer to . . .*
ordonner de *to order to . . .*
oublier de *to forget to . . .*
permettre de *to allow to . . .*
prier de *to beg to . . .*
promettre de *to promise to . . .*
refuser de *to refuse to . . .*
regretter de *to be sorry for . . .*

Certain other words apart from verbs also require a preposition before a following infinitive:

beaucoup à (faire) *a lot to (do)*
le dernier à *the last to . . .*
prêt à *ready to . . .*
le premier à *the first to . . .*
rien à *nothing to . . .*
certain de *certain to . . .*
content de *pleased to . . .*
le droit de *the right to . . .*
étonné de *surprised to . . .*
heureux de *happy to . . .*
obligé de *obliged to . . .*
l'occasion de *the opportunity to . . .*
la permission de *the permission to . . .*
surpris de *surprised to . . .*
le temps de *the time to . . .*

Note also the preposition **pour** before an infinitive:
Je suis allé en ville **pour** rencontrer des amis. *I went to town to meet some friends.*
Il est trop malade **pour** venir. *He is too ill to come.*
Vous êtes assez intelligent **pour** comprendre. *You are intelligent enough to understand.*

Some verbs need the preposition **à** before an indirect object:
acheter à quelqu'un *to buy from someone*
cacher à quelqu'un *to hide from someone*
conseiller à quelqu'un *to advise someone*
défendre à quelqu'un *to forbid someone*
donner à quelqu'un *to give someone*
dire à quelqu'un *to tell someone*
emprunter à quelqu'un *to borrow from someone*
envoyer à quelqu'un *to send (to) someone*
se fier à quelqu'un *to trust someone*
montrer à quelqu'un *to show (to) someone*
obéir à quelqu'un *to obey someone*
offrir à quelqu'un *to offer (to) someone*
ordonner à quelqu'un *to order someone*
penser à quelqu'un *to think about someone*
plaire à quelqu'un *to please someone*
prendre à quelqu'un *to take from someone*
prêter à quelqu'un *to lend someone*
promettre à quelqu'un *to promise someone*
raconter à quelqu'un *to tell someone*
répondre à quelqu'un *to reply to someone*
réfléchir à quelque chose *to think (ponder) about something*
ressembler à quelqu'un *to resemble someone*
voler à quelqu'un *to steal from someone*

Some verbs need the preposition **de** before an object:
s'approcher de *to approach . . .*
dépendre de *to depend on . . .*
jouir de *to enjoy . . .*
se moquer de *to make fun of . . .*
remercier de *to thank for . . .*
se servir de *to use . . .*
se souvenir de *to remember . . .*

31 IMPERSONAL VERBS

You should be able to use the following accurately:

(a) **Il y a** + all tenses
Il y a beaucoup de monde en ville. *There are a lot of people in town.*
Il y avait une grande foule devant la mairie. *There was a large crowd in front of the town hall.*
Il y a eu un accident. *There has been an accident.*
Il y aura un jour de congé la semaine prochaine. *There will be a day's holiday next week.*

(b) **Il faut** it is necessary
Il fallait it was necessary (*continuous*)
Il a fallu it was necessary (*event*)
Il faudra it will be necessary
Il me faut rentrer. *I must go home.*
Il lui fallait travailler dur. *He had to work hard.*
Il m'a fallu acheter une nouvelle robe. *I had to buy a new dress.*

Remember that you may use **devoir** (*to have to*) in sentences similar to those above, but with a personal subject:
J'ai dû acheter une nouvelle robe.

For **Il faut que** . . . see section 26 on the subjunctive (p. 22).

(c) **Il reste** . . . there remains . . .
Il me reste vingt francs. *I have twenty francs left.*
Il restait . . . there remained . . .
Il lui restait deux pommes. *He had two apples left.*

You should be able to recognize the following impersonal verbs:

(a) **Il s'agit de** . . . It is a question of . . .
De quoi s'agit-il? Il s'agit d'un vol. *What's it about? It's about a theft.*

(b) **Il vaut mieux** . . . It's better . . .
Il vaut mieux rentrer tout de suite. *It's better to return home straightaway.*

32 TENSES WITH 'SI'

Check the following rule carefully.
Si + present tense . . ., (future).
Si + imperfect tense . . ., (conditional).
Si + pluperfect tense . . ., (conditional perfect).

(a) S'il vient, je te téléphonerai. *If he comes, I shall telephone you.*

(b) S'il venait, je te téléphonerais. *If he were to come, I should telephone you.*

(c) S'il était venu, je t'aurais téléphoné. *If he had come, I should have telephoned you.*

33 VENIR DE

This expression means 'to have just' (done something).

Remember to use the *present* tense in such expressions as:
I have just arrived. **Je viens** d'arriver.

Use the *imperfect* tense in such expressions as:
They had just gone out. **Ils venaient de** sortir.

34 NEGATIVES

ne . . . pas (*not*)
ne . . . point (*not at all*)
ne . . . jamais (*never*)
ne . . . personne (*nobody*)
ne . . . plus (*no more, no longer*)
ne . . . que (*only*)
ne . . . rien (*nothing*)

Check carefully
ne . . . aucun (*not one, not any*)
ne . . . guère (*scarcely*)
ne . . . ni . . . ni . . . (*neither . . . nor*)
ne . . . nulle part (*nowhere*)

The position of the negative in the sentence

(a) Present tense:
Je **ne joue pas** au tennis. *I don't play tennis.*

(b) Perfect tense:
Je **n'**ai **pas** joué au tennis. *I didn't play tennis.*
NB exception with 'ne . . . personne':
Je **n'**ai vu **personne.** *I saw nobody.*

(c) Reflexive verbs:
Je **ne** me lève **pas** de bonne heure. *I don't get up early.*
Je **ne** me suis **pas** levé de bonne heure. *I didn't get up early.*

(d) With object pronouns:
Je **ne** le vois **pas.** *I don't (can't) see him (it).*
Je **ne** l'ai **pas** vu. *I didn't see him (it).*

Remember that certain negatives may be inverted to become the subject of a sentence:
Rien n'est arrivé. *Nothing has happened.*
Personne n'a gagné. *Nobody won.*
Aucun avion **n'**a décollé. *No plane took off.*

Words like **rien**, **personne** and **jamais** may be used on their own:
Qu'a-t-il vu? **Rien.** *What did he see? Nothing.*
Y êtes-vous allés? **Jamais.** *Did you ever go there? Never.*
Qui avez-vous vu? **Personne.** *Whom did you see? Nobody.*

Combination of negatives

(a) **Plus** before **rien**:
Ils ne font plus rien. *They no longer do anything.*

(b) **Jamais** before **rien**:
Il ne nous donnent jamais rien. *They never give us anything.*

(c) **Plus** before **personne**:
Je n'y recontre plus personne. *I don't meet anyone there now.*

(d) **Jamais** before **personne**:
Je n'y recontre jamais personne. *I never meet anyone there.*

Negatives before an infinitive

Except for **ne** . . . **personne**, both parts of the negative precede the present infinitive:
J'ai décidé de **ne jamais** retourner. *I decided never to return.*
J'ai décidé de **ne** voir **personne.** *I decided to see nobody.*

Remember that **si**=*yes* after a negative question or statement:
Ne l'avez-vous pas vu? Si, je l'ai vu. *Haven't you seen it (him)? Yes, I've seen it (him).*

N'est-ce pas?

This is a most useful phrase which translates a variety of negative expressions at the end of questions, e.g. . . . haven't we? . . . didn't they? . . . wasn't he? . . . can't she? etc.

Nous avons réussi, n'est-ce pas? *We succeeded, didn't we?*
Ils ont gagné, n'est-ce pas? *They won, didn't they?*
Il était malade, n'est-ce pas? *He was ill, wasn't he?*
Elle peut venir, n'est-ce pas? *She can come, can't she?*

35 QUESTIONS

There are various ways of asking a question in French.

(a) One of the easiest ways is to use **Est-ce que** . . . at the beginning of the sentence:
Est-ce qu'il vient? *Is he coming?*

(b) Except for the first person singular of many verbs, inversion may be used:
Vient-il? *Is he coming?*

(c) Vocal intonation is frequently used in conversation:
Il vient? *Is he coming?*

Care must be taken when a noun is the subject of a question. Remember that, in writing, a pronoun should also be used:
Votre frère est-il à la maison? *Is your brother at home?*

In conversation, however, vocal intonation might be used:
Votre frère est à la maison?

Words used to introduce questions

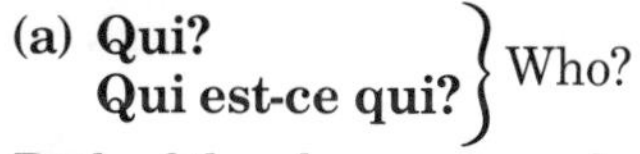
(a) **Qui?** / **Qui est-ce qui?** } Who?

Both of the above are used as the *subject* of the question:

Qui a dit cela? / Qui est-ce qui a dit cela? } *Who said that?*

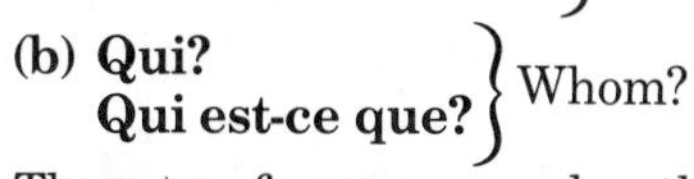
(b) **Qui?** / **Qui est-ce que?** } Whom?

These two forms are used as the *object* of the sentence:

Qui as-tu vu? / Qui est-ce que tu as vu? } *Whom did you see?*

Note that when **est-ce** is used in any question-form the verb and subject are not inverted.

(c) **Qu'est-ce qui?** What? (as the subject)
Qu'est-ce qui est arrivé? *What has happened?*

(d) **Que?** / **Qu'est-ce que?** } What? (as the object)

Qu'as-tu vu? / Qu'est-ce que tu as vu } *What have you seen?*

(e) m. **Quel** + noun / f. **Quelle** + noun / m.pl. **Quels** + noun / f.pl. **Quelles** + noun } What? which?

Quels livres? *What (which) books?*
Quelle maison? *What (which) house?*

(f) **Où?** Where?
Où habitez-vous? *Where do you live?*
Combien? How much?
Combien as-tu gagné? *How much did you earn (win)?*
Comment? How?
Comment vas-tu? *How are you?*
Pourquoi? Why?
Pourquoi es-tu venu? *Why did you come?*
Quand? When?
Quand rentres-tu? *When are you going back (home)?*

36 INVERSION

Remember that inversion is required in the following circumstances:

(a) After direct speech:
'Asseyez-vous', a-t-il dit. *'Sit down,' he said.*

(b) After **peut-être** at the beginning of a sentence:
Peut-être viendra-t-il. *Perhaps he will come.*
However, inversion can be avoided by using **peut-être que**:
Peut-être qu'il viendra.

(c) In certain subordinate clauses:
Voici la maison où habite ma grand'mère. *Here is the house where my grandmother lives.*

(d) Note also the translation of the following English inversion:
Qu'elle est jolie! *How pretty she is!*

2 FUNCTIONS

Given below is a list of the *functions* which a candidate should be able to carry out, with examples of useful expressions.

1 Asking for/giving advice and help

Advice: Excusez-moi, Monsieur/Madame, pourriez-vous me dire . . .?
Je vous conseille de . . . (conseiller=*to advise*)
Help: Excusez-moi, Monsieur/Madame, pourriez-vous m'aider? Puis-je vous aider?

For emergencies: AU SECOURS!

2 Seeking accommodation

See **vocabulary topic areas: hotel** and **camping** (p. 36).

Hotel: Vous avez des chambres libres, Monsieur/Madame?
Camping: Vous avez une place libre pour une tente, Monsieur/Madame?

3 Agreeing/disagreeing

Agreeing: D'accord. Je veux bien. Moi aussi.

Disagreeing: Pas du tout. Je ne suis pas d'accord. Non, merci.

4 Apologizing

(Oh) Pardon! Excusez-moi! Je regrette . . .

5 Responding to apologies

Ça ne fait rien. Ne t'en fais pas. Ne vous en faites pas.

6 Expressing appreciation

For a meal: C'est vraiment délicieux

General: C'est bien agréable. (C'est) formidable! Génial! C'est bien amusant.
C'est bien intéressant. Ça me plaît beaucoup. Je l'aime bien.

7 Attracting attention

Pardon, Monsieur/Madame. Excusez-moi, Monsieur/Madame. Dis donc! Dites donc! (*I say!*)

In case of fire: AU FEU!
To summon help: AU SECOURS!
To stop a thief: AU VOLEUR!

8 Simple banking procedures

See **vocabulary topic areas** and **role play** (pp. 47 and 71).

To change a travellers' cheque: Je voudrais toucher un chèque de voyage.
To change money: Je voudrais changer . . . (e.g., des livres sterling) en francs.

9 Expressing certainty/uncertainty

Je suis certain(e) que . . . Je ne suis pas certain(e). Je suis sûr(e) que . . . Je doute que . . .*

10 Congratulating

Bravo! Formidable! Félicitations!

11 Seeking/giving directions

Pour aller à . . ., s'il vous plaît? Il faut tourner à droite/à gauche. Allez tout droit. (*straight on*)
Prenez la première rue à droite/à gauche. Allez jusqu'à. . . . (*as far as*)

* Avoid this expression unless you know how to use the subjunctive.

12 Expressing disappointment

C'est dommage. Je suis vraiment déçu(e).

13 Expressing fear/worry

J'ai peur (de . . .) Je crains que . . .*

Je m'inquiète de . . . Cela m'inquiète. Ne vous en faites pas! (*Don't worry!*)

14 Forgetting/remembering

J'ai oublié de . . . N'oublie pas de . . . /N'oubliez pas de . . .
Donne(z) mon bon souvenir à . . . (*Remember me to . . .*)

15 Expressing hope

Je l'espère bien. J'espère que . . .

16 Seeking/giving information

Pourriez-vous me dire . . .? Y a-t-il . . .? A quelle heure . . .? etc.

Voici . . . Voilà . . . Il faut . . . D'abord . . .

17 Expressing intention

Je vais (+ infinitive) Je compte (+ infinitive) J'ai l'intention de . . .

18 Expressing interest/lack of interest

Je m'intéresse beaucoup à . . . Je me passionne pour . . . C'est bien intéressant.

Je n'aime pas tellement . . . Cela ne m'intéresse pas beaucoup.

19 Giving/accepting invitations

Veux-tu . . .?/Voulez-vous . . .? Je t'invite à . . ./Je vous invite à . . .

Je veux bien. Oui, merci. Avec plaisir.

20 Introducing/greeting people

Voici . . . Je te/vous présente . . . Permettez-moi de vous présenter . . .

Enchanté(e), Monsieur/Madame. Bonjour, Monsieur/Madame. Salut (Eve-Marie).

21 Taking leave of people

Au revoir, Monsieur/Madame. A bientôt. (*See you soon*) A demain. (*See you tomorrow*)
A la semaine prochaine. (*See you next week*)

22 Expressing likes/dislikes

J'aime bien . . .

Je n'aime pas du tout . . . Je déteste . . .

23 Expressing need/necessity

J'ai besoin de . . . Je dois . . . Il me faut . . .

24 Offering

Puis-je . . .? Je peux . . .? Permets-moi de . . ./Permettez-moi de . . .
Tu permets?/Vous permettez? Veux-tu . . .?/Voulez-vous . . .?

25 Ordering

Donne moi . . ./Donnez-moi . . . Je voudrais . . .

26 Asking for/giving permission

See also **offering**, section 24.

C'est possible? Il est possible de . . .?

Avec plaisir. Bien sûr. D'accord.

* Avoid this expression unless you know how to use the subjunctive + **ne**.

27 Expressing possibility/impossibility

C'est possible.   On peut . . .   Peut-être.

Ce n'est pas possible.   C'est impossible.

28 Expressing preference

J'aime mieux . . .   Je préfère . . .

29 Refusing

Je regrette mais je ne peux pas accepter.   Non merci.   Je ne veux pas.

30 Expressing regret

Je regrette . . .   Je suis désolé.

31 Reporting

On m'a dit que . . .   On dit que . . .

32 Requesting

Peut-on . . .?   Puis-je . . .?   C'est possible?   . . . s'il te plaît?/. . . s'il vous plaît?

33 Expressing satisfaction/dissatisfaction

J'en suis très content(e).   Très bien.   Ça va bien.

Ça ne va pas (du tout).   Je n'en suis pas content(e) (du tout).

34 Socializing

Agreed, all right!	D'accord.
Cheer up!	Courage!
Come now!	Allons donc! Voyons donc!
Good morning **Good afternoon**	Bonjour
Goodbye	Au revoir
Good evening	Bonsoir
Good night	Bonne nuit
Good health!	Santé!
Good luck!	Bonne chance!
Happy birthday!	Bon anniversaire!
Happy Christmas!	Joyeux Noël!
Happy New Year!	Bonne Année!
How are you?	Comment vas-tu?/Comment allez-vous?
Have a good trip!	Bon voyage!
Have a good meal!	Bon appétit!
Sleep well!	Dors bien!/Dormez bien!

35 Expressing surprise

Tiens!/Tenez!   Quelle idée!   Quelle surprise!   Ça m'étonne(ra) beaucoup.   Vraiment?

36 Expressing sympathy

Quel dommage!   Je suis désolé(e).   Mes condoléances. (For a bereavement.)

37 Expressing thanks/gratitude

Merci beaucoup/bien.   Je te/vous remercie de . . .   J'en suis très reconnaissant.

38 Acknowledging thanks

Tu es/vous êtes bien aimable.   Je t'en prie./Je vous en prie.   De rien.

39 Expressing understanding/misunderstanding

Ah oui, je comprends.   D'accord.   Je regrette mais je ne comprends pas.
Je n'ai pas bien compris.

40 Warning

Attention!   Il est interdit de . . .   Il ne faut pas . . .   Prenez garde!

3 NOTIONS

1 DIRECTION/DISTANCE LA DIRECTION/LA DISTANCE

bottom *(end)* le fond
corner le coin
in the distance au loin
in the direction of du côté de
east l'est (m)
elsewhere ailleurs
end le bout
everywhere partout
far loin
here ici
in front devant
inside dedans, à l'intérieur
kilometre le kilomètre
left gauche
on/to the left à gauche
long (de) long
lower *(e.g. floor)* inférieur
metre le mètre
mile le mille
near (tout) près
near to près de
neighbouring voisin
next to à côté de, auprès de
north le nord
nowhere nulle part
outside dehors, à l'extérieur
place le lieu, l'endroit (m)
right droite
on/to the right à droite
side le côté
on all sides de tous côtés
on one side d'un côté
on the other side de l'autre côté
situated (at) situé à
somewhere quelque part
south le sud
space l'espace (m)
straight on tout droit
there là
here and there çà et là
over there là-bas
up there là-haut
upper *(e.g. floor)* (à l'étage supérieur)
west l'ouest (m)
wide (de) large
NB La maison se trouve **à** 3 kms de l'école.
Le jardin a 30 mètres **de long.**
Le jardin a 25 mètres **de large.**
Le bâtiment a 20 mètres **de haut.**
Le jardin **est long de** 30 mètres.
Le jardin **est large de** 25 mètres.
Le bâtiment **est haut de** 20 mètres.

2 PLACE/POSITION LES ENDROITS/LES SITUATIONS

before devant
behind derrière
bottom le bas, le fond
centre le centre
elsewhere ailleurs
end le bout, l'extrémité (f)
everywhere partout
here and there çà et là
inside dedans, à l'intérieur (m)
middle le centre, le milieu
nearby tout près
nowhere nulle part
on sur
outside dehors, à l'extérieur (m)
over dessus, par-dessus
place l'endroit (m); le lieu (un bel endroit: son lieu de naissance)
side le côté
space l'espace (m)
together ensemble
top le haut
under sous, au-dessous de

3 QUALITY

See **Grammar section: adjectives and adverbs** (pp. 2-5)

Colours Les couleurs
black noir
blue bleu
brown brun
dark foncé
dark brown marron (invariable)
green vert
grey gris
light clair
orange orange
pink rose
purple pourpre
red rouge
red (of hair) roux
white blanc/blanche
yellow jaune
NB When using a compound adjective of colour (e.g. light blue, dark green) do NOT make the adjectives agree with the noun.

e.g. la robe **verte**
but: la robe **vert foncé**

Materials Les matières
acrylic acrylique
bronze (le) bronze (e.g., de bronze/en bronze de cuivre/en cuivre etc.)
copper (le) cuivre
cotton (le) coton
glass (le) verre
gold l'or
lace la dentelle
lead le plomb
leather le cuir
metal (le) métal
nylon le nylon

ovenproof (plat) allant au four
silver l'argent
stainless steel l'acier inoxydable
wood le bois
wool la laine

4 NUMBER/QUANTITY LES NOMBRES/LES QUANTITES

1 un
2 deux
3 trois
4 quatre
5 cinq
6 six
7 sept
8 huit
9 neuf
10 dix
11 onze
12 douze
13 treize
14 quatorze
15 quinze
16 seize
17 dix-sept
18 dix-huit
19 dix-neuf
20 vingt
21 vingt et un
22 vingt-deux, etc.
30 trente
31 trente et un
32 trente-deux, etc.
40 quarante
41 quarante et un
42 quarante-deux, etc.
50 cinquante
51 cinquante et un
52 cinquante-deux, etc.
60 soixante
61 soixante et un
62 soixante-deux, etc.
70 soixante-dix
71 soixante et onze
72 soixante-douze, etc.
80 quatre-vingts
81 quatre-vingt-un, etc.
90 quatre-vingt-dix
91 quatre-vingt-onze, etc.
99 quatre-vingt-dix-neuf
100 cent
200 deux cents
300 trois cents
301 trois cent un
450 quatre cent cinquante

NB The 's' is omitted in the plural hundreds when another number follows.

1000 mille
3000 trois mille
NB An 's' is never added to **mille** (=*thousand*)
Milles=*miles*
1,000,000 un million

about 10 une dizaine (de)
about 20 une vingtaine (de)
about 100 une centaine (de)
a dozen une douzaine (de)
a quarter un quart
a half une moitié
half demi(e)
three-quarters trois-quarts
a third un tiers
two-thirds deux tiers
a fifth un cinquième, etc.

1 kilo=1000g=2.2 lb
1 litre=1¾ pints

first premier, première
second second, deuxième
third troisième, etc.

Note particularly the spelling of **cinquième** and **neuvième**.

When expressing the date, remember to use:
le premier avril *the first of April*
le trois décembre *the third of December*
le vingt-trois février *the twenty-third of February, etc.*

Expressions of quantity

a bar of ... une tablette (de chocolat)
un lingot (d'or) (*gold*)
un pain (de savon) (*soap*)
a bottle of ... une bouteille de ...
a box of ... une boîte de ...
enough of ... assez de ...
a jar of ... un pot de ...
a kilo of ... un kilo de ...
a little of ... un peu de ...
so much of ... tant de
too much of ... trop de ...
a packet of ... un paquet de ...
a pound of ... un demi-kilo de ... une livre de ...
a tin of ... une boîte de ...

5 EMOTIONS/FEELINGS LES EMOTIONS/LES SENTIMENTS

to admire admirer
to be afraid avoir peur
anger la colère
to get angry se mettre en colère; se fâcher
to annoy ennuyer
anxiety l'inquiétude (f)
to be anxious s'inquiéter
to boast se vanter
to bore ennuyer
boredom l'ennui (m)
care le soin: (*worry*) le souci
to care for, to look after soigner
confidence la confiance
to complain se plaindre
to console consoler
to cry pleurer
to delight enchanter, charmer, ravir
despair le désespoir
to despise mépriser
to disappoint décevoir
to discourage décourager
to disturb déranger
doubt le doute
to doubt douter
to encourage encourager
to endure supporter
to enjoy jouir de

to enjoy (doing something) se plaire à (faire quelque chose)
to enjoy oneself s'amuser
enthusiasm l'enthousiasme (m)
envy l'envie (f)
NB avoir envie de *to feel like (doing . . .)*
to expect s'attendre à
to fear craindre
fear la crainte, la peur
to forgive pardonner à
friendship l'amitié (f)
to frighten effrayer; faire peur à
frightened effrayé
grateful reconnaissant
gratitude la reconnaissance
groan le gémissement
to groan gémir
happy heureux (m), heureuse (f)
to hate détester
hatred la haine
to hope espérer
hope l'espoir (m)
horror l'horreur (f)
to be interested in s'intéresser à
joy la joie
to laugh at se moquer de
laughter les rires (mpl)
to laugh rire
to like, love aimer
love l'amour (m)
to mistrust se méfier de
to be in a good mood être de bonne humeur
to be in a bad mood être de mauvaise humeur
nice (*of a person*) sympathique, aimable, gentil(le)
to pity plaindre
pity la pitié
What a pity! Quel dommage!
to please plaire à
pleasure le plaisir
to prefer aimer mieux, préférer
pride l'orgueil (m)
proud fier (m), fière (f)
to relieve soulager
sad triste
sadness la tristesse
to satisfy satisfaire à
to scold gronder
shame la honte
to be ashamed avoir honte (de)
to shout crier
shudder le frémissement
to shudder frémir, frissonner
to sigh soupirer
to sob sangloter
to be sorry regretter
to suffer souffrir
surprise la surprise, l'étonnement
to surprise étonner, surprendre
to be surprised s'étonner
to suspect soupçonner
sympathy la compassion, la sympathie
tears les larmes (fpl)
to burst into tears fondre en larmes
to tease taquiner
terror la terreur
to terrify effrayer, épouvanter, terrifier
to thank remercier
to threaten menacer
to trouble gêner
to trust se fier à
to warn avertir, prévenir
to welcome accueillir

6 TIME L'HEURE/LE TEMPS

after après
at first d'abord
at last enfin
again de nouveau, encore une fois
ago il y a
already déjà
always toujours
at once aussitôt, tout de suite
before avant
to begin commencer
beginning le commencement, le début
century le siècle
clock la pendule (*house*); l'horloge (f) (*public building*)
day le jour, la journée
day before la veille
day before yesterday avant-hier
early de bonne heure
end la fin
to end finir, terminer
eve la veille
evening le soir, la soirée
formerly jadis
fortnight quinze jours, une quinzaine
from time to time de temps en temps
future l'avenir
in the future à l'avenir
half an hour une demi-heure
hour l'heure (f)
immediately immédiatement, tout de suite
to last durer
late tard, en retard
later plus tard
midday midi (m)
midnight minuit (m)
minute la minute
moment le moment, l'instant (m)
month le mois
morning le matin, la matinée
next prochain (*adj.*); ensuite (*adv.*)
never ne . . . jamais
night la nuit
at nightfall à la nuit tombante, à la tombée de la nuit
now de nos jours; maintenant
often souvent
once une fois
to pass (*of time*) s'écouler
in the past autrefois
period (*of time*) l'époque (f)
precisely (à cinq heures) précises
at present à présent, actuellement
presently tout à l'heure
previously auparavant
a quarter of an hour un quart d'heure
quickly vite
rarely rarement
to remain rester

second la seconde
since depuis
soon bientôt
so soon si tôt
a stay un séjour
still encore, toujours
straightaway immédiatement, tout de suite
suddenly tout à coup
time (*by the clock*) l'heure (f)
time (*occasion*) la fois
a long time longtemps
during this time pendant ce temps
in time à temps
then puis
today aujourd'hui
tomorrow demain
up till now jusqu'ici
usually d'habitude
week la semaine
weekend le weekend
when quand, lorsque
year l'an (m), l'année (f)
yesterday hier
yesterday morning hier matin
yesterday evening hier soir
every day tous les jours
every afternoon tous les après-midi
every evening tous les soirs
every morning tous les matins
every month tous les mois
every week toutes les semaines
every year tous les ans
the next day le lendemain
the next morning le lendemain matin
next week la semaine prochaine
next month le mois prochain
last month le mois dernier
last week la semaine dernière

7 DATES/FESTIVALS LES DATES/LES FÊTES

anniversary; birthday l'anniversaire (m); la fête
birthday party la réunion d'anniversaire
bank holiday la fête légale, le jour férié
baptism le baptême
Christmas Noël (m)
at Christmas à Noël
congratulations félicitations (fpl)
to congratulate féliciter
Easter Pâques (m)
first of April le jour des poissons d'avril
first of May la fête du muguet; la fête du travail
Hallowe'en la veille de la Toussaint
14th July la Fête Nationale
Shrove Tuesday le mardi gras
New Year's Day le Jour de l'An
New Year's Eve la veille du Jour de l'An
wedding le mariage; les noces (fpl)

Days of the week Les jours de la semaine
Sunday dimanche
Monday lundi
Tuesday mardi
Wednesday mercredi
Thursday jeudi
Friday vendredi
Saturday samedi

All the days of the week in French are masculine, and are written with small letters.

on Monday lundi
on Mondays le lundi
Never use **'sur'** with days of the week

Months of the year Les mois de l'année
January janvier
February février
March mars
April avril
May mai
June juin
July juillet
August août
September septembre
October octobre
November novembre
December décembre

All the months of the year in French are masculine, and are written with small letters.

in January en janvier, au mois de janvier.

4 VOCABULARY TOPIC AREAS

The following lists contain key words for a number of topics which will be of use to you when preparing for the GCSE examination in French. Try to learn a set number of key words each week from each section. You must begin this preparation work well in advance of the GCSE exam in order to increase your knowledge and confidence in the subject. Vocabulary learning cannot be left until the last minute. These vocabulary topic lists are all based on the everyday subjects which may be included in the examination. Remember that your success depends on . . .

PREPARATION PRACTICE REVISION

CAFÉ/HOTEL/RESTAURANT LE CAFÉ/L'HÔTEL/LE RESTAURANT

See also **Food** and **Drink**

aperitif un apéritif
bar (counter) le comptoir
with bathroom avec salle de bains
bill (hotel) la note
bill (restaurant) l'addition (f)
boarding-house la pension
boarder le(la) pensionnaire
full-board la pension complète
half-board la demi-pension
breakfast le petit déjeuner
chambermaid la femme de chambre
cook le cuisinier, la cuisinière
head cook le chef de cuisine
cover charge le couvert
cup la tasse
dessert le dessert
dining-room la salle à manger
dinner le dîner
dish le plat
drink la boisson
to drink boire
to eat manger
fork la fourchette
glass le verre
guest un(e) invité(e)
hotelier un hôtelier
inn une auberge
inn-keeper un aubergiste
lift un ascenseur
lunch le déjeuner
to have lunch déjeuner
(to have a meal) prendre un repas
manager le patron
menu le menu, la carte
napkin la serviette
to order commander
plate une assiette
proprietor le patron
pub le bistrot, le cabaret, l'estaminet (m)
room la chambre
double-room la chambre à deux personnes
single room une chambre à un lit
service charge included service compris
shower la douche
spoon la cuiller
stairs l'escalier (m)
supper le souper
table cloth la nappe
to lay the table mettre le couvert
tea (drink) le thé
tea (meal) le goûter
waiter le garçon
head waiter le maître d'hôtel
waitress la serveuse
VAT le TVA (taxe à la valeur ajoutée)

CAMPING LE CAMPING

to boil faire bouillir
to go camping faire du camping
camp bed le lit de camp
camping equipment le matériel de camping
camp fire le feu de camp
camping gas le camping-gaz
campsite le terrain de camping
camping stove le réchaud
to cook faire cuire
dustbin la poubelle
full complet/complète
gamesroom la salle de jeux
ground sheet le tapis de sol
hammer le marteau
lantern la lanterne
(tent) **peg** le piquet
pitch un emplacement
to pitch a tent dresser/monter la tente
reception la réception, le bureau d'acceuil
rucksack le sac à dos
shower la douche
sleeping-bag le sac de couchage
tent la tente
to take down the tent démonter la tente
torch la torche électrique
water-container le bidon à eau

CLOTHES LES VÊTEMENTS/LES HABITS

apron le tablier
belt la ceinture
beret le béret
blazer le blazer
blouse le chemisier
boot la botte, la bottine
braces les bretelles (fpl)
button le bouton
cap le casque, le képi (police, army)
cardigan le tricot, la veste
cashmere le cachemire

coat le manteau
cotton le coton
dress la robe
dressing-gown la robe de chambre
dressmaker le couturier, la couturière
dungarees les bleus (mpl), la salopette
embroidery la broderie
fur la fourrure
glove le gant
handkerchief le mouchoir
hat le chapeau
helmet le casque
jacket le veston, la veste
jeans le blue-jean
lace la dentelle
leather le cuir
linen le lin
made-to measure sur mesure
material l'étoffe (f), le tissu
nightdress la robe de nuit
nylon le nylon
overcoat le pardessus
overall la blouse
pinafore dress la chasuble
plastic la (matière) plastique
pocket la poche
pullover le pull (over)
pyjamas le pyjama
rags les haillons (mpl)
raincoat un imperméable
ready-made prêt-à-porter
sandal la sandale
scarf une écharpe (long), le foulard (square)
shirt la chemise
shoe la chaussure, le soulier
shorts le short
silk la soie
size la taille
collar size l'encolure (f)
shoe size la pointure
skirt la jupe
sleeve la manche
slipper la pantoufle
sock la chaussette
stocking le bas
suit le complet, le costume, le tailleur
sweater le chandail
terylene le térylène, le tergal
tie la cravate
tights le collant
trainers les baskets (mpl)
trousers le pantalon
short trousers la culotte
trouser-suit un ensemble-pantalon
velvet le velours
waistcoat le gilet
windcheater le blouson
wool la laine

COUNTRIES/NATIONALITIES LES PAYS ET LES NATIONALITÉS

Countries	**Les pays**	**Inhabitants/Les habitants**
America	l'Amérique (f)	un(e) Américain(e)
USA	les États-Unis (mpl)	un(e) Américain(e)
Asia	l'Asie (f)	un(e) Asiatique
Austria	l'Autriche (f)	un(e) Autrichien(ne)
Belgium	la Belgique	un(e) Belge
Canada	le Canada	un(e) Canadien(ne)
China	la Chine	un(e) Chinois(e)
Denmark	le Danemark	un(e) Danois(e)
England	l'Angleterre (f)	un(e) Anglais(e)
Europe	l'Europe (f)	un(e) Européen(ne)
Germany	l'Allemagne (f)	un(e) Allemand(e)
Great Britain	la Grande-Bretagne	un(e) Britannique
Greece	la Grèce	un Grec, une Grecque
Holland	la Hollande	un(e) Hollandais(e)
Italy	l'Italie (f)	un(e) Italien(ne)
India	l'Inde (f)	un(e) Indien(ne)
Ireland	l'Irlande (f)	un(e) Irlandais(e)
Japan	le Japon	un(e) Japonais(e)
Luxembourg	le Luxembourg	un(e) Luxembourgeois(e)
Mexico	le Mexique	un(e) Mexicain(e)
Netherlands	les Pays Bas (mpl)	un(e) Néerlandais(e)
New Zealand	la Nouvelle Zélande	un(e) Néozélandais(e)
Norway	la Norvège	un(e) Norvégien(ne)
Poland	la Pologne	un(e) Polonais(e)
Portugal	le Portugal	un(e) Portugais(e)
Russia	la Russie	un(e) Russe
USSR	l'URSS (f)	un(e) Russe
Scotland	l'Écosse (f)	un(e) Écossais(e)
S Africa	l'Afrique (f) du Sud	un(e) Sud-Africain(e)
Spain	l'Espagne (f)	un(e) Espagnol(e)
Sweden	la Suède	un(e) Suédois(e)
Switzerland	la Suisse	un Suisse, une Suissesse
UK	le Royaume-Uni	un(e) habitant(e) du Royaume-Uni
Wales	le Pays de Galles	un(e) Gallois(e)
Yugoslavia	la Yougoslavie	un(e) Yougoslave

COUNTRYSIDE LA CAMPAGNE

bank (of a river) le bord, la rive
bird un oiseau
e.g., **blackbird** le merle
crow le corbeau
cuckoo le coucou
dove la colombe
duck le canard
eagle un aigle
feather la plume
kingfisher le martin-pêcheur
nest le nid
nightingale le rossignol
owl le hibou
robin le rouge-gorge
skylark une alouette
sparrow le moineau
swallow une hirondelle
swan le cygne
thrush la grive
bridge le pont
cave la caverne
cottage la chaumière
countryman le paysan
countrywoman la paysanne
current le courant
farm la ferme
e.g., **barley** l'orge (f)
barn la grange
cart la charrette
cattle le bétail
combine-harvester la moissonneuse-batteuse
corn le blé
cowshed une étable
crop la récolte
dairy la laiterie
farmer le fermier
farmer's wife la fermière
farmyard la basse-cour
fertilizer l'engrais(m)
flock le troupeau
fork la fourche
gate la barrière
goose une oie
harvest la moisson
hay le foin
hen la poule
henhouse le poulailler
loft le grenier
milk le lait
mill le moulin
oats l'avoine (f)
orchard le verger
pigsty la porcherie
plough la charrue
to plough labourer
to reap faucher
shepherd le berger
to sow semer
stable une écurie
straw la paille
tractor le tracteur
turkey le dindon, la dinde
field le champ, la prairie, le pré
to flow couler
flower la fleur
e.g., **buttercup** le bouton d'or
clover le trèfle
daisy la marguerite
dandelion le pissenlit
nettle une ortie
thistle le chardon
wild flowers les fleurs sauvages
forest la forêt
hamlet le hameau
hayrick la meule de foin
hill la colline
insect un insecte
e.g., **ant** la fourmi
bee une abeille
butterfly le papillon
cicada la cigale
fly la mouche
grasshopper la sauterelle
mosquito le moustique
spider une araignée
wasp la guêpe
lake le lac
landscape le paysage
mountain la montagne
mud la boue
path le sentier, le chemin
pebble le caillou (pl: cailloux)
picnic le pique-nique
to picnic pique-niquer
pond un étang, la mare
river le fleuve, la rivière
road la route
slope la pente
spring (water) la source
stone la pierre
stream le ruisseau
tree un arbre
e.g., **ash** le frêne
beech le hêtre
branch la branche
bush le buisson
(horse) **chestnut** le marronier
(sweet) **chestnut** le châtaignier
copse le taillis
elm un orme
fir le sapin
hawthorn l'aubépine (f)
hedge la haie
holly le houx
ivy le lierre
lime le tilleul
oak le chêne
pine le pin
poplar le peuplier
trunk le tronc
willow le saule
wood le bois
waterfall la cascade, la fontaine
wooded boisé
valley la vallée
village le village

DAILY ROUTINE LA ROUTINE JOURNALIÈRE

to get up se lever
to have a shower prendre une douche

to have a bath prendre un bain
to get washed se laver
to brush one's teeth se brosser les dents
to go down(stairs) descendre (l'escalier)
to go into the kitchen aller dans la cuisine
to have breakfast prendre le petit déjeuner
to leave for school partir pour l'école
to catch the bus attraper l'autobus
to arrive at school arriver à l'école
to chat with one's friends bavarder avec ses amis
to go to class aller en classe
to have lunch in the canteen déjeuner dans la cantine
to go back to class retourner en classe
to go back home rentrer à la maison
to have tea prendre le goûter
to do homework faire les devoirs
to watch television regarder la télévision
to have supper souper
to go out sortir
to go to bed se coucher
to go to sleep s'endormir

EDUCATION L'ENSEIGNEMENT

art le dessin
assembly l'assemblée (f)
biology la biologie
chemistry la chimie
civics l'instruction civique
college une École Normale
commerce le commerce
comprehensive school le CES (Collège d'Enseignement Secondaire)
computer science l'informatique
corporal punishment le châtiment corporel
to take a course suivre un cours
craft les travaux pratiques
detention la colle (fam.)/la retenue
domestic science les arts ménagers/les études ménagères
to draw dessiner
economics l'économie politique
exam un examen
to take an exam passer un examen
to pass an exam réussir/être reçu à un examen
English l'anglais
essay une composition/une rédaction/une dissertation
experiment une expérience
free period une leçon de perme
geography la géographie
geology la géologie
German l'allemand
Greek le grec
gymnastics la gymnastique
gymnasium la salle de gymnastique
head le directeur/la directrice (primary school) le proviseur (secondary school)
deputy **head** (pastoral) le censeur
history l'histoire
home economics les cours ménagers
laboratory le laboratoire
Latin le latin
to learn apprendre
lesson la leçon/le cours
Italian l'italien
maths les mathématiques
metalwork le travail des métaux
music la musique
natural science les sciences naturelles
nursery school l'école maternelle
PE l'éducation physique
physics la physique
private school une école privée/une école libre
Russian le russe
scripture les études religieuses
secondary school le collège
sewing la couture
shorthand/typing la sténodactylographie
social sciences les sciences humaines
Spanish l'espagnol
studies les études
to study étudier
supervisor le surveillant
to swot potasser/piocher (e.g. mon français)
technical drawing le dessin industriel
teacher (primary school) un instituteur/une institutrice, (secondary school) un professeur
time-table un emploi du temps
translation la version
uniform l'uniforme scolaire
university l'université
Welsh le gallois
woodwork le travail du bois

FOOD/DRINK LA NOURRITURE/LES BOISSONS

bacon le bacon/le lard
beef le boeuf
beer la bière
pint of **beer** un demi
bread le pain
bread roll le petit pain
butter le beurre
cake le gâteau (pl: les gâteaux)
champagne le champagne
cheese le fromage
chips les (pommes) frites (fpl)
crescent roll le croissant
crisps les chips (mpl), les pommes (fpl) chip
chocolate le chocolat
chop la côtelette
cider le cidre
coffee le café
cream la crème
crumb la miette
egg un oeuf
fish le poisson
fruit le fruit
e.g., **apple** la pomme
apricot un abricot
banana la banane
blackberry la mûre
cherry la cerise
(red) **currant** la groseille
gooseberry la groseille à maquereau
grapefruit le pamplemousse
grapes les raisins (mpl)
lemon le citron
melon le melon

orange une orange
peach la pêche
pear la poire
pineapple un ananas
plum la prune
raspberry la framboise
rhubarb la rhubarbe
strawberry la fraise
fruit juice le jus de fruit
ham le jambon
ice cream la glace
jam la confiture
lamb l'agneau (m)
lemonade la limonade
lemon squash le citron pressé
marmalade la confiture d'oranges
meat la viande
milk le lait
mushroom le champignon
mustard la moutarde
omelette une omelette
pancake la crêpe
pepper le poivre
pork le porc
potato la pomme de terre
preserves les conserves (fpl)
roast rôti
salt le sel
sandwich le sandwich
sausage la saucisse (large), le saucisson (small)
slice la tranche
snail un escargot
soup le potage, la soupe
starter un hors d'oeuvre
steak le bifteck, le steak
e.g., **well cooked** bien cuit
medium à point
rare saignant
sugar le sucre
tea (drink) le thé
tea (meal) le goûter
today's speciality (in a restaurant) le plat du jour
toast le pain grillé
trout la truite
veal le veau
vegetables les légumes (mpl)
e.g., **artichoke** un artichaut
asparagus les asperges (fpl)
bean le haricot
runner bean le haricot vert
beetroot la betterave
Brussels sprouts les choux (mpl) de Bruxelles
cabbage le chou
carrot la carotte
cauliflower le chou-fleur
celery le céléri
cress le cresson
cucumber le concombre
garlic l'ail (m)
leek le poireau
lettuce la laitue
onion un oignon
parsley le persil
parsnip le panais
peas les petits pois
potato la pomme de terre
radish le radis
salad la salade
spinach les épinards (mpl)
sweetcorn le maïs
tomato la tomate
turnip le navet
vinegar le vinaigre
water l'eau (f)
mineral/spa water l'eau minérale
wine le vin (e.g. rouge, blanc, rosé)
table wine le vin du pays, ordinaire, vin de table
guaranteed vintage appellation contrôlée
yoghurt le yaourt
flavoured **yoghurt** le yaourt parfumé

HEALTH/ILLNESS LA SANTÉ/LES MALADIES

ambulance une ambulance
antiseptic cream la crème antiseptique
aspirin l'aspirine (f)
bandage/dressing le pansement
to be better aller mieux
to feel better se sentir mieux
to be cold avoir froid
to be hot avoir chaud
to be hungry avoir faim
to be thirsty avoir soif
blind aveugle
blindness la cécité
(a) **boil** un furoncle
bruise un bleu
to bruise se faire un bleu (se meurtrir)
to burn (oneself) se brûler
capsule (tablet) le cachet
chemist le pharmacien
chemist's shop la pharmacie
chicken-pox la varicelle
a cold un rhume
to catch cold prendre froid, attraper un rhume, s'enrhumer
to have a cold être enrhumé(e)
cough la toux
to cough tousser
to cure/heal guérir
to be cured/healed se guérir
to cut (se) couper
deaf sourd(e)
deafness la surdité
diarrhoea la diarrhée
dizzy (e.g., *I feel dizzy*) Ma tête me tourne
doctor le médecin
dumb muet(te)
dumbness (physical) le mutisme
to faint s'évanouir
to fall ill tomber malade
to feel ill se sentir souffrant(e)
first aid post le poste de secours
'flu la grippe
German measles la rubeole
harm/injury le mal
health la santé
to be in bad health se porter mal
to be in good health se porter bien
headache le mal de tête
to have a headache avoir mal à la tête

help l'aide (f), le secours
to have hiccups avoir le hoquet
to hurt oneself se blesser, se faire mal
ill malade
to be ill être malade
illness la maladie
to look after soigner
measles la rougeole
medicine le médicament
misfortune le malheur
mumps les oreillons (mpl)
nurse un infirmier, une infirmière
pain la douleur
prescription une ordonnance
pulse le pouls
to take one's pulse tâter le pouls
to recover se remettre, se récupérer
to be sick vomir
to feel sick avoir mal au coeur
to be air sick avoir le mal de l'air
to be sea sick avoir le mal de mer
serious grave
to sneeze éternuer
spots les boutons (mpl)
to sprain se fouler, se faire une entorse
sticking plaster le sparadrap
sting la piqure
to be stung être piqué par . . .
(e.g., **une abeille** bee
une guêpe wasp
un frelon hornet
un moustique mosquito)
sunstroke un coup de soleil
swollen enflé
tablet le comprimé
to have a high temperature avoir de la fièvre
bad tooth la dent gâtée
to have a tummy upset avoir une crise de foie
to be fit and well être en forme
wound une blessure
to wound (se) blesser
NB also 'to hurt' in various parts of the body:
avoir mal à . . .
e.g., **avoir mal au bras** to have a pain in the arm
avoir mal aux dents to have toothache
avoir mal au dos to have backache
avoir mal à l'oreille to have earache,
etc.

HUMAN BODY
LE CORPS HUMAIN

ankle la cheville
arm le bras
back le dos
beard la barbe
blood le sang
bone un os
breath l'haleine (f), le souffle
cheek la joue
chest la poitrine
chin le menton
complexion le teint
ear une oreille
elbow le coude
eye(s) un oeil, les yeux (m)
eyebrow le sourcil
eyelash le cil
eyelid la paupière
face la figure, le visage
finger le doigt
fist le poing
flesh la chair
foot le pied
forehead le front
hair les cheveux (mpl)
hand la main
head la tête
heart le coeur
heel le talon
hip la hanche
knee(s) le(s) genou(x)
leg la jambe
lip la lèvre
lung le poumon
mouth la bouche
moustache la (les) moustache(s)
nail un ongle
neck le cou
nose le nez
shoulder une épaule
skin la peau
stomach l'estomac (m), le ventre
thigh la cuisse
throat la gorge
thumb le pouce
tongue la langue
tooth la dent
toe un orteil
voice la voix
waist la taille
wrinkle la ride
wrist le poignet

ACCIDENT/INJURY
LES ACCIDENTS

ambulance l'ambulance (f)
to bandage bander
to break briser/casser
to break one's arm/leg se casser le bras /la jambe
to bump into heurter
to collide (with a person) heurter
to collide (with a vehicle) heurter/entrer en collision avec
to crush écraser
to be crushed s'écraser/être écrasé(e)
to cut (e.g. one's finger) se couper (le doigt)
to damage abîmer
to drown (se) noyer
a fatal accident un accident mortel
Help! Au secours!
to help aider
to hit frapper
to hurt (se) faire mal à
to injure (se) blesser
to jostle/push bousculer
to knock down/over renverser
a motor accident un accident de voiture
to have (e.g. a leg) **in plaster** avoir (la jambe) dans le plâtre
a road accident un accident de la route

a serious accident un accident grave
to be shipwrecked faire naufrage
to sprain se fouler
stretcher le brancard
to be stung by . . . être piqué par . . .
to tear déchirer
to trap (se) coincer
to twist one's ankle se fouler la cheville/se faire une entorse

HOME LA MAISON

attic le grenier
basement le sous-sol
bathroom la salle de bains
bedroom la chambre à coucher
bell la sonnette
block of flats un immeuble
bolt le verrou
building le bâtiment
bungalow le bungalow, le pavillon
caretaker le (la) concierge
caretaker's room / **porter's lodge** la loge (du concierge)
ceiling le plafond
cellar la cave
central heating le chauffage central
to clean nettoyer
corridor le couloir
cupboard une armoire, le placard
curtains les rideaux (mpl)
dining-room la salle à manger
door la porte
entrance-hall une entrée
flat un appartement
council flat une HLM (Habitation à Loyer Modéré)
floor le plancher
floor (i.e. storey) un étage
front door la porte d'entrée
furniture les meubles (mpl)
garage le garage
gate la grille, la porte
ground floor le rez-de-chaussée
guest room la chambre d'amis
household le ménage
kitchen la cuisine
key la clé, la clef
landing le palier
lavatory le cabinet de toilette
lift un ascenseur
living-room la salle de séjour
lock la serrure
to lock fermer à clé
lounge le salon
to overlook donner sur
rent le loyer
to rent louer
roof le toit
room la pièce, la salle, la chambre (*bedroom*)
second home une résidence secondaire
shutter le contrevent, le volet
stairs un escalier
study le cabinet de travail
tenant le (la) locataire
threshold le seuil
utility/laundry room la buanderie
villa une villa
wall le mur
window la fenêtre
window-sill le rebord de la fenêtre
yard la cour

Bathroom La salle de bains

bath la salle de bains
to bathe se baigner
bidet le bidet
razor-point la prise du rasoir
shower la douche
soap le savon
sponge une éponge
tap le robinet
toothbrush la brosse à dents
toothpaste le dentifrice
towel la serviette (de toilette)
washbowl le lavabo

Bedroom La chambre (à coucher)

alarm-clock le réveil, le réveille-matin
bed le lit
bedside-table le chevet
bedside lamp la lampe de chevet
blanket la couverture
bolster le traversin
chest of drawers la commode
comb le peigne
drawer le tiroir
dressing-table la table de toilette
duvet le duvet
hairbrush la brosse à cheveux
hand mirror la glace à main
to make one's bed faire son lit
mattress le matelas
mirror la glace, le miroir
pillow un oreiller
rug la descente du lit
sheet le drap
shelf le rayon
wardrobe une armoire, la garde-robe, la penderie

Dining-room La salle à manger

chair la chaise
cup la tasse
fork la fourchette
glass le verre
knife le couteau
to lay the table mettre le couvert
mustard la moutarde
napkin la serviette
oil l'huile (f)
pepper le poivre
place-setting le couvert
plate une assiette
salt le sel
saucer la soucoupe
sideboard le buffet
silver (adj.) d'argent, en argent
spoon la cuiller
stainless steel (adj.) d'acier inoxydable, en acier inoxydable, (frequently) en inox
table la table
tablecloth la nappe
tray le plateau
vinegar le vinaigre

Kitchen La cuisine

broom le balai
bucket le seau
coffee-pot la cafetière
cooker la cuisinière
dishwasher le lave-vaisselle
duster le torchon
electric mixer le batteur (électrique)
freezer le congélateur
fridge le frigo, le réfrigerateur
frying-pan la poêle
iron le fer à repasser
to iron repasser
to do the ironing faire le repassage
jug la cruche (large), le cruchon (small), le pot
kettle la bouilloire
micro-wave oven le four à micro-ondes
oven le four
pressure-cooker un auto-cuiseur
saucepan la casserole
sink un évier
spin-dryer une essoreuse
stew-pan la marmite
stool le tabouret
stove le fourneau, le poêle
tap le robinet
teapot la théière
vacuum-cleaner un aspirateur
to wash clothes faire la lessive
washing-machine la machine à laver
to wash dishes faire la vaisselle

Living-room/lounge Le salon/la salle de séjour

armchair le fauteuil
bookcase la bibliothèque
carpet le tapis
clock la pendule
curtains les rideaux (mpl)
cushion le coussin
hi-fi la chaîne hi-fi
nest of tables la table cigogne
occasional table la petite table de salon
picture le tableau
radio la radio
transistor radio le transistor
record-player un électrophone, le tourne-disque(s)
settee le canapé
shelf le rayon
standard lamp le lampadaire
stereo le système stéréo
tape-recorder le magnétophone
TV le poste de télévision, le téléviseur
video-recorder le magnétoscope

Garden Le jardin

bench le banc
to dig bêcher
flower la fleur
e.g., **carnation** un oeillet
  clover le trèfle
  daisy la marguerite
  daffodil la jonquille
  hyacinth la jacinthe
  pansy la pensée
  rose la rose
  rose bush le rosier
  tulip la tulipe
  wallflower la giroflée des murailles
flowerbed la plate-bande, le parterre
foliage le feuillage
fork la fourche
grass l'herbe (f)
greenhouse la serre
to grow pousser (intransitive), cultiver (transitive)
hedge la haie
kitchen garden le jardin potager
ladder une échelle
lawn le gazon, la pelouse
lawn-mower la tondeuse
leaf la feuille
path une allée
plant la plante
rake le rateau
seed la graine
see-saw la balançoire
spade la bêche
sundial le cadran solaire
(child's) **swing** une escarpolette
tree un arbre
e.g., **ash** le frêne
  beech le hêtre
  chestnut (horse) le marronier
  chestnut (sweet) le châtaignier
  elm un orme
  fir le sapin
  hawthorn une aubépine
  holly le houx
  ivy le lierre
  lime le tilleul
  oak le chêne
  plane tree le platane
  poplar le peuplier
  willow le saule
  yew un if
vegetables les légumes (mpl)
(see also **'food'** topic area)
weed la mauvaise herbe
wheelbarrow la brouette

JOBS/PROFESSIONS LES MÉTIERS/LES PROFESSIONS

accountant le(la) comptable
air-hostess une hôtesse de l'air
antique-dealer un(e) antiquaire
apprentice un(e) apprenti(e)
auctioneer le directeur de la vente
auctioneer-valuer le commissaire-priseur
baker le boulanger
barrister un avocat
blacksmith le forgeron
bookseller le (la) libraire
boss le patron
bricklayer le maçon en briques
builder le constructeur
businessman le commerçant, l'homme d'affaires
businesswoman la femme d'affaires
butcher le boucher
caretaker le (la) concierge
carpenter le charpentier, le menuisier

cashier le caissier, la caissière
chemist (medical) le pharmacien
chemist (industrial) le chimiste
civil servant le (la) fonctionnaire
clerk un(e) employé(e)
commercial traveller le commis-voyageur
computer scientist un(e) informaticien(ne)
conductor le receveur
customs officer le douanier
daily help la femme de ménage, la femme de journée
dentist le (la) dentiste
doctor le médecin, la femme médecin
driver le chauffeur
dustman le boueur
electrician un électricien
engineer un ingénieur
farmer le fermier
farmer's wife la fermière
fireman le sapeur-pompier
fisherman le pêcheur
foreman le chef d'équipe, le contre-maître
gardener le jardinier
garage-owner le garagiste
grocer un épicier
greengrocer le marchand de légumes
hairdresser le coiffeur, la coiffeuse
headmaster le directeur, le proviseur
hotel-keeper un hôtelier
housekeeper la femme de charge
housewife la ménagère
interpreter un(e) interprète
journalist un(e) journaliste
judge le juge
librarian le (la) bibliothécaire
lorry-driver le routier
maid la bonne
manager le gérant
managing director le P.D.G. (le Président Directeur General)
manufacturer le fabricant
mason le maçon
mayor le maire
mechanic le mécanicien
MP le Député (France), le Membre de la Chambre des Communes (UK)
miner le mineur
musician le (la) musicien(ne)
nurse un(e) infirmier/ière
painter le (la) peintre
painter/decorator le peintre-décorateur
photographer le (la) photographe
pilot le pilote
plumber le plombier
poet le (la) poète
policeman un agent de police, le policier, le gendarme (country)
policewoman la femme-agent
politician l'homme politique, la femme politique
postman le facteur
priest le prêtre
Prime Minister le Premier Ministre
railway worker le cheminot
receptionist le (la) réceptionniste
representative le représentant
sailor le marin, le matelot
sales-assistant le commis, le vendeur, la vendeuse
second-hand dealer le brocanteur, la brocanteuse
second-hand book dealer le (la) bouquiniste
secretary le (la) secrétaire
servant le (la) domestique
shoe-mender le cordonnier
shop-keeper le (la) marchand(e)
soldier le soldat
solicitor un avoué, le notaire
staff le personnel
tailor le tailleur
teacher le professeur
junior school teacher un instituteur, une institutrice
telephonist le (la) standardiste
trade unionist le (la) syndicaliste
traffic warden la 'pervenche'
typist le (la) dactylo
unemployed person le chômeur, la chômeuse
usherette une ouvreuse
vicar le curé
waiter le garçon
waitress la serveuse
worker un ouvrier, une ouvrière
writer un écrivain

LEISURE LES LOISIRS

aerobics l'aérobic (m)
amusement le divertissement, la distraction
athletics l'athlétisme
badminton le badminton
ballet le ballet
to play basketball jouer au basket-ball
to collect beermats collectionner les dessous de bocks de bière
to play billiards jouer au billard
boating le canotage
boxing la boxe
camera un appareil (photographique)
to go canoeing faire du canoë
cassette une cassette
cine-camera la caméra
to go camping faire du camping
carpentry la menuiserie
to play cards jouer aux cartes
to play chess jouer aux échecs
classical music la musique classique
cinema le cinéma
actor un acteur
actress une actrice
to applaud applaudir
applause les applaudissements
balcony (circle) le balcon
to book a seat louer/retenir une place
box la loge
cartoon un dessin animé
character le personnage
comedy une comédie
concert le concert
detective film un film policier
documentary le documentaire
entrance une entrée
exit la sortie
film le film

the 'gods' la galerie
horror film le film d'horreur
interval un entr'acte
love film le film d'amour
opera un opéra
orchestra stalls les fauteuils (mpl) d'orchestre
performance la répresentation
play la pièce
to be present at assister à
programme le programme
radio/tv programme une émission
scenery le décor
science fiction film le film de science-fiction
screen un écran
seat le fauteuil, la place
show le spectacle
spy film le film d'espionnage
stage la scène
star la vedette, la star
thriller le film à suspens
ticket le billet
tip le pourboire
usherette une ouvreuse
war film le film de guerre
wings les coulisses (fpl)
cricket le cricket
cross country running faire du cross
crosswords les mots croisés
cycling le cyclisme
dance le bal
to play darts jouer aux fléchettes
detective story le roman policier
disco la discothèque, le dancing
do-it-yourself le bricolage
draughts le jeu de dames
to enjoy oneself s'amuser
to fish pêcher
fishing la pêche
game le jeu (e.g. cards), la partie (e.g. game of cards), le sport (outdoor game), le match (competitive game)
girl guide une éclaireuse
golf le golf
gymnastics la gymnastique
hang-gliding le delta-plane, le sport de l'aile libre
hockey le hockey
horse-racing la course de chevaux
horse-riding l'équitation (f)
to go horse-riding monter à cheval
jazz le jazz
jogging le jogging, le footing
karate le karate
kite le cerf-volant
to knit tricoter
to listen to the radio écouter la radio
magazine le magazine, la revue
model-making faire des maquettes
mountaineering l'alpinisme
netball le netball
to paint peindre
painting la peinture
party la (sur) boum, la soirée, la surprise partie
a play une piece de théâtre
to play a musical instrument jouer de . . .
e.g., **cello** jouer du violoncelle
clarinet . . . de la clarinette
drums . . . de la batterie
flute . . . de la flûte
guitar . . . de la guitare
oboe . . . du hautbois
organ . . . de l'orgue
piano . . . du piano
trumpet . . . de la trompette
violin . . . du violon
to take photos prendre des photographies
'pop' music la musique pop, la musique disco
potholing la spéléologie
race la course
racket la raquette
record le disque
record-player un électrophone, le tourne-disque(s)
to read a novel lire un roman
rock-climbing la varappe
roller-skating le patin à roulettes
rugby le rugby
scouting le scoutisme
to sew coudre
sewing-machine la machine à coudre
to sing chanter
skating le patinage
to skate patiner
skate-board la planche à roulettes
snooker (une sorte de) jeu de billard
sportsman le sportif
sportswoman la sportive
squash le squash
stadium le stade
to collect stamps collectionner les timbres-poste
surfboard la planche à voile
swimming la natation
swimming-pool la piscine
to play table-football jouer au baby-foot
to play table-tennis jouer au ping-pong
tape-recorder le magnétophone
tape (for recording) la bande (magnétique)
team une équipe
tennis le tennis
theatre le théâtre
toboggan la luge, le toboggan
toy le jouet
track (e.g. running) la piste
training l'entraînement
transistor radio le transistor
TV la télévision
TV set le téléviseur
to go for a walk se promener
to take the dog for a walk promener le chien
video games les jeux vidéos
volleyball le volleyball
waterskiing le ski nautique
wrestling la lutte
Youth Club le Club des Jeunes, la Maison des Jeunes

THE MEDIA LES MÉDIA

advert (newspaper) une annonce
advert (on TV) un spot publicitaire
announcer le speaker/la speakerine

cartoon (strip) une bande dessinée
cartoon (film) un dessin animé
channel la chaîne
comedy une comédie
comic un journal de bandes dessinées
daily paper un quotidien
documentary un documentaire
headline le titre
magazine un magazine/une revue/un illustré
monthly mensuel
news les informations/les actualités/les nouvelles/Journal (TV)
newspaper le journal
opinion poll un sondage
programme une émission
quizzes les jeux-concours
radio la radio
transistor radio un transistor
serial un feuilleton
sports page la page des sports
TV la télévision
TV set le téléviseur
variety show les variétés
video-recorder un magnétoscope
walkman les écouteurs
weather forecast la météo
weekly hebdomadaire

Current affairs

Here are some useful words which you might encounter in passages of a journalistic nature.

news les actualités
the French Assembly (the equivalent of the British House of Commons) l'Assemblée Nationale
House of Commons la Chambre des Communes
immigrant un immigré
mayor le maire
minister le ministre
prime minister le premier ministre
party le parti
politics la politique
percentage le pourcentage
queen la reine
king le roi
rise une augmentation
strike la grève
trade union le syndicat
unemployment le chômage
unemployed person le chômeur, la chômeuse
war la guerre

PERSONAL IDENTIFICATION

name: **Je m'appelle** . . .
age: **J'ai** (e.g. seize) . . . **ans**
address: **J'habite** (à) . . .
date of birth: **Je suis né(e)** . . . (e.g. vingt-trois novembre dix-neuf cent soixante et onze)
telephone number: **Mon numéro de téléphone est** . . .
nationality: **Je suis** (e.g. Anglais/e, Ecossais/e, Gallois/e, Irlandais/e).

Descriptions Les descriptions

build la taille
medium build la taille moyenne (e.g. Je suis de taille moyenne)
big grand(e)
little petit(e)
fat gros(se)
thin mince
eyes les yeux
blue eyes les yeux bleus (e.g. J'ai les yeux bleus)
brown eyes les yeux bruns
green eyes les yeux verts
grey eyes les yeux gris
hair les cheveux
blond hair les cheveux blonds (e.g. J'ai les cheveux blonds)
brown hair les cheveux bruns
red hair les cheveux roux
curly hair les cheveux frisés
long hair les cheveux longs
short hair les cheveux courts
straight hair les cheveux plats
handsome beau
pretty joli(e)/belle
ugly laid(e)

THE FAMILY LA FAMILLE

adult un(e) adulte
aunt la tante
baby le bébé
bride la nouvelle mariée
bridegroom le nouveau marié
brother le frère
cousin le (la) cousin(e)
daughter la fille
daughter-in-law la belle-fille
elder aîné(e)
father le père
father-in-law le beau-père
granddaughter la petite-fille
grandfather le grand-père
grandmother la grand'mère
grandson le petit-fils
grown-ups les grandes personnes
husband le mari, l'époux
kids les gosses (m and f pl)
mother la mère
mother-in-law la belle-mère
nephew le neveu
niece la nièce
parents les parents
relatives les parents
sister la soeur
sister-in-law la belle-soeur
son le fils
son-in-law le beau-fils, le gendre
uncle l'oncle
widow la veuve
widower le veuf
wife la femme, l'épouse
young people les jeunes gens
younger (e.g. sister, brother) cadet(te)

FRIENDS LES AMIS

friend un ami/une amie
friend un camarade/une camarade

pal/chum un copain/une copine
best meilleur(e) (e.g. ma meilleure amie)

PETS
LES ANIMAUX DOMESTIQUES

budgie la perruche inséparable
cat le chat/la chatte
dog le chien/la chienne
alsatian le berger allemand
poodle le (la) caniche
sheepdog le chien de berger
spaniel un épagneul
dove la colombe
donkey un âne
fish les poissons
gerbil la gerbille
goldfish le(s) poisson(s) rouge(s)
goat le bouc, la chèvre
guinea pig le cobaye, le cochon d'Inde
hamster le hamster
horse le cheval
mare la jument
mouse la souris
parrot le perroquet
pony le poney
rabbit le lapin
stick insect le phasme
tortoise la tortue

SEASIDE AU BORD DE LA MER

anchor un ancre
to bathe se baigner
bay la baie
beach la plage
beachball le ballon de plage
boat le bateau
bucket le seau
cliff la falaise
coast la côte
crab le crabe
crossing la traversée
deckchair le transa(t)
dinghy le canot
to disembark débarquer
to dive plonger
to drown (se) noyer
to embark s'embarquer
first aid post le poste de secours
to fish pêcher
fisherman le pêcheur
fishing-boat la barque (de pêcheur)
fishing-rod la canne à pêche
holiday-maker un estivant, le vacancier
ice-cream la glace
jellyfish la méduse
jetty/pier la jetée
life-buoy la bouée de sauvetage
life-guard le gardien de plage
lighthouse le phare
mast le mât
to moor amarrer
motor-boat le canot automobile
navy la marine
oar un aviron
paddle la pagaie
to paddle pagayer (e.g. a canoe), patauger (=to wade)
passenger le passenger
passenger-boat le paquebot
rock le rocher, la roche
rowing-boat le bateau à rames
sailing la voile
to go sailing faire de la voile
sailing-boat le voilier, le bateau à voiles, le canot à voile
sailor le marin, le matelot
sand le sable
sandcastle le château de sable
seagull la mouette
ship le navire
shipwreck le naufrage
to be shipwrecked faire naufrage
shore le littoral
shrimp la crevette
spade la pelle
steamer le vapeur
to sunbathe prendre des bains de soleil, se bronzer
sunburn le coup de soleil
sun-lounger le lit de plage
suntan le bronzage
sun umbrella une ombrelle, le parasol
surfboard la planche de surfing
surfing le surfing
to swim nager
swimming costume le maillot de bain
swimming trunks le caleçon de bain
tide la marée
at high tide à marée haute
at low tide à marée basse
water-skiing le ski nautique
to go water-skiing faire du ski nautique
to go wind-surfing faire de la planche à voile
yacht le yacht

SERVICES LES SERVICES

Bank La banque

bank card la carte bancaire/la plaque d'identité bancaire
bank note le billet de banque
cheque un chèque
cheque book un carnet de chèques
travellers' cheques des chèques de voyage
to cash a cheque toucher un chèque
counter le guichet
cash counter la caisse
(loose) change la monnaie
money l'argent
notes les billets
pound sterling la livre sterling
to sign signer

Lost property office
Le bureau des objets trouvés

to lose perdre
lost perdu
camera un appareil
handbag le sac à main
passport le passeport
purse le porte-monnaie
ring la bague
wallet le portefeuille
watch la montre

Post Office Le bureau de poste

(by) airmail par avion
counter le guichet
envelope une enveloppe
form la fiche, la formule, le formulaire
letter la lettre
letter-box la boîte aux lettres
mail le courrier
packet le paquet
parcel le colis
to post a letter mettre une lettre à la poste
postal order le mandat (postal)
postman's bag la sacoche
post card la carte postale
postman le facteur
registered recommandé
stamp le timbre-poste
telegram le télégramme

Telephone kiosk La cabine téléphonique

button le bouton
code l'indicatif
country code l'indicatif du pays
regional code l'indicatif du département
coin la pièce
dial le cadran
to dial composer le numéro
dialling tone la tonalité
directory un annuaire
fire brigade les pompiers
number le numéro
numbers les chiffres
operator le/la standardiste
police la police
rate le tarif
cheap rate le tarif réduit
the receiver le récepteur/le combiné
to replace the receiver raccrocher
slot la fente
subscriber un abonné
to transfer a call téléphoner en PCV (payer chez vous)

Tourist information office Un office de tourisme/Le syndicat d'initiative

brochure la brochure
information les renseignements
leaflet le dépliant
list la liste
. . . **of campsites** des terrains de camping
. . . **of future events** des événements à venir
. . . **of hotels** des hôtels
. . . **of walks** des randonnées
map la carte

SHOPPING LES ACHATS

bag le sac
baker's la boulangerie
bank note le billet de banque
basement le sous-sol
basket le panier
bookshop la librairie
box la boîte
butcher's la boucherie
to buy acheter
cake shop la pâtisserie
(loose) change la monnaie
cash desk la caisse
cheap bon marché
chemist's la pharmacie
cheque le chèque
cheque-book le carnet de chèques
traveller's cheque le chèque de voyage
clothes shop la boutique, le magasin de vêtements
consumer le consommateur
to cost coûter
counter le comptoir
customer le (la) client(e)
dairy la crémerie, la laiterie
delicatessen la charcuterie
department store un grand magasin
draper's la mercerie, le magasin de nouveautés
dry cleaner's le pressing
drugstore la droguerie
floor (storey) un étage
greengrocer's le marchand de légumes
grocer's une épicerie
groceries les provisions (fpl)
How much? C'est combien? Ça fait combien?
hypermarket un hypermarché, une grande surface
ironmonger's la quincaillerie
jeweller's la bijouterie
launderette la blanchisserie automatique, la laverie
market le marché
money l'argent (m)
newspaper stand le kiosque à journaux
to owe devoir
to pay payer
pork butcher's la charcuterie
pound (weight and money) la livre
price le prix
purse le porte-monnaie
sales les soldes (mpl)
to save économiser
scales la balance
to sell vendre
shelf le rayon
shop assistant le vendeur, la vendeuse
shop window la vitrine, la devanture
to go shopping faire des achats, faire des courses, faire des emplettes
shoe shop le magasin de chaussures
size l'encolure (f) (shirts), la pointure (shoes), la taille (clothes)
special offer une offre spéciale/promotionelle, Promotion
to spend dépenser
stall un étalage
stainless steel (adj.) en inox/d'acier inoxydable
stationer's la papeterie
supermarket le supermarché
sweetshop la confiserie
till la caisse
tobacconist's le débit de tabac
trolley le chariot
wallet le portefeuille
watchmaker's une horlogerie
to weigh peser
weight le poids

to go window-shopping faire du lèche-vitrine
to wrap emballer, envelopper

TOWN LA VILLE

avenue une avenue, le boulevard
bank la banque
branch (of a bank) la succursale
bridge le pont
building le bâtiment
bus station la gare routière
busy (e.g. street) animé(e)
campsite le terrain de camping
car park le parking
cathedral la cathédrale
church une église
cinema le cinéma
civic centre le centre civique
concert hall la salle des concerts
crossroads le carrefour, le croisement
district le quartier
factory une usine
fire station la caserne des sapeurs-pompiers
hospital un hôpital
industrial estate la zone industrielle
information centre le syndicat d'initiative
lamppost le réverbère
law court le palais de justice, le tribunal
letter-box la boîte aux lettres
level crossing le niveau à passage
library la bibliothèque
lost property office le bureau des objets trouvés
market le marché
museum le musée
newspaper stand le kiosque à journaux
outskirts les environs (mpl)
park le jardin public
pavement le trottoir
pedestrian le piéton
pedestrian crossing le passage clouté
pedestrian precinct la voie piétonne, la zone piétonne
police station le commissariat de police, la gendarmerie, le poste de police
public conveniences les toilettes (fpl)
railway station la gare
recreation / **sports** } **centre** le centre/complexe sportif
roundabout le rond-point
rush hour les heures d'affluence
school une école, le collège, le lycée
sign le panneau
square la place
sports ground le terrain de sport
sports stadium le stade
street la rue
suburbs la banlieue, les faubourgs (mpl)
subway le passage souterrain
supermarket le supermarché
swimming-pool la piscine
telephone kiosk la cabine téléphonique
theatre le théâtre
town clock une horloge
town hall l'Hôtel de Ville (large town), la Mairie (small town)
traffic la circulation
traffic jam un embouteillage
traffic lights les feux (mpl)
traffic warden la 'pervenche'
travel agent's une agence de voyages
underground railway le métro
workshop un atelier
Youth Centre le Centre des Jeunes

TRAVEL LES VOYAGES

Airport L'aéroport

air hostess l'hôtesse de l'air
air sickness le mal de l'air
air terminal une aérogare
control-tower la tour de contrôle
to fly voler
helicopter un hélicoptère
hijacker le pirate de l'air
hijacking le détournement d'avion
jet un avion à réaction
to land atterrir
loudspeaker le haut-parleur
(airport) lounge la salle d'attente
pilot le pilote
plane un avion
runway la piste d'atterrissage
to take off décoller

Bus station La gare routière

bus un autobus
bus stop un arrêt d'autobus
coach le car

Car La voiture

bonnet le capot
boot le coffre
brake le frein
to brake freiner
breakdown la panne
to break down être en panne
breathalyser l'alcotest (m)
bumper le pare-chocs
car une auto, la voiture
to check vérifier
clutch l'embrayage (m)
door la portière
driver le chauffeur
driving-licence le permis de conduire
driving mirror le rétroviseur
engine le moteur
headlamp le phare
garage-owner le garagiste
gear-lever le (levier de) changement de vitesse
to change gear changer de vitesse
horn un avertisseur, le klaxon
to sound the horn klaxonner
indicator light le feu clignotant
lorry le camion
mechanic le mécanicien
moped le cyclomoteur, le vélomoteur
motorbike la motocyclette
motorway une autoroute
mudguard le garde-boue, le pare-boue
number plate la plaque d'immatriculation
oil l'huile (f)
to park garer, stationner
petrol l'essence (f)

petrol-pump le poste d'essence
to fill up with petrol faire le plein d'essence
petrol-tank le reservoir à essence
puncture la crevaison, le pneu crevé
radiator le radiateur
to repair (after a breakdown) dépanner
roof rack la galerie
safety belt la ceinture de sécurité
seat le siège
bench-seat la banquette
scooter le scooter
second-hand car la voiture d'occasion
service station la station-service
side light le feu de position
spare wheel la roue de secours
speed la vitesse
steering-wheel le volant
step le marchepied
toll le péage
tyre le pneu
to pump up a tyre gonfler un pneu
van la camionette
window la glace
windscreen le pare-brise
windscreen wiper un essuie-glace

Railway Le chemin de fer

arrival une arrivée
booking-office le guichet
compartment le compartiment
first-class compartment un compartiment de première classe
second-class compartment un compartiment de seconde classe
non-smoking compartment un compartiment non-fumeur
smoking compartment un compartiment pour fumeurs
connection la correspondance
departure le départ
dining-car le wagon-restaurant
door la portière
engine la locomotive
entrance une entrée
exit la sortie
French railway network la SNCF (Société des Chemins de Fer Français)
guard le chef de train
high speed train le TGV (train à grande vitesse)
information bureau le bureau de renseignements
journey le voyage
(short) **journey** le trajet
left-luggage office la consigne
level-crossing le passage à niveau
line/track la voie
luggage les bagages (mpl)
luggage-rack le filet à bagages, le porte-bagages
luggage-van le fourgon à bagages
to miss (e.g. a train) manquer (le train)
passenger le voyageur
platform le quai
porter le porteur, un employé
railway station la gare
rate/price le tarif
reduced rate le tarif réduit
refreshment-room le buffet
to reserve réserver
sleeping-car le wagon-lit
to date stamp composter
station master le chef de gare
suitcase la valise
ticket le billet
single ticket un aller simple, le billet d'aller
return ticket un aller et retour, le billet d'aller et retour
ticket collector le contrôleur
time-table un indicateur
train le train
commuter train le train de banlieue
express train le rapide
non-stop train le train direct
trolley le chariot
trunk la malle
underground railway le Métro
underground station la station de métro
waiting-room la salle d'attente

General terms

abroad à l'etranger
bicycle la bicyclette, le vélo
English Channel la Manche
customs la douane
customs officer le douanier
customs scanner le détecteur
ferry le ferry
frontier la frontière
to hitch-hike faire de l'auto-stop
hovercraft un aéroglisseur, un hovercraft
identity card la carte d'identité
luggage trolley le chariot
passenger le voyageur, le passager (air/sea travel)
passport le passeport
passport control le contrôle des passeports
to set off se mettre en route
taxi le taxi
ticket le billet
travel agency une agence de voyages
youth hostel une auberge de jeunesse

WEATHER LE TEMPS

What's the weather like? Quel temps fait-il?
It's cold. Il fait froid.
It's dark. Il fait nuit/noir.
It's foggy. Il fait du brouillard.
It's freezing. Il gèle.
It's hot. Il fait très chaud.
It's light. Il fait jour.
It's raining. Il pleut.
It's pouring with rain. Il pleut à verse.
It's snowing. Il neige.
It's sunny. Il fait du soleil.
It's thawing. Il dégèle.
It's thundering. Il tonne.
It's warm. Il fait chaud.
It's windy. Il fait du vent.
The weather is bad. Il fait mauvais temps.
autumn l'automne (m)
in autumn en automne
breeze la brise

bright intervals des éclaircies (fpl)
climate le climat
cloud le nuage
cloudy nuageux, ciel couvert
cold froid
cool frais, fraîche
dawn l'aube (f), le point du jour
dew la rosée
frost la gelée
heat la chaleur
ice la glace
lightning les éclairs (mpl), la foudre
to melt fondre
mist la brume
moon la lune
moonlight le clair de lune
rain la pluie
to rain pleuvoir
shower of rain une averse
rainbow un arc-en-ciel
season la saison
snow la neige
spring le printemps
in spring au printemps
star une étoile
storm la tempête
summer l'été (m)
in summer en été
sunrise le lever du soleil
sunset le coucher du soleil
thunder le tonnerre
thunderstorm un orage
clap of thunder le coup de tonnerre
twilight le crépuscule
weather forecast la météo
wind le vent
winter l'hiver (m)
in winter en hiver

Core Section Summary

In the GCSE examination in French you will be asked to carry out certain tasks which will require certain skills. The core section of this book provides you with the basic information which you will need to carry out these tasks. The later sections which contain examination practice will help you to develop the skills required.

Thorough revision of Grammar/Structures/Notions/Functions/Vocabulary is essential for . . .

UNDERSTANDING written and spoken French

MAKING YOURSELF UNDERSTOOD in French

and of course . . . gaining a high grade in your exam!

5 SELF-TEST UNIT

5.1 Structures and Grammar Revision

ARTICLES AND NOUNS

Give the plural forms of . . .

l'animal le cadeau le cheval le fils le journal l'oeil l'oiseau monsieur madame le timbre-poste

ADJECTIVES

What is the French for . . .? (give both masculine and feminine singular forms)
old pretty big white dear first sweet favourite beautiful new

ADVERBS

What is the French for . . .?
badly happily too much really better often

PRONOUNS

What is the French for . . .?
Who? of which each one anybody someone

CONJUNCTIONS

What is the French for . . .?
when because so since (giving a reason) as soon as

PREPOSITIONS

What is the French for . . .?
amongst before (place) before (time) on the right on foot until on the other side on holiday

VERBS

Present tense

Give the correct form of the following verbs:

1 Il (finir)
2 Nous (manger)
3 Vous (appeler)
4 Je (venir)
5 Elles (aller)
6 Tu (jeter)
7 Elle (vouloir)
8 Nous (commencer)
9 Ils (être)
10 Elles (avoir)
11 Vous (faire)
12 Il (écrire)
13 Tu (savoir)
14 Vous (dire)
15 Nous (se coucher)
16 Je (recevoir)
17 Elles (s'asseoir)
18 Elle (devoir)
19 Ils (connaître)
20 Vous (prendre)

Future tense

Give the correct form of the following verbs:

1 Ils (avoir)
2 Je (pouvoir)
3 Elle (s'asseoir)
4 Vous (venir)
5 Tu (vouloir)
6 Ils (appeler)
7 Nous (faire)
8 Il (falloir)
9 Tu (être)
10 Elles (recevoir)
11 Je (courir)
12 Elle (devoir)
13 Vous (envoyer)
14 Tu (finir)
15 Il (pleuvoir)
16 Elles (répéter)
17 Je (savoir)
18 Nous (apercevoir)
19 Tu (tenir)
20 Nous (cueillir)

Imperfect tense

Give the correct form of the following verbs:

1 Nous (finir)
2 Il (être)
3 Ils (avoir)
4 Vous (aller)
5 Je (faire)
6 Elles (pouvoir)
7 Elle (envoyer)
8 Il (vouloir)
9 Je (jeter)
10 Vous (dire)

Conditional tense

Give the correct form of the following verbs:

1 Je (vouloir)
2 Ils (aller)
3 Nous (être)
4 Tu (pouvoir)
5 Vous (demander)
6 Elle (dire)
7 Elles (avoir)
8 Je (venir)
9 Il (faire)
10 Vous (envoyer)

Perfect tense

Give the correct form of the following verbs:

1 Il (devoir)
2 Elle (s'asseoir)
3 Vous (mettre)
4 Je (suivre)
5 Tu (retourner)
6 Nous (descendre)
7 Elles (voir)
8 Il (prendre)
9 Je (devenir)
10 Nous (vivre)
11 Il (se souvenir)
12 Vous (ouvrir)
13 Tu (connaître)
14 Ils (recevoir)
15 Nous (vouloir)
16 Je (rentrer)
17 Elles (avoir)
18 Elle (craindre)
19 Vous (être)
20 Il (pouvoir)

Past historic tense

Give the English for . . .

1 Ils mirent
2 Je dus
3 Nous prîmes
4 Ils eurent
5 Elle sut
6 Ils virent
7 Elles vinrent
8 Il fut
9 Il fit
10 Elle but

IMPERATIVE AND PRESENT PARTICIPLE

What do the following mean?

1 sachant
2 étant
3 ayant
4 Finis!
5 Sois!

NEGATIVES

Give the French for . . .

I don't like homework.
I never go there.
No one has arrived.
She hasn't eaten anything.

5.2 Functions

1 What would you shout in an emergency if calling for help?

2 What would you say in French if you were agreeing to a suggestion?

3 How would you say to someone that it does not matter?

4 What would you say if you were congratulating someone?

5 If you were giving someone directions in French, how would you tell them to go straight on?

6 How would you say to someone in French 'It's a pity'?

7 How would you tell someone in French that you are very interested in . . .?

8 What would you say in French to an adult to whom you have just been introduced?

9 What would you say in French to express 'See you soon'?

10 How would you tell someone in French that something is not possible?

11 What would you say in French to tell someone that you are very sorry?

12 Give the French for . . . Happy birthday! Cheer up!
Happy New Year! Sleep well!

13 What would you say in French to tell someone that you are sorry but that you don't understand?

14 What would you say in French to tell someone that something is forbidden?

5.3 Notions

Direction/Distance

Give the French for . . .

in the distance
everywhere
on the left
on the right
the north
on the other side
straight on
over there

Place/Position

Give the French for . . .

together
under
nearby

Quality

Give the French for . . .

red (of hair)
leather
stainless steel
wool
lace

Number/Quantity

Say the following aloud in French . . .

13
39
63
64
101

What is the French for . . .?

a bottle of
a jar of
a pound of
a tin of
a packet of

Emotions/Feelings

What is the French for . . .

to be afraid
to bore
to disturb
to enjoy oneself
happy
to laugh
sad
to scold

Time

at last
before (time)
from time to time
half an hour
already
the next morning
later
soon
tomorrow
a long time

Dates/Festivals

to congratulate
Easter
New Year's Day
birthday

5.4 Vocabulary Topic Areas

Give the French for the following words.

Café/hotel/restaurant

breakfast
cup
lift
single room
shower
plate
full board
drink
guest
lunch

Camping

camping equipment
dustbin
pitch
rucksack
water-container
sleeping-bag
camping gas
hammer
tentpeg
campsite

Clothes

belt
jeans
nightdress
pocket
size (clothes)
sleeve
socks
shirt
cardigan
jacket

Countries/nationalities

Belgium
Great Britain
Scotland
Switzerland
Wales
UK
an Austrian (f)
a German (m)
an Indian (f)
a Greek (m)

Countryside

a robin
a swan
the barn
the farmer's wife
a flock
the orchard
the shepherd
the ant
the pebbles
the stream

Daily routine

to have a shower
to brush one's teeth
to catch the bus
to have tea
to go to sleep

Education

chemistry
comprehensive school
computer science
head
(of a secondary school)
to learn
to draw
time-table
uniform
to study
to pass an exam

Food/drink

bread roll
crisps
grapes
fruit juice
chop
well-cooked steak
veal
Brussels sprouts
yoghurt
salt

Health/illness

a boil
chicken-pox
to have a cold
I feel dizzy
to faint
first aid post
'flu
to sprain
to feel sick
to have a high temperature

Human body

ankle
face
heart
back
wrist
lip
tongue
shoulder
thumb
chin

Accident/injury

Help!
a road accident
to be stung by
to knock over
to break
to cut
a serious accident
stretcher
to trap
to hurt

Home/rooms

block of flats
cupboard
ground floor
caretaker
living room
tenant
to rent
to lock
storey
to clean
tap
soap
bedside table
blanket
shelf
place setting
vacuum-cleaner
record-player
video-recorder
to wash dishes

Garden

path
flowerbed
greenhouse
wheelbarrow
see-saw

Jobs/professions

customs officer
engineer
accountant
housewife
manager
lorry driver
hairdresser
solicitor
staff
unemployed person

Leisure

to play cards
do-it-yourself
hang-gliding
horse-riding
a party (teenage)
potholing
skating
surfboard
video games
swimming

The media

weather forecast
serial
opinion poll
daily paper
a TV channel

Personal identification

green eyes
red hair
thin
medium build
short hair
ugly
blond hair

Family/friends

granddaughter
nephew
younger
aunt
best friend

Pets

rabbit
tortoise
donkey
spaniel
guinea pig
mouse

Seaside

cliff
deckchair
ice cream
lighthouse
rock
to go sailing
bucket and spade
sun umbrella
to go water-skiing
to sunbathe

Services

to cash a cheque
traveller's cheques
the counter
wallet
camera
letter-box
to post a letter
stamp
to dial
directory
tourist information office
a list of walks

Shopping

bookshop
consumer
jeweller's
newspaper stand
butcher's
basement
How much?
shop window
stationer's
to weigh

Town

information centre
bus station
lost property office
pedestrian crossing
sports centre
district
subway
traffic lights
square
roundabout

Travel

plane
bus stop
air terminal
roof rack
tyre
number plate (of car)
platform
suitcase
return ticket
luggage trolley

Weather

It's snowing
bright intervals
dawn
rainbow
a shower of rain
cloudy
weather forecast
in spring
heat
moonlight

6 EXAMINATION PRACTICE

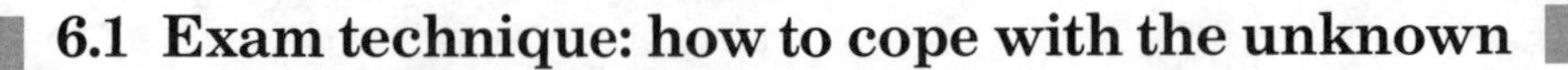

6.1 Exam technique: how to cope with the unknown

WHEN READING

It is highly unlikely that an exam candidate will know all the vocabulary required in the GCSE examination. Candidates must therefore learn to cope successfully with the five per cent (approx.) of vocabulary not included in the defined content syllabus of their particular Examining Group. Time must be set aside each week, in the months prior to the exam itself, in order to learn and revise all the words that you know may be included in the GCSE examination for your Examining Group.

To cope successfully with those words in the exam which you do *not* know, you should:

1 Use your common sense to put the word(s) into the context of the question being attempted.

2 Remember that titles to questions are there to 'give you a clue' to the content of the questions.

3 Realize that, for comprehension purposes, it is not necessary to know the meaning of every word, so long as you understand the gist of the passage.

4 Try to deduce the grammatical function of the unknown word, e.g. is it a noun, adjective, adverb or verb? It is linked to a phrase, whose meaning you *do* understand?

5 Relate the unknown word(s) to what you *do* understand in the question/passage and imagine what you yourself would include in that particular context.

6 Learn certain standard patterns used in the formation of words in French:

Prefixes

in-, *im-* often suggest the word 'not':
e.g. *possible/impossible* (as in English)
attendu expected/*inattendu* unexpected
utile useful/*inutile* useless
etc.

Dé- often has the meaning 'dis-':
e.g. *débarquer* to disembark
découvrir to discover

Re- at the beginning of a word often has the meaning 'again':
e.g. *commencer/recommencer* to begin again
prendre/reprendre to retake
etc.

Mi- at the beginning of a word means 'half':
e.g. *temps/mi-temps* half time
chemin/mi-chemin half-way
vitesse/mi-vitesse half-speed
etc.

Sous- adds the meaning 'under(neath)':
e.g. *chef/sous-chef* assistant chief/manager/chef
directeur/sous-directeur assistant manager
dévéloppé/sous-dévéloppé under-developed

Endings

-et/ette often signifies 'little':
e.g. *fille/fillette* little girl
livre/livret small book
etc.

-able—as in English—'able to be . . .':
e.g. *réparer* to repair *réparable* able to be repaired
manger to eat *manageable* edible

NB *potable* drinkable (derived from the Latin verb)

-eur often indicates the 'doer' of an action:
e.g. *vendre* to sell — *vendeur* sales assistant
déménager to move house — *déménageur* removal man
voler to steal — *voleur* thief

-aine added to a number means 'about . . .':
e.g. *une vingtaine* about twenty
une trentaine about thirty
une centaine about one hundred

Many words which end in *-é/-ée* in French often end in '-y' in English:

e.g. *armée* army
liberté liberty
solidarité solidarity

Similarly, words ending in French in *-i/ie* often end in '-y' in English:

e.g. *parti* party
monotonie monotony
etc.

It is often easy to guess correctly the meaning of words which are similar to English words, even when one or two letters have been changed:

e.g. *-que-* in French '-c/ck/k-' in English
attaquer to attack
risquer to risk

-ou- in French '-o-/-u-' in English
gouvernement government
mouvement movement

-o- in French '-u-' in English
fonction function
nombre number
etc.

Remember also that a ^ over a letter usually indicates that the letter 's' has been eliminated . . .

e.g. *hôpital* hospital
forêt forest
intérêt interest
etc.

WHEN LISTENING

All the above points for reading also apply, but remember, too, the following:

1 The 'h' at the beginning of a word is silent;

2 the final consonant of a word is often not pronounced;

3 'th' is not pronounced as in English, but usually sounds like a 't' in French;

4 in natural speech, words will 'run together'.

Careful listening techniques must be adopted. As always, plenty of practice in listening to authentic French is very important. Try to listen to French radio for 10-15 minutes each day.

WHEN SPEAKING

In the oral exam, you may be faced with a situation where you have not understood the question which you have just been asked. In this situation, you should ask the examiner either to repeat the question: *Voulez-vous répéter la question, s'il vous plaît?*; or, if you think that you have heard the question, but wish to confirm it, *Vous voulez savoir . . .?*;

or, if you have no idea what you have been asked, be honest and say: *Je regrette, monsieur(madame), mais je ne comprends pas la question.* The examiner will then either rephrase the question or move on to a different question.

WHEN WRITING

The key to success is 'use what you know, understand and can do'. Always be prepared to paraphrase, use alternatives or explain in a different way, using what you know to be correct. After all, this is what we do with our own native language each day.

However, by revising all the core sections in this book you should be able to reduce considerably much of the potentially 'unknown'.

7 THE ORAL EXAM: CONVERSATION

All GCSE Examining Groups set a test in French conversation, both at Basic and Higher levels. All candidates must attempt the Basic Speaking test–'to respond to unprepared questions on a limited range of clearly defined topic areas; the questions should be unprepared in the sense that they are not specified in advance, although the close definition of the topic areas to be dealt with will make it possible for candidates to practise the types of question which are likely to be asked'. (National Criteria)

For candidates aiming at the award of Grade D and above, additional objectives are necessary. One of these is the Higher-level speaking test–'to demonstrate the skills listed under Basic Speaking over a wider range of clearly defined topic areas. They should be expected to ask, and respond to, questions relating to a wider range of clearly defined situations which are within the experience and scope of a sixteen-year-old and to conduct a sustained free conversation (i.e. a conversation which has not been rehearsed) on one or more subjects, as specified in the syllabus.' (National Criteria)

7.1 Preparation

1 Check the syllabus requirements for your Examining Group for the level which you will be taking.

2 Check the Topic Areas carefully and learn all the new words given in the Topic Areas section of this book.

3 Prepare a few sentences on each of the topics on which you know that you may be tested. Imagine that you are speaking to a new acquaintance in French. He/she will probably want to know about your home and family, the area where you live, what you like doing in your spare time, where you go on holidays, what you study at school, as well as asking about your name, age, likes and dislikes, etc. . . .

4 Make sure that you can answer the questions listed below but also be prepared to add extra information. In a conversation many questions/answers will depend on what you have already said, and should follow on naturally from what has just been said. The questions below are not the only ones that you might be asked but they represent the variety of questions which may be asked.

7.2 Pronunciation/Intonation

To achieve the highest grades in the Speaking Tests in the GCSE examination, candidates will have to score high marks for pronunciation and intonation as well as to show variety and precision of vocabulary and grammar.

There are several things that you can do to improve your French pronunciation and intonation. Practise the following in the weeks/months before the examination.

1 Listen to as much authentic French as possible–on radio, television, or to any native speaker you know–and try to imitate the sounds that you hear.

2 Remember that French has a rising intonation in a sentence and that the voice does not fall until the end of the sentence. However, do remember also that the voice continues to rise at the end of a question. Practise this by asking questions aloud.

e.g. Tu as quel âge? Tu as froid? etc.

3 Remember that in French the final consonant at the end of a word is rarely pronounced, unless the following word in the same sentence begins with a vowel or 'h' and providing that there is no comma in between.

e.g. Les garçons —here the final 's' on both words should *not* be pronounced.
Les hommes—the 's' of 'les' should be pronounced here, but that of 'hommes' should not. (Remember also that the letter 'h' is never pronounced when it is the first letter of the word.)

4 Practise the French 'u' sound by placing the tip of the tongue near the top of your lower teeth and making your mouth into a perfect closed 'o' shape; do not move the lips whilst producing the 'u' sound.

5 Practise the French 'r' sound by opening the mouth and saying aloud 'ah-ara-ra'. This should sound similar to gargling at the back of the throat.

6 Practise nasal sounds by holding your nose and saying 'un', 'on', etc. Then try to make the same sounds without holding your nose.

As for all parts of the examination, the emphasis is on *practice*. It will be *your* voice that will be heard in the examination. Make sure that what you say sounds as authentically French as possible.

7.3 Conversation Topics

PERSONAL IDENTIFICATION

Basic level and Higher level

Name: Q Comment t'appelles-tu? Comment vous appelez-vous?
A Je m'appelle . . .

Age: Q Quel âge as-tu? Quel âge avez-vous?
A J'ai . . . ans

Birthday: Q Quelle est la date de ton/votre anniversaire?
A (e.g. Le vingt-sept avril).

Address: Q Quelle est ton/votre adresse?
A J'habite (e.g. au numéro onze, rue Pasteur, . . .)

Nationality: Q De quelle nationalité es-tu/êtes-vous?
A Je suis (e.g. Anglais/e, Gallois/e, Ecossais/e, etc.)

FAMILY

Basic level

1 Combien de personnes y a-t-il dans ta/votre famille?

2 Avez-vous/as-tu des frères ou des soeurs?

For physical descriptions of members of your family see **vocabulary topic area: descriptions** (p. 46).

Higher level

You will be expected to answer all the Basic level questions about members of your family and also give information about their personalities.

e.g. Mon frère est très distrait (*absent-minded*).

Ma soeur est très élégante.
. . . égoïste (*self-centred*).
. . . gâté(e) (*spoilt*).
. . . impoli(e).
. . . intelligent(e).
. . . paresseux/paresseuse (*lazy*).
. . . patient(e).
. . . sympathique.
. . . timide, etc.

and to answer such questions as . . .

1 Qui est l'aîné(e)? (*older/oldest*).

2 Qui est le cadet/la cadette? (*younger/youngest*)

3 Tes (vos) frères ont déjà quitté l'école? Que font-ils?

4 Tu as des nièces et des neveux?

as well as give extra information . . .

e.g. Mon père est grand et mince. Il a les cheveux gris coupés très courts. Il est de taille moyenne. Son visage est rectangulaire et il a les yeux sombres. Il porte des lunettes et il a toujours un air renseigné . . .

FAMILY PETS

See **vocabulary topic area:** Pets

Basic level

1 Q As-tu/avez-vous des animaux domestiques?

2 Comment s'appelle-t-il?

3 Comment est-il?

4 Qu'est-ce qu'il aime manger?

Higher level

You should be able to answer the above questions and give more details about your pets.

e.g. Depuis quand as-tu/avez-vous un chien?
Je l'ai depuis trois ans.

1 Pourquoi préfères-tu/préférez-vous les épagneuls? (*spaniels*).

2 Pourquoi préfères-tu/préférez-vous les poissons rouges?

3 Pourquoi n'aimes-tu pas les chats?

DAILY ROUTINE

See **vocabulary topic areas**

You should be able to give/ask for information about:

times of getting up/going to bed
times of meals
what you do before leaving for school
what you do when you get home from school
what you do at weekends, etc.

Basic level

1 A quelle heure te lèves-tu/vous levez-vous?

2 Qu'est ce que tu as fait/vous avez fait hier soir?

3 Qu'est-ce que tu as fait/vous avez fait samedi dernier?

4 Qu'est-ce que tu as fait/vous avez fait dimanche dernier?

5 Qu'est-ce que tu feras/vous ferez samedi prochain?

6 Où fais-tu/faites-vous vos devoirs?

7 Combien de devoirs as-tu/avez-vous chaque soir?

8 A quelle heure te couches-tu/vous couchez-vous?

9 Est-ce qu'on te/vous donne de l'argent de poche?

10 Comment dépenses-tu/dépensez-vous ton/votre argent de poche?

Higher level

More detailed information is required on the above topic:

e.g. Q Que fais-tu/faites-vous généralement le weekend?
A Je sors avec mes amis. Nous allons souvent en boîte (*night-club*) ou dans une discothèque. Je

passe rarement le samedi soir chez moi. Mais si je rentre tard, mes parents ne sont pas contents. La semaine dernière, par exemple, je suis rentré vers minuit et voilà mon père sur le point d'appeler la police!

1 Que fais-tu/faites-vous généralement avant d'aller à l'école?

2 As-tu/avez-vous un petit emploi pour gagner de l'argent de poche?

EDUCATION

See **vocabulary topic areas**

Candidates should be able to give and ask for information about schools, lessons, activities, facilities and their plans for the future.

Basic level

1 Habites-tu/habitez-vous loin de l'école?

2 Quelles sont les matières que tu étudies/vous étudiez à l'école?

3 Quelle est ta/votre matière préférée?

4 . A quelle heure arrives-tu/arrivez-vous à l'école le matin?

5 A quelle heure quittes-tu/quittez-vous l'école?

6 Quels jours de la semaine vas-tu/allez-vous en classe?

7 Quand as-tu/avez-vous l'intention de quitter l'école?

8 Depuis combien de temps apprends-tu/apprenez-vous le français?

9 Combien d'élèves y a-t-il dans ta/votre classe?

10 Combien de cours as-tu/avez-vous le matin à l'école?

Higher level

1 Qu'as-tu/avez-vous l'intention de faire quand tu auras/vous aurez quitté l'école?

2 Veux-tu/voulez-vous me décrire une journée typique à l'école?

3 Comment est ton/votre collège?

FOOD AND DRINK

See **vocabulary topic areas**

Candidates should be able to state their likes and dislikes about food and drink. They should be able to describe typical meals and places where they normally eat, e.g. school canteen, restaurants etc., what they like eating on holiday and to explain to a French visitor the nature of the meal on a menu.

Basic level

1 Qu'est-ce que tu as/vous avez mangé pour le petit déjeuner aujourd'hui?

2 Qu'est-ce que tu as/vous avez bu au petit déjeuner aujourd'hui?

3 Quels sont les repas que tu prends/vous prenez chaque jour et à quelle heure?

4 Quels fruits aimes-tu/aimez-vous?

5 Quels légumes préfères-tu/préférez-vous?

6 Tu rentres/vous rentrez à la maison pour déjeuner?

7 Quand tu étais/vous étiez en vacances en France, qu'est-ce que tu as/vous avez mangé?

8 Qu'est-ce qu c'est qu'un 'pudding'?

Higher level

1 Si tu préparais/vous prépariez un pique-nique, qu'est-ce que tu achèterais/achèteriez?

2 Si tu n'avais/vous n'aviez presque plus d'argent, qu'est-ce que tu pourrais préparer à manger?

3 As-tu/avez-vous jamais suivi un régime? (*go on a diet*).

4 Quel est ton/votre repas favori?

See **role play section** for further practice (p. 66).

FREE TIME

Candidates should be able to talk about their hobbies and leisure pursuits and to inquire about those of other people. They should be able to give and ask for information about leisure facilities and to express opinions about TV programmes, films, books, etc.

See **vocabulary topic area:** les loisirs

Basic level

1 Comment occupes-tu/occupez-vous tes/vos moments de loisir?

2 Quel est ton/votre passe-temps favori?

3 Quel genre de livres préfères-tu/préférez-vous?

4 Quel genre de musique préfères-tu/préférez-vous?

5 Quel genre de films préfères-tu/préférez-vous?

6 Vas-tu/allez-vous souvent au cinéma?

7 Tu joues/vous jouez d'un instrument musical?

8 Que fais-tu/faites-vous le soir après avoir fini les devoirs?

9 Quel est ton/votre sport préféré?

10 Quels sports peut-on pratiquer à l'école?

Higher level

1 Que fais-tu/faites-vous pour te/vous distraire?

2 Si tu sors/vous sortez le weekend, où vas-tu/allez-vous?

3 Tu es/vous êtes sportif/sportive?

4 Qu'est-ce qui t'/vous intéresse à la télé?

HOLIDAYS

See **vocabulary topic areas**

Candidates should be able to talk about where and how they spend their holidays and to ask others about their holidays. They should be able to talk about holiday plans for the future. If you have already been to France, you should be prepared to give details and your impressions of the area in which you stayed.

Basic level

1 Aimes-tu/aimez-vous voyager? Pourquoi?/Pourquoi pas?

2 Préfères-tu/préférez-vous passer les vacances au bord de la mer ou à la campagne? Pourquoi?

3 Aimes-tu/aimez-vous faire du camping? Pourquoi?/Pourquoi pas?

4 Où es-tu/êtes-vous allé(e)(s) en vacances l'année dernière?

5 As-tu/avez-vous fait des vacances avec un groupe scolaire?

6 Où iras-tu/irez-vous en vacances cette année?

7 Quel pays étranger voudrais-tu/voudriez-vous visiter?

8 Quels pays as-tu/avez-vous visités?

9 Combien de semaines de vacances as-tu/avez-vous par an?

See **role-play section** for further practice on this topic (p. 66).

Higher level

1 Que feras-tu/ferez-vous pendant les grandes vacances?

2 Pourquoi préfères-tu/préférez-vous les auberges de jeunesse?

3 Es-tu/êtes-vous jamais allé en France?

HOME

Basic level

See **vocabulary topic areas**

1 Tu habites/vous habitez une maison ou un appartement?

2 Comment est ta maison?

3 Comment est ta chambre?

You should also be able to describe, in a similar way, the other rooms in your house/flat and the furniture in them.

Higher level

You should be able to answer all the questions at Basic level and also add extra details.

e.g. Combien de pièces y a-t-il au rez-de-chaussée?
Il y en a cinq. Il y a le salon, la salle à manger, la cuisine, la buanderie (*utility room*) et le cabinet de travail de mon père.

1 Si l'on te donnait la permission d'aménager* ta chambre, qu'est-ce que tu ferais?

You should also be able to state preferences and give reasons for your choice.

e.g., Q Tu aimes/vous aimez faire le ménage?
Pourquoi/pourquoi pas?
A J'aime me débrouiller (*doing things for yourself/coping*).
J'aime faire la cuisine mais je déteste faire la vaisselle.
Je préfère repasser (*to iron*) le linge que de nettoyer les vitres (*clean the windows*).
Je n'aime pas voir la maison en désordre mais ce que je préfère vraiment c'est passer la journée à ne rien faire!

FURTHER USEFUL VOCABULARY

ranger la chambre/le salon, etc. to tidy up
cirer les planchers to polish the floors
épousseter to dust
éplucher les légumes to peel the vegetables
travailler dans le jardin to work in the garden
tondre la pelouse to cut the grass
balayer to sweep
faire les lits make the beds
laver la voiture wash the car

GARDEN

At both Basic and Higher levels you should be able to describe your garden and also ask about other people's gardens. The amount of detail required for the Higher level will, of course, be greater.

See **vocabulary topic areas**

1 Tu travailles dans le jardin?
2 Que fais-tu pour aider tes parents dans le jardin?

* aménager = *to furnish/decorate.*

SHOPPING

Candidates should be able to talk about different kinds of shops and the facilities they offer and to express personal opinions and preferences for shopping.

See **vocabulary topic areas**

Basic level

1 Quels magasins y a-t-il près de chez toi/vous?

2 A quelle heure se ferment les magasins en Grande Bretagne? En France?

3 Tu préfères/vous préférez faire des achats chez les petits commerçants ou dans un hypermarché? Pourquoi?

4 Qu'est-ce qu'on peut acheter dans les grands magasins en Grande Bretagne?

Higher level

1 Y a-t-il une grande surface près de chez toi/vous? (*superstore*).
Si oui, qu'est-ce qu'on peut y acheter?

2 Quels sont les avantages ou les désavantages de la grande surface pour le consommateur? (*consumer*).

TIME AND DATE

See **vocabulary topic areas**

You should be able to give/ask for information about the time of day, opening and closing times, market days, public holidays, etc.

Basic level

1 A quelle heure te lèves-tu/vous levez-vous le samedi?

2 A quelle heure te lèves-tu/vous levez-vous le dimanche?

3 A quelle heure te couches-tu/vous couchez-vous le samedi?

4 A quelle heure quittes-tu/quittez-vous la maison le matin?

5 A quelle heure dois-tu/devez-vous rentrer à la maison le soir?

6 La banque est ouverte à quelle heure?

7 Le magasin se ferme à quelle heure?

8 Quel est le jour de marché à Valréas?

9 Que fais-tu/faites-vous le jour de Noël?

10 Que fais-tu/faites-vous pendant les vacances de Pâques?

11 Quelle est la date de ton anniversaire?

12 Comment vas-tu/allez-vous fêter ton/votre anniversaire?

Higher level

At this level, you should be able to deal with more complex ideas of time and date, e.g., to answer questions with ease in the present, perfect and future tenses.

1 Que fais-tu/faites-vous pendant les grandes vacances?

2 Qu'as-tu fait/qu'avez-vous fait pendant les grandes vacances l'année dernière?

3 Que feras-tu/ferez-vous pendant les vacances de mi-trimestre? (*half-term*)

TOWN AND REGION

See **vocabulary topic areas**

Candidates should be able to give information about their home town or village and region. They should also be able to ask others about towns, regions and local amenities. At the Higher level candidates should be able to offer information about regions other than their own and to recommend places of interest to visit.

Basic level

1 Comment est ton/votre village?

2 Comment est ta/votre ville?

3 Tu préfères/vous préférez habiter la ville ou à la campagne?

4 Quels moyens de transport y a-t-il dans ta/votre région?

5 Qu'est-ce qu'il y a d'intéressant à voir dans ta/votre région?

Higher level

1 Comment est la région où tu habites/vous habitez?

2 Si on veut passer une après-midi intéressante dans ta/votre ville, qu'est-ce qu'il faut voir?

3 Quelles sont les régions touristiques de la Grande-Bretagne qu'il faut visiter?

4 Quelle région préfères tu/préférez-vous en France? Pourquoi?

TRAVEL/TRANSPORT

See **vocabulary topic areas**

All candidates should be able to say how they get to and from school, what means of transport they prefer for journeys other than those to and from school, and to ask for information about public/private transport in France as well as give information about public/private transport in their own country.

Basic level

1 Comment vas-tu/allez-vous à l'école?

2 Tu habites/vous habitez loin de l'école?

3 Tu préfères/vous préférez voyager en voiture?

4 Comment peut-on traverser la Manche? (*English Channel*)

5 Peut-on faire du stop (*hitch-hiking*) en Grand Bretagne?

Higher level

1 Sais-tu/savez-vous faire un trajet en métro?

2 Pourquoi préfères-tu/préférez-vous voyager en avion?

3 Pourquoi préfères-tu/préférez-vous faire des trajets en métro?

See **role-play section** for further practice on this topic (p. 66).

WEATHER

See **vocabulary topic areas**

Candidates should be able to describe and comment on weather conditions at home and abroad and to inquire about weather conditions and climates.

Basic level

1 Quel temps fait-il dans ta/votre région en été/en hiver/en automne/au printemps?

2 Quel temps a-t-il fait quand tu étais/vous étiez en vacances l'année dernière?

Higher level

1 Fait-il toujours du brouillard en Angleterre?

2 Quel temps va-t-il faire demain?

3 Quel climat préfères-tu/préférez-vous?

4 Quel temps a-t-il fait quand tu étais en France l'année dernière?

8 THE ORAL EXAM: ROLE-PLAY

8.1 Introduction

In this type of oral test the candidate is presented with a situation which he or she would be likely to meet when visiting France. The examiner plays the role of, for example, a stallholder in a market, a petrol-pump attendant or a booking-office clerk, and the candidate is given written instructions (in English) concerning his or her role, e.g. buying fruit, petrol, a railway ticket, etc.

The test will be in the form of a conversation with the examiner. You will be given several minutes before the actual examination to prepare, but part of the examination may be spontaneous, depending on the answers you give. You must be prepared to sustain a conversation in French according to the situation given.

It is very likely that the 'character' with whom you must hold a conversation will need to be addressed in the polite 'vous' form; but always check your instructions carefully in case the 'tu' form is required, i.e. for talking to a member of your family, or friend of your own age.

Remember to use the words 'monsieur' or 'madame' when addressing a stranger in French.

Check carefully Grammar Revision section 35 (pp. 27–8) to make sure that you know how to form questions in French. Many of the role-playing situations require you to ask someone for information.

You may also be asked to give an order in French in certain situations, e.g. sending for the doctor or policeman. Check the Grammar Revision section for this also.

The following phrases will be useful for many different role-play situations:

Pour aller à . . .?	How do I get to . . .?
Y a-t-il . . .?	Is (Are) there . . .?
J'ai besoin de . . .	I need . . .
Il me faut . . .	I need . . .
Je dois . . .	I must . . .
Je peux . . .	I can . . .
Je ne peux pas . . .	I can't . . .
Puis-je . . .	Can I/May I . . .?
Pouvez-vous . . .?	Can you . . .?
Pouvez-vous me dire . . .?	Can you tell me . . .?
Pouvez-vous me dire où se trouve . . .	Can you tell me where . . . is?
Pourriez-vous . . .?	Could you . . .?
Je voudrais . . .	I would like . . .
Je veux/Je voudrais . . .	I want . . .
Je ne veux pas . . .	I don't want . . .
Attendez!	Wait!
D'accord!	All right!
Bien sûr.	Of course.
Entendu.	Of course.
Certainement.	Of course.
Avec plaisir.	With pleasure.
Malheureusement.	Unfortunately;
Excusez-moi.	Excuse me.
Je suis désolé(e).	I am sorry.
Quel dommage!	What a pity!
Quelle chance!	What luck!
Formidable!	Great!
Chouette!	Great!

De rien, monsieur (madame). **Je vous en prie, monsieur (madame).** **Il n'y a pas de quoi, monsieur (madame)**	These expressions are used as a reply when you have been thanked for something. They are the equivalent of 'Don't mention it' or 'My pleasure' or 'Not at all'.

For each of the following situations a list of useful expressions is given, plus some examination role-play questions and specimen answers.

8.2 Basic Level

SEEKING ACCOMMODATION – CAMPSITE/HOTEL/YOUTH HOSTEL

Useful expressions

Camping

See **vocabulary topic areas**
Avez-vous une place libre, monsieur, pour une tente/une caravane?
Do you have any room for a tent/caravan?
la carte d'identité *identity card*
Où sont les WC et les lavabos? *Where is the toilet and washroom block?*

Hotel

See **vocabulary topic areas**

Est-ce que vous avez des chambres libres, monsieur? *Do you have any vacant rooms, sir?*
une chambre à deux lits (personnes) *a double room*
une chambre à une personne *a single room*
avec salle de bains *with bathroom*
avec douche *with shower*
service compris *service charge included*
le petit déjeuner compris *breakfast included*
la demi-pension *half board*
la pension complète *full board*

Youth hostel (L'auberge de jeunesse)

l'aubergiste/le gardien *the warden*
Avez-vous des lits pour ce soir? *Have you any beds for tonight?*
Est-ce que je peux louer un sac de couchage et des couvertures?
May I hire a sleeping-bag and some blankets?

C'est combien la nuit? }
C'est combien par nuit? } *How much is it per night?*

C'est combien par personne? *How much is it per person?*

1 Au terrain de camping

The examiner, who will be playing the role of the campsite warden, will speak first. This is not a translation exercise. Try to make your conversation as fluent and as natural as possible. Wait for the reply in between each part.

Full marks can be obtained in this section only if a suitable form of the verb is used in each part. You must not consult other sources of information nor write anything down.

(a) Ask if there is any room on the campsite for one night.
(b) Say that you are on your own with just a tent.
(c) Ask where the toilets and washrooms are.
(d) Ask where you will be able to buy some bread in the morning.

2 A l'auberge de jeunesse

You arrive at a youth hostel. The examiner is the warden.

(a) Ask the warden if there is any room.
(b) Say that there are three of you.
(c) Say that you would like to hire sleeping-bags.
(d) Ask if the breakfast is included.

3 A l'hôtel

You arrive at a hotel in the evening. The examiner is the hotel proprietor.

(a) Ask if there are any rooms vacant for the night.
(b) Say that you would like a single room with a bathroom.
(c) Ask the price of the room for the night, and when told ask if the breakfast is included.

ASKING FOR INFORMATION/ASKING THE WAY

Useful expressions

See **vocabulary topic areas**

Le Syndicat d'Initiative *Tourist Information Office*
un plan de la ville *a plan of the town*

une carte de la région *a map of the region*
Pour aller à . . . s'il vous plait? *How does one get to . . . please?*
tournez à droite *turn to the right*
tournez à gauche *turn to the left*
la première rue à droite *the first street on the right*
la première rue à gauche *the first street on the left*
allez tout droit* *go straight on*
allez jusqu'à . . . *go as far as . . .*
Pouvez-vous m'aider? *Can you help me?*
au bout de . . . *at the end of . . .*
. . . minutes d'ici . . . *minutes from here*
. . . mètres d'ici . . . *metres from here*
de l'autre côté *on the other side*
tout près *quite near*

1 At the Information Bureau

You have just arrived with your family in a small French town where you have rented a cottage for a fortnight. You go to the Syndicat d'Initiative. The examiner will play the part of the person on duty.

(a) Ask if the shops are open every day of the week.
(b) Ask what there is to see in and around the town.
(c) Say that you are very interested in castles and ask if there is one nearby.
(d) Ask how you can get to it.

2 Dans la rue

You are in the street and trying to get to your hotel. The examiner is a passer-by.

(a) Ask the passer-by if he/she can help you.
(b) Ask him/her to tell you the way to the Hôtel Moderne.
(c) Ask if you have to catch a bus to get there.

MEETING PEOPLE/INVITATIONS

Useful expressions

présenter *to introduce*
heureux (hereuse) de faire votre connaissance *pleased to meet you*
enchanté(e) *delighted (to meet you)*
Salut! *Hello!*

'Bonjour/au revoir' should always be accompanied by the person's name or 'monsieur/madame'.

(a) Comment allez-vous?	*How are you?*	**(a)** Polite form used when addressing an adult.
(b) Comment vas-tu?		**(b)** For a person of your own age, or younger.
(c) Ça va?		**(c)** Colloquial form.

A bientôt
A tout à l'heure } *See you soon*

A ce soir. *Till this evening*
A demain. *Till tomorrow*
inviter *to invite*

Voulez-vous . . .?
Veux tu . . .? } *Will you?*

Voudriez-vous . . .? *Would you like . . .?*
Je voudrais . . . *I would like . . .*

1 Imagine you have just arrived at the home of your pen-friend in France. His/her mother/father is there to welcome you. Your teacher will play the part of your pen friend's mother/father.

(a) Say you are pleased to meet her/him.
(b) Say you have two suitcases.
(c) Say you would like lemonade.
(d) Say you are not very hungry.
(e) Thank her/him and say you are very tired.

2 A French friend invites you to go to a party in the evening. The examiner is the friend.

(a) Thank your friend for the invitation and say you would like to go.
(b) Ask your friend at what time the party begins.
(c) Ask him/her where you should meet before the party.

* You must be very careful with the pronunciation of 'droit'. The 't' should not be pronounced, unlike 'droite' where the 't' is pronounced.

ILLNESS/INJURY

Useful expressions

See **vocabulary topic areas**

NB especially 'J'ai mal à . . .' *I have a pain . . .*
e.g. J'ai mal à la tête. *I have a headache.* J'ai mal aux dents. *I have toothache, etc.*

1 You are staying with your French correspondent and wake up in the morning with toothache. The examiner is your correspondent's mother/father.

(a) Tell your correspondent's mother/father that you do not feel well and that you have toothache.
(b) Tell him/her that you had to take some aspirins during the night.
(c) Ask him/her to telephone the dentist.

2 Imagine you are taken ill on holiday in France. The doctor comes to see you. Your teacher will play the part of the doctor.

(a) You return the doctor's greeting.
(b) Say you have a headache.
(c) Say you are not eating.
(d) When the doctor prescribes tablets ask when you should take them.
(e) Thank the doctor for the prescription and say goodbye.

GARAGE

Useful expressions

See **vocabulary topic areas**

1 A la station-service
The examiner, who will be playing the role of the petrol-pump attendant, will speak first.

(a) Ask the assistant to fill up the tank.
(b) Ask how much you owe.
(c) Ask if they also sell maps.
(d) Say that you want one of the North of France.

2 Imagine you have just arrived at a garage to say your father's car has broken down on the road. Your teacher will play the part of the person at the garage.

(a) Say the car is on the Paris road.
(b) Say it's three kilometres away.
(c) Say it's green and black.
(d) Say it's a Ford.
(e) When you are asked the registration number, say you don't know.

TRAVEL

Useful expressions

See **vocabulary topic areas**

en auto *by car*
en autobus *by bus*
en avion *by plane*
en bateau *by boat*
par le train *by train*
A quelle heure arrive le train de . . .? *When does the train from . . . arrive?*
A quelle heure arrive l'avion de . . .? *When does the plane from . . . arrive?*
A quelle heure part le prochain train pour . . .? *When does the next train for . . . leave?*
Combien de temps faut-il pour aller à . . .? *How long does it take to get to . . .?*
Faut-il changer de train (d'avion)? *Does one have to change trains (planes)?*

1 A la gare

(a) Say that you want a single, second class ticket to Paris.
(b) Say that you only have a 100 franc note.
(c) Ask what time the train leaves.
(d) Ask where the waiting room is.

2 Imagine you have just got on a bus in Paris with a friend and you are talking to the driver.

(a) Ask if the bus goes to Notre Dame.
(b) Ask for two tickets, please.
(c) Explain you are students.
(d) Say you haven't any change.
(e) Say you are sorry.

RESTAURANT/CAFÉ

Useful expressions

See **vocabulary topic areas**

un steak-frites *Steak and chips*
Qu'est-ce que vous avez comme dessert? *What is there for dessert?*
retenir une table *to reserve a table*

NB Use 'prendre' when you wish to say 'have' in French when speaking of food and drink:
Je prends le petit déjeuner à huit heures. *I have breakfast at eight o'clock.*
Je prendrai un café-crème. *I'll have a white coffee.*

1 A la terasse d'un café

(a) Say that you would prefer to sit outside.
(b) Ask your friend if he/she would like some croissants.
(c) Call the waiter and order one black and one white coffee.
(d) Agree with your friend and ask how long he/she has been living there.

2 In a restaurant

You enter a restaurant with three friends. Your examiner will play the part of the waiter or waitress and your friends.

(a) Ask if there is a table for four.
(b) Ask your friends what they would like to eat.
One it seems would like a salad which is not on the menu.
(c) Order the meal and ask the waiter/waitress if it is possible to have a salad.
(d) You have finished your meal. Ask the waiter/waitress for the bill and then ask if the service is included.

CINEMA/THEATRE

Useful expressions

See **vocabulary topic areas**

les comédies *comedies*
les dessins animés *cartoons*
les films d'amour *romantic films*
les films d'aventure *adventure films*
les films d'espionnage *spy films*
les films de guerre *war films*
les films d'horreur *horror films*
les films policiers *thrillers*
les westerns *cowboy films*
un film doublé *a 'dubbed' film*
un film en noir et blanc *a black and white film*
un film sous-titré *a film with subtitles*
une pièce de théâtre *a play*
une pièce de Shakespeare *a Shakespearian play*
la séance a commencé *the film/play has begun.*

1 The examiner, who will be playing the role of your friend, will speak first.

(a) Suggest you and your friend go to the pictures.
(b) Ask your friend to pass the paper. Then say that there is a good film on at the Rex.
(c) Say that you will have to hurry as it starts at 21h.30.
(d) Ask if your friend has enough money.

2 Imagine you and your penfriend are planning to go to the cinema. Your teacher will play the part of your penfriend.

(a) Say you would like to go very much.
(b) Say you would like to see a French film.
(c) Ask if you are going this evening.
(d) Ask what time it begins.
(e) Say 'All right', and repeat the time.

POST OFFICE/TELEPHONING

Useful expressions

See **vocabulary topic areas**

P et T (Postes et Télécommunications) *Post Office*
le jeton *token required when using a phone in a café*
Qui est à l'appareil? *Who is speaking?*
Allô *Hello!* (Used when answering the phone, but not when greeting someone in the street. 'Bonjour' or 'Salut' is then used.)
Ici . . . *This is . . . speaking*
NB téléphoner **à** quelqu'un *to telephone someone*

1 The examiner, who will be playing the role of the post-office assistant, will speak first.

(a) Say you would like to telephone your friend.
(b) The number is Lisieux 62-03-24.
(c) Ask what booth to go to.
(d) Thank him/her and ask how much it costs for three minutes.

2 You are at the post office in France. The examiner is the counter-clerk.

(a) Tell the clerk you would like to send some postcards to England.
(b) Ask how much it is to send a postcard to England.
(c) Ask for five stamps at this price.

SHOPPING

Useful expressions

See **vocabulary topic areas**

1 You are at a fruit and vegetable stall in the market. The examiner is the stallholder.

(a) Tell the stallholder you would like to buy half a kilo of grapes.
(b) Ask if the small peaches are good to eat.
(c) Ask if the oranges are more expensive than the peaches.

2 Chez le boulanger-pâtissier

The examiner, who will be playing the role of a shop assistant, will speak first.

(a) Ask the assistant to give you two large loaves.
(b) Ask how much the strawberry tarts cost.
(c) Say that they are dear, but that you will take one.
(d) Answer 'yes' to the examiner's question and say that you did not have any breakfast.

BANK/LOST PROPERTY

Useful expressions

un bureau de change *foreign exchange office*
une livre sterling } *a pound (£)*
une livre anglaise }
toucher un chèque de voyage *to cash a traveller's cheque*
une récompense *a reward*

1 You are at the bank. The examiner is the bank-clerk.

(a) Say you would like to change a traveller's cheque.
(b) Show the clerk your passport and say that the cheque is for £20.
(c) Agree to sign the form and ask where the cash desk is.

2 You are at the Lost Property Office. Your father has lost his wallet. The examiner is the employee at the counter.

(a) Tell the employee that your father has lost his wallet.
(b) Tell the employee that your father lost it this afternoon, outside the town hall.
(c) Tell the employee that it contained 500 francs, some photos and a driving licence.

8.3 Higher Level

GARAGE

1 You are at a garage in France. The examiner will play the part of the attendant.

(a) Say hello and ask for 25 litres of 4-star petrol.
(b) Ask the attendant to check the oil.
(c) Ask him/her to check the water-level.
(d) Say that you have a puncture in the spare wheel and ask if they can repair it today.
(e) Ask how much you owe.

2 Your car has broken down in France and you have to telephone a garage.

(a) Say that the car has broken down and ask if they can send someone.
(b) Say where exactly you have broken down.
(c) Say that you haven't had an accident.
(d) But that you can't start the car.
(e) Ask if they can send a breakdown lorry.

SEEKING ACCOMMODATION

Candidates should be able to perform all the tasks set for Basic level and also perform more complex tasks, for example, make a complaint, suggest payment by credit card, etc.

Extra vocabulary

porter plainte *To complain (about)*

une carte de garantie bancaire (*bank*) } *a credit card*
une carte de crédit }

Hotel

You have arrived at your hotel in France. The examiner will play the part of the receptionist.

(a) Give your name and say that you have reserved a room.
(b) Say that you reserved it by telephone, two days ago.
(c) Say that it is a double room with shower.
(d) Ask if you may pay by credit card.
(e) Ask what floor the room is on.
(f) Thank the receptionist.

Camping

You are staying at a campsite which is below the standard that was advertised. You wish to make a complaint to the warden.

(a) Say good-morning to the warden.
(b) Say that you are sorry but that you must make some complaints about the campsite.
(c) Say that your pitch is too near the dustbins.
(d) Say that the showers are dirty, and that there is no hot water.
(e) Say that there is so much noise at night that you cannot sleep.
(f) Say that you will be leaving tomorrow.

Youth hostel

(a) Say hello to the warden.
(b) Ask if there is any room for tonight.
(c) Say that there are four of you, two boys and two girls.
(d) Ask if you can hire sleeping-bags and blankets.
(e) Ask where you can leave your bicycles.
(f) Ask at what time the evening meal is and if there is a telephone.

ILLNESS/INJURY

1 You have witnessed a street accident in France. The examiner will play the part of the policeman.

(a) Say that you were at the corner of the street when the accident happened.
(b) Say that a cyclist turned left without looking where he was going.
(c) Say that he knocked over a lady who was crossing the street.
(d) Give your name and the address of the hotel where you are staying.
(e) Say that the accident happened half an hour ago.

2 You are at the doctor's because you have sprained your wrist. The examiner will play the part of the doctor.

(a) Tell the doctor that you have sprained your wrist.
(b) Say that it is hurting a lot.

(c) Say that you were playing tennis when it happened.
(d) Ask if you need to go to hospital.
(e) Say that you will be returning home next week.

ASKING FOR INFORMATION/DIRECTIONS

1 You are travelling by car in France. You stop in a town for directions. The examiner will play the part of a passer-by.

(a) Say 'Excuse me' to the passer-by.
(b) Say that you are almost out of petrol and ask if there is a petrol station nearby.
(c) Ask if it is open all day.
(d) Ask how far it is from Paris.
(e) Thank the passer-by.

2 You are in Paris and trying to find your way back to your hotel.

(a) Say 'Excuse me' to the passer-by.
(b) Say that you are looking for the Rue St Honoré, and ask if it is far.
(c) Ask if you should return on foot or by the metro.
(d) Ask if the taxis are expensive, and where you can find one, please.
(e) Thank the passer-by.

LOST PROPERTY

You are on holiday in France. You have lost your camera. You go to the Lost Property Office. The examiner will play the part of the assistant.

(a) Say good-morning to the assistant.
(b) Say that you have lost your camera.
(c) Say that you lost it in the market square, yesterday evening.
(d) Say that it is a Kodak.
(e) Give the assistant your name and the address of your hotel.

MEETING PEOPLE/INVITATIONS

1 It is your first evening staying with your penfriend's family in France. The examiner will play the part of your penfriend's mother/father.

(a) Say that you hope to speak a lot of French during your stay.
(b) Say that you hope to improve your French.
(c) Say that you are very tired after your long journey.
(d) Say that you met some French people called Vermorel on the train.
(e) Say that you would like to go to bed and ask at what time you should get up tomorrow.

2 Your French friend (played by the examiner) invites you to go to the cinema.

(a) Say that you would like to go very much.
(b) Say that you have never seen a French film.
(c) Ask if you are going this evening.
(d) Ask at what time the film begins.
(e) Ask if the cinema is far.

RESTAURANT/CAFÉ

1 You are at a café/restaurant on a hot summer's day. The examiner will play the part of the waiter.

(a) When the waiter shows you to a table say that you would prefer to sit outside in the shade.
(b) Thank the waiter and say that that will do nicely.
(c) Say that you would like something cool to drink.
(d) Say that you will have lemon squash.
(e) Say that you are too hot to eat at the moment.

2 You are at a café in France and think that there is a mistake when given your bill.

(a) Call the waiter.
(b) Ask for the bill.
(c) Say that you think that he has made a mistake.
(d) Say that you only had a white coffee and a cake.
(e) Ask him to check the bill, please.

SHOPPING

1 You are in a music shop in France. The examiner will play the part of the assistant.

(a) Say good-morning to the assistant and ask where the record section is.
(b) Say that you are looking for the pop records.

(c) Ask what is at the top of the charts this week.
(d) Ask what is the most popular French singer/group.
(e) Ask if you may listen to the record.

2 You are in a department store in France. The examiner will play the part of the assistant.

(a) Say good-morning to the assistant and ask where the T-shirts are.
(b) Ask if they have any T-shirts in yellow.
(c) Ask for your size.
(d) Ask if they have anything cheaper.
(e) Thank the assistant and ask where you should pay.

TELEPHONING

You are on holiday in France and need to phone home to Great Britain. You go to the post office to make your call. The examiner will play the part of the assistant.

(a) Say good-morning to the assistant.
(b) Ask if you can telephone to Great Britain from there.
(c) Say that you wish to transfer charges.
(d) Give your name and the number you wish to phone.

POST OFFICE

(a) Say good-morning to the assistant.
(b) Say that you wish to send some letters to England.
(c) Ask how much it is for a letter.
(d) Ask how much it is for a postcard also.
(e) Ask for three stamps for your letters and five stamps for postcards.

AT THE TOURIST OFFICE

1 You have gone to the tourist office in a French town. The examiner will play the part of the assistant.

(a) Say good-morning to the assistant.
(b) Ask for a list of the hotels.
(c) Ask if they can recommend a good hotel.
(d) Say that you would like a quiet hotel not far from the town centre.
(e) Ask the assistant how far the hotel is.

2 You are in a tourist office in a French town. You are enquiring about the local area. The examiner will play the part of the assistant.

(a) Say good-morning to the assistant.
(b) Ask if he/she has any information about the local area.
(c) Ask if there are any guided tours.
(d) Ask at what time the castle opens.
(e) Ask if you can get there on foot.

TRAVEL

1 You are going through French customs. The examiner will play the part of the customs' officer.

(a) Say that you have two suitcases.
(b) Say that you have nothing to declare but a bottle of whisky.
(c) Say that it is a present for your penfriend's father.
(d) Say that it cost £6.
(e) Say that you are going to stay in France for three weeks.

2 You are boarding a plane at a French airport. The examiner will play the part of the air-hostess.

(a) Say good-morning and ask where seat 68 is.
(b) Ask at what time the plane will take off.
(c) Ask at what time you will arrive in London.
(d) Ask where you should put your hand-luggage.
(e) Thank the air-hostess.

AT THE TRAVEL AGENCY

You are at a travel agency in France. The examiner will play the part of the assistant.

(a) Say good-morning to the assistant.
(b) Say that you would like to visit the Loire valley.
(c) Say that you would like to go by coach.
(d) Say that you would like a list of comfortable hotels which are not too dear.
(e) Say that you would like to stay for about five days.

9 THE ORAL EXAM: ORAL COMPOSITION

9.1 General Advice

Oral narrative composition based on a series of connected pictures may be tested by your GCSE examining group, at the **Higher Level**. This type of test will usually consist of a set of four or six pictures which relate an incident which you are to imagine that you witnessed or in which you were personally involved. You will be asked to describe in French what happened. You will not be allowed to make any notes but you will be given about ten minutes in which to prepare your narrative. You should use the past tenses (e.g. perfect tense, imperfect tense, but NOT the past historic tense in spoken French).

If you are told that you are to relate the incident as a witness, then the third person parts of the verbs should be used for the main narrative (i.e., il/elle, ils/elles).

If you are personally involved in the incident then you will need to use the je/nous forms for the main part of the narrative.

9.2 Preparation

You must use your preparation time wisely to prepare ALL of the pictures and not just the beginning of the composition. Always prepare a good ending as well as a good beginning since the ending will be fresh in the examiner's mind when awarding you a mark. You should prepare about three or four sentences on each picture, using linking phrases between the pictures in order to produce a continuous narrative and avoid a disjointed effect. Always remember that you are relating a kind of story, so do not use such phrases as 'Dans la première image nous voyons . . .'

Keep the French simple and above all be accurate in your use of verbs. Do not work out the story in English and then try to put it into French. Candidates who try to do this often 'dry up' searching for words and phrases in French. Think in French at all times. Accurate simple French will earn you more marks than complicated but incomplete or innacurate sentences.

Although you will not know beforehand the topic for the oral composition, it is possible for you to do some preparation in the weeks before the examination. The topic chosen for narrative composition often includes an accident or theft, and police, firemen or doctors are often involved. Check that you know the basic vocabulary for those topic areas. Check also words to do with losing one's way, missing trains, breaking an arm or leg, telephoning the police, taking someone to hospital, etc. The topic areas that you should revise especially are . . . accident/injury, café/hotel/restaurant, camping, countryside, house, railway, seaside, shopping, town, travel, weather.
You should also prepare some of the following elements for inclusion in your oral narrative:

(a) a season of the year
e.g. pendant les grandes vacances
au mois de janvier
l'année dernière
au printemps

(b) a day of the week
e.g. lundi dernier
samedi matin
hier soir

(c) a time of day
e.g. à dix heures et demie
à trois heures de l'après-midi

(d) a reference to the weather where relevant
e.g. par un beau jour d'été/
par un mauvais jour d'hiver

(e) a French location if suitable
e.g. à Paris, à Calais, etc.

(f) 'link' words for linking the pictures together
e.g. puis, quelques minutes plus tard,
au bout d'une demi-heure, bientôt

Look at the following sets of pictures and prepare them for oral composition. Time yourself to complete your preparation in ten minutes.

1.
LOCATION DE BATEAUX
10F ½ heure

2.
6

3.
6

4.

5.

6.
6

1.
HOTEL BELLEVUE

2.

3.

4.

5.

6.

9.3 Set Questions on Single Pictures

Some Examination Groups may set questions based on a picture (or pictures) which are to be answered orally. When this type of test is used you must not only study the picture(s) carefully but also pay careful attention to the questions. There will often be a useful piece of information given in the question, usually in the form of the verb. The specific questions will vary according to the picture, but there are several types of question which can apply to almost any picture:

Quel temps fait-il? What is the weather like?
Quelle heure est-il? What time is it?
Comment est . . .? What is . . . like?
Comment sont . . .? What are . . . like?
Combien de . . .? How many (much) . . .?
Où est (sont) . . .? Where is (are) . . .?
Pourquoi . . .? Why . . .?
Qu'est-ce que . . .? What . . .?
Que fait . . .? What is (someone) doing . . .?
Que font . . .? What are (they) doing . . .?
Où se passe cette scène Where is this taking place?
A qui est . . .? To whom does (something) belong?

Look at the following pictures and answer the questions orally, remembering that you will not see the questions in the examination itself.

1 The port

(a) Où se passe cette scène?
(b) Quel temps fait-il?
(c) Quelle heure est-il?
(d) Que vend l'homme au centre?
(e) Combien d'oiseaux voyez-vouz?
(f) Que fait l'homme à droite?
(g) Combien de bateaux voyez-vous?
(h) Que fait l'homme à gauche?
(i) Où se trouve l'agence de voyages?
(j) Que font les enfants?

2 Preparing for the holidays

(a) Où est la voiture?
(b) Où est le chat?
(c) Qu'est-ce qu'il y a dans le coffre de la voiture?
(d) En quelle saison se passe cette scène?
(e) Qu'est-ce qu'il y a à droite de la maison?
(f) Combien de raquettes de tennis y a-t-il?
(g) Qu'est-ce que l'homme tient à la main droite?
(h) Qu'est-ce que la petite fille prend?
(i) Où est le garçon?
(j) Où va la famille?

3 At the swimming pool

(a) Où se passe cette scène?
(b) Quel temps fait-il?
(c) Que fait la dame à droite?
(d) Que fait la dame au premier plan?
(e) Que font les deux filles à gauche?
(f) Que fait-on dans une piscine?
(g) Qu'est-ce qu'on porte pour nager?
(h) Sur quoi la dame s'est-elle couchée?
(i) Qu'est-ce que le garçon (A) va faire?
(j) Savez-vous nager?

4 Snowscene

(a) En quelle saison se passe cette scène?
(b) Quel temps fait-il?
(c) Que font les enfants à gauche?
(d) Que font les enfants près de l'arbre à droite?
(e) Que font les enfants sur la colline?
(f) Décrivez les vêtements de l'enfant (A).
(g) Qu'est-ce qui est arrivée à l'enfant (B)?
(h) Où se trouve la forêt?
(i) Comment vous amusez-vous dans la neige?

Sometimes you are asked to describe a picture, without any questions to prompt you. Say as much as you can about these pictures:

9.4 Other Visual Material

Some candidates may be asked questions in the oral exam on other visual/written stimuli. Check the exam syllabus for your examining group to see if you will have to answer such questions.

Here are some examples . . .

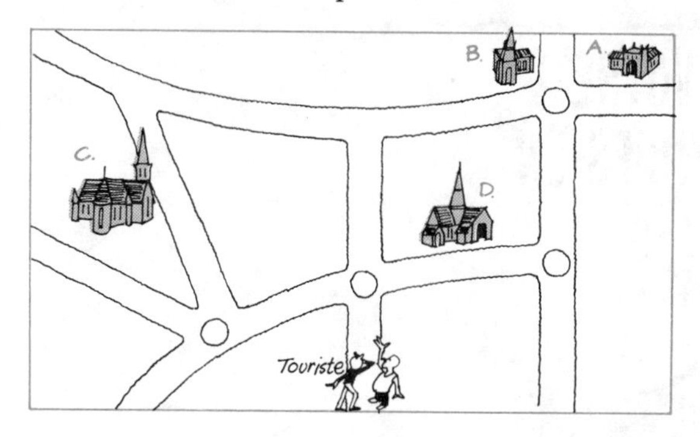

1. A French tourist has asked you the way to Church A. Give him the necessary details in French. *Or*
2. Direct him to Church B. *Or*
3. Direct him to Church C. *Or*
4. Direct him to Church D.

5 Combien de villages y a-t-il sur l'Ile de Ré?
Comment peut-on traverser de La Rochelle à l'Ile de Ré?
Sur quelle île y a-t-il des forêts?
Est-ce que l'Ile D'Aix est plus grande que l'Ile D'Oléron?

ILE D'AIX	ILE D'OLÉRON	ILE DE RÉ
la plus petite des 3 îles 1 village–plages et criques rocheuses Bateau entre Fouras et Aix	30 km de long Plages–Massifs forestiers Port de pêche Port entre ORS et CHAPUS	30 km de long 10 villages–grandes plages et landes sauvages Bac entre La Rochelle et Ré

6 Qu'est-ce qu'on peut voir au théâtre de Châteadun le 18 octobre?
Quand y aura-t-il des promenades guidées dans la région d'Orléans?
Les deux récitals de piano auront lieu où?
Qu'est-ce qu'il y a d'intéressant à Orléans pour ceux qui aiment les fleurs?

CHÂTEAUDUN	ORLÉANS
● Concerts à la Salle des Gardes du Château; rens. (37) 45.22.46. —Orchestre de Chambre Bernard Thomas–**21 septembre**. –Récital piano et violoncelle–**12 octobre**. ● Grand Ballet argentin de Cordoba–Théâtre **18 octobre**; rens. (37) 45.22.46. ● "Lorsque l'enfant paraît" d'A. Roussin–Théâtre–**20 octobre**; rens. (37) 45.11.91.	● Récital piano–Bach, Schumann, Liszt. Salle de l'Institut–**13 Octobre**; rens. (38) 54.02.41. ● Parc Floral: rens. (38) 63.33.17. –Critérium des roses à massif–**Septembre** –Critérium des dahlias–**Octobre**. ● Randonnées découvertes de la nature avec guide: rens. (38) 62.04.88. –le Pithiverais–**20 et 21 juillet**

7 Regardez cet emploi du temps.
A quelle heure commencent les cours du matin?
Combien de leçons a-t-on le samedi matin?
Que fait-on entre midi et deux heures?
Quel jour de la semaine a-t-on une classe de gymnastique?

	lundi	**mardi**	**mercredi**	**jeudi**	**vendredi**	**samedi**
8-9h	maths	anglais	histoire	français	travaux pratiques	maths
9-10h	anglais	sciences naturelles	maths	histoire	gymnastique	anglais
10-11h	travaux manuels	géographie	français	dessin	français	français
11-12h	travaux manuels	français	géographie	dessin	instruction civique	
			L'HEURE DU DÉJEUNER			
2-3h	français	maths	—	maths	anglais	
3-4h	chimie	physique	—	travaux pratiques	maths	
4-5h	chimie	physique	—	musique	perme	

8 Connaissez-vous ces régions de la France?
Où êtes-vous allé en France?
Où se trouvent les Pyrénées
Qu'est-ce que c'est qu'une roulotte?
Où se trouve la Côte Atlantique?

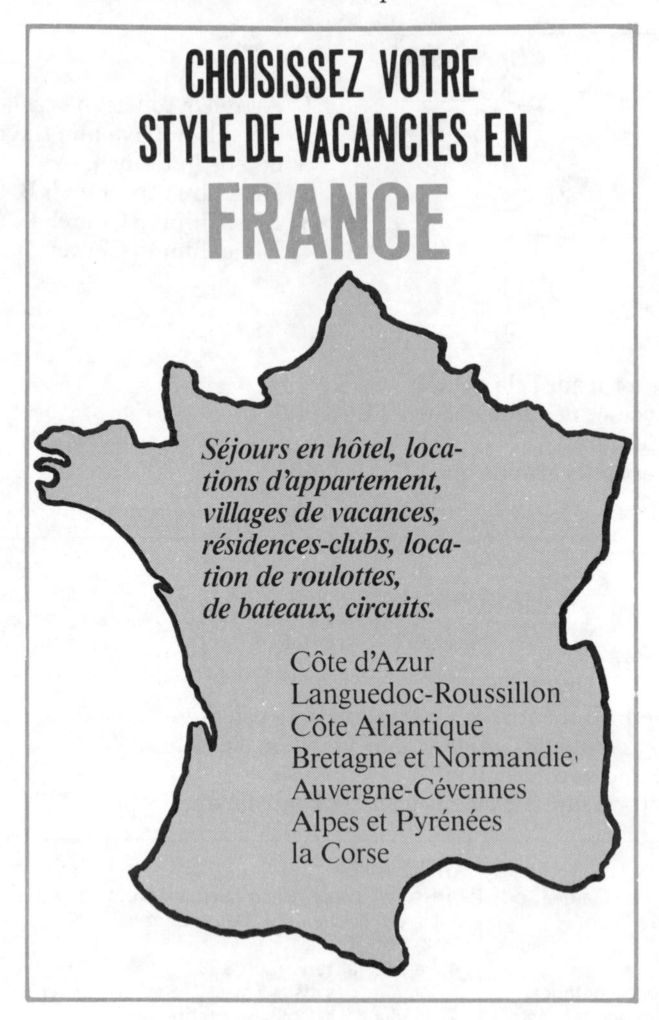

CHOISISSEZ VOTRE
STYLE DE VACANCIES EN
FRANCE
Séjours en hôtel, locations d'appartement, villages de vacances, résidences-clubs, location de roulottes, de bateaux, circuits.
Côte d'Azur
Languedoc-Roussillon
Côte Atlantique
Bretagne et Normandie
Auvergne-Cévennes
Alpes et Pyrénées
la Corse

9 Peut-on aller à l'Office de Tourisme pour chercher un hôtel?
Qu'est-ce qu'on peut faire du 12 au 15 mai?
Qu'est-ce qu'on va faire le 9 avril?
A quoi peut-on assister au mois de juillet?
Quel sera une date importante pour les fanatiques de cyclisme?

L'Office de Tourisme

est à votre disposition pour:

—ACCUEIL–INFORMATION
—RÉSERVATION HOTEL
—VISITES GUIDÉES ET CONFÉRENCES SUR LA VILLE ET LA RÉGION
—ORGANISATION DE CONGRÉS

GRANDES DATES 1988

FEVRIER
Du 10 au 20–Holiday on Ice

MARS
Le 19–Concours de Belote
Du 25 au 28–"4 Jours de l'Automobile"

AVRIL
Le 9–Bal de l'Élection de la Reine

MAI
Du 12 au 15 et de 21 au 23 Semaine de la Voile
Le 29–Cavalcade

JUIN
Le 12–4ème Prix Cycliste du Mail

JUILLET
Festival d'Art Contemporain

AOÛT
Du 26 au 4 septembre
Foire Exposition Commerciale

SEPTEMBRE
Du 15 au 19–Grand Pavois

OCTOBRE
Du 14 au 20–"6 Jours de Course à Pied"
Du 28 au 31–Festival du Film de la Voile

10 Comment est la ville d'Orange?
Quels bonbons peut-on acheter à Montélimar?
Qu'est-ce qu'il y a d'intéressant à voir à Crussol?
Qu'est-ce que c'est qu'un pictogramme?
On quitte les autoroutes à droite ou à gauche en France?

panneaux touristiques

Vous allez rencontrer sur votre trajet des panneaux à fond brun.

Ils se présentent généralement sous la forme :

- *D'un symbole dessiné (pictogramme) précédant un texte message écrit.*
Vous avez quelques secondes pour deviner la signification du pictogramme précédant le texte.

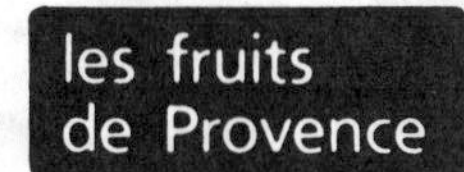

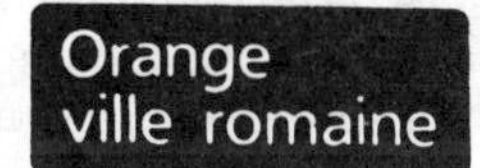

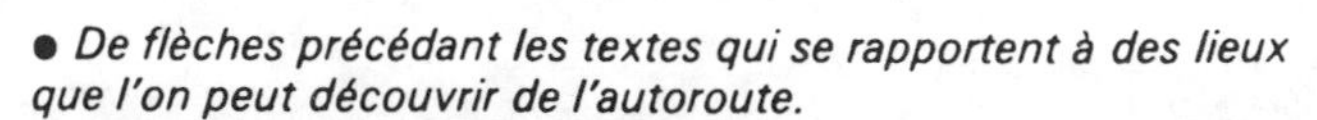

- *De flèches précédant les textes qui se rapportent à des lieux que l'on peut découvrir de l'autoroute.*

le Massif Central
mont Pilat

vallée
du Rhône

château
de Crussol

Les panneaux sont destinés :

- *A vous expliquer les régions traversées, les paysages aperçus, les particularités...*
- *A vous annoncer les principaux centres d'intérêt touristique, les grandes réalisations d'intérêt national, les centres d'information touristique.*

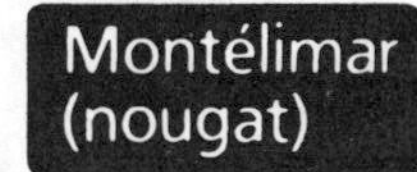

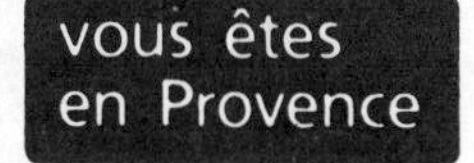

information
touristique

9.5 Photographs

Some examining groups may include a question in the oral exam based on a photograph. You will be asked questions about the photograph which you must answer in French.

Here are some examples but remember that in an oral exam you will not see the questions but only hear them.

1 Quel jour est-ce?
Quel temps fait-il?
Que fait-on?
En quelle saison se passe cette scène?
Qu'est-ce qu'on voit derrière les arbres?

2 Où se passe cette scène?
Quel temps fait-il?
Qu'est-ce que la jeune fille demande?
Que fait l'homme?
Comment peut-on traverser la rue?

3 Qu'est-ce qu'on peut faire ici?
Peut-on y entrer le dimanche?
A quelle heure s'ouvre le magasin le matin?
A quelle heure se ferme-t-il le samedi soir?
Comment s'appelle le supermarché?

CAMPING CARAVANING
Les Dunes ★★★★
arrete de classement n° 82 DIR 1/4 du 5/1/82

TARIF 85	PRIX PAR JOUR HAUTE SAISON 1/07 AU 31/08	PRIX PAR JOUR BASSE SAISON 1/09 AU 30/06
PAR ADULTE	10,50	7,00
PAR ENFANT DE MOINS DE 7 ANS	6,50	4,50
PAR EMPLACEMENT 100m² une voiture comprise	61,00	47,00
PAR EMPLACEMENT DOUBLE 160m²	91,10	70,00
GARAGE MORT sur l'emplacement	51,50	2,00
TAXE DE SEJOUR PAR PERSONNE	1,10	
MACHINES A LAVER le jeton	12,00	12,00
TENNIS l'heure	38,00	28,00

4 Comment s'appelle le camping?
C'est combien pour jouer au tennis par jour en haute saison?
C'est combien la machine à laver par jour en basse saison?
C'est combien la taxe de séjour par personne?
Peut-on prendre des douches chaudes ici?

9.6 The Oral Exam: Summary

The key to success in this part of the exam is . . . PRACTICE. You will not suddenly be able to speak French well by practising for a few days before the exam only.

Begin your revision programme EARLY. Practise . . . EVERY DAY.

Hold imaginary conversations with yourself in FRENCH.

Try to include some new words each time you practise and then REMEMBER them.

If possible, try to find a native speaker who will ask you questions on a regular basis.

Above all . . . BE PREPARED.

10 LISTENING COMPREHENSION

10.1 Preparation

One of the most difficult sections of the GCSE exam to revise on your own is the Listening Comprehension section. You should try to listen to as much authentic French as possible but . . . this is not easy. If possible, try to ask a native speaker to put the following extracts on to tape so that you can actually hear French when you are revising for this part of the exam. Some examining groups may have specimen tapes, which you can obtain, which will give you some idea of the tests which you will have to take.

The best way to prepare for this part of the exam is to spend some time in France, speaking only French. However, you can do quite a lot to revise for this type of test even if you are not able to go to France.

Always LISTEN carefully.

Learn the VOCABULARY TOPICS section carefully.

Use your COMMON SENSE when answering.

Here is an extract from the National Criteria . . .
BASIC LISTENING
'Candidates should be expected . . . to demonstrate understanding of . . . announcements, instructions, requests, monologues (e.g. weather forecasts, news items) interviews and dialogues.'

Here are some specimen questions. Answer them in English.

10.2 Basic Level

A l'aéroport

1 You are on a plane to France when you hear the following announcement:
'Nous survolons la Manche à deux mille mètres. Nous atterrirons à Heathrow dans un quart d'heure. Le temps à Londres est nuageux.'

(a) What are you flying over?
(b) How high are you flying?
(c) Where will you land?
(d) What is the weather like in London?

2 You are at an airport in France and hear the following announcement:
'Le vol Air France numéro deux cent quarante. Embarquement immédiat, porte numéro onze.'

(a) What is the flight number? (Answer in English)
(b) What is about to happen?
(c) Where do you have to go?

3 You are in an airport lounge in France. You hear the following announcement.
'Les passagers du vol numéro trente, destination Londres, sont priés de se rendre à la porte numéro dix. L'avion va décoller dans trente minutes à neuf heures cinq.'

(a) Where is the flight for?
(b) What are the passengers told to do?
(c) At what time will the plane take off?

Au terrain de camping

1 You are at a campsite in France when you hear the following announcement. Explain to your parents, who do not understand French, what is being said.
'Les campeurs sont informés que le boucher passe tous les mercredis à neuf heures et demie.'

2 You ask for a brochure at a campsite. The warden asks you . . .
'En français, anglais ou allemand?'
What are you being asked?

3 When enquiring about vacancies at a campsite in France, you are asked . . .
'C'est pour une tente ou une caravane?'
What are you being asked?

4 You are then told . . .
'Votre emplacement est au fond du champ.'
Where is your pitch?

5 When you ask where the showers are, you are told . . .
'Les douches se trouvent là-bas, à côté de la piscine.'
Where are the showers?

A la douane

You are going through Customs in France. The Customs officer asks you the following questions. Explain to your parents, who do not understand French, what you are being asked.
'Votre passeport, s'il vous plaît.'
'Vous n'avez rien à déclarer?'

Au bureau des objets trouvés

You have gone to the lost property office to enquire about a camera that you have lost. The assistant asks you . . .
'Où l'avez-vous perdu?'
'Il est de quelle marque?'
What two questions are you asked?

A la banque

You have gone to a bank in France to change some traveller's cheques. You are told . . .
'Pour toucher un chèque de voyage, il faut aller au guichet marqué "change".'
What do you have to do?

Directions

1 You are in France looking for a museum. When asking for directions, you hear . . .
'Pour aller au musée, il faut prendre la première rue à droite.'
What instruction are you given?

2 You are in France looking for the cathedral. When asking for directions, you hear . . .
'Pour aller à la cathédrale, il faut continuer tout droit.'
What instruction are you given?

3 You are looking for the record department in a store.
You are told . . .
'C'est au troisième étage.'
Where is it to be found?

4 You are looking for the nearest metro station in Paris. You are told . . .
'La station la plus proche est à cinq minutes à pied. Descendez cette rue, puis tournez à gauche.'
(a) How far away is it?
(b) What two directions are you given?

Les visites

1 You are in France on holiday and are in front of a museum. You hear the following announcement.
'Visite guidée du musée, tous les mercredis à quatorze heures. Vous pouvez acheter votre ticket à l'entrée du musée. Durée de la visite: une heure et demie.'
(a) On what days can you visit the museum?
(b) At what time?
(c) How long will the guided tour last?
(d) Where can you buy your ticket?

2 You are about to visit a castle and hear the following announcement.
'Le château est ouvert tous les jours entre quatorze heures et vingt heures.'
(a) On what days is the castle open?
(b) At what times can you visit?

3 You are on a guided tour of Paris and have arrived at the Arc de Triomphe. Your guide tells you . . .
'L'Arc de Triomphe a été construit pour célébrer les victoires de Napoléon.'
Explain to your friend, who does not understand French, what you are told.

4 When visiting the cathedral of Notre-Dame, you are told . . .
'Les tours s'élèvent à soixante-neuf mètres.'
How high are the towers?

A l'hôtel/en vacances

1 You arrive at a hotel in France which you have booked in advance. The receptionist speaks to you. What is she saying?
'Votre chambre est au troisième étage. C'est la chambre numéro quarante-deux.'

2 What answer are you given when you enquire about an evening meal?
'Nous n'avons pas de restaurant ici mais il y a un bon restaurant en face de l'hôtel.'

3 The next morning, you switch on the radio to hear the weather forecast. What will the weather be like?
'Aujourd'hui il fera encore froid. Le ciel sera couvert toute la journée.'

4 The hotel receptionist speaks to you as you are leaving the hotel. What is she saying?
'Au revoir. Bonne promenade.'

5 While sight-seeing, you ask a passer-by how to get to the cathedral. What does he tell you?
'Je regrette, mais je ne sais pas. Je ne suis pas d'ici.'

6 A little later in the morning, you realize that you have lost your bag. You go to the lost property office. What does the assistant ask you?
'Où l'avez-vous perdu? Qu'est-ce qu'il y avait dans votre sac?'

7 When you return to your hotel, the receptionist has a message for you. Who is the message from?
'Votre agence de voyages nous a téléphoné.'

8 What problem has arisen?
'Il y aura un délai à l'aéroport demain. L'avion partira à midi au lieu de dix heures.'

Medical situations

1 You want to make an appointment to see the doctor. The receptionist asks.
'C'est urgent? Qu'est-ce que vous avez?
. . . Vous pouvez voir Monsieur le docteur dans un quart d'heure.'

(a) What does the receptionist ask you?
(b) When can you see the doctor?

2 Having consulted the doctor, you are told . . .
'Ce n'est pas grave. Voici une ordonnance. Vous trouverez la pharmacie au coin de la rue.'

(a) Is it serious?
(b) What does he give you?
(c) What does he say you will find? Where?

3 You are at the chemist's. When he has made up your prescription the chemist tells you . . .
'Voilà des comprimés. Prenez-en trois par jour.'
What do you have to take and when?

4 You have gone to the dentist's in France because you have toothache. He tells you . . .
'Je vais vous faire un plombage.'
What is the dentist going to do?

Social situations

1 You are arranging to meet a friend, who tells you . . .
'On se recontre à huit heures devant le cinéma.'

(a) Where are you going to meet?
(b) At what time?

2 You are at the ticket office at the cinema. The assistant says to you . . .
'Quel âge avez-vous? Il est interdit aux moins de dix-huit ans.'

(a) What are you being asked?
(b) Why?

3 In the cinema you hear the following announcement . . .
'Mesdames et messieurs, vous pouvez acheter des glaces et des bonbons dans le foyer.'

(a) What can be bought?
(b) Where?

4 You receive a phone call from your French penfriend . . .
'Allô . . . J'arriverai mardi matin à dix heures à l'aéroport de Heathrow au lieu de lundi après-midi. Il y a une grève à l'aéroport de Lyon.'

(a) When will your penfriend arrive? (Give day and time.)
(b) Where will he arrive?

5 While staying with your penfriend in France, the telephone rings. You answer the phone. This is what you hear . . .
'Allô . . . Ici Jean-Pierre. Tu as envie de sortir ce soir? Dis à Bruno de venir nous rencontrer au café à neuf heures.'

(a) Who is the call from?
(b) What message does he give you?

A la gare

1 You are at a railway station in France. You hear the following announcement.
'Le rapide en provenance de Lille est annoncé au quai numéro cinq.'

(a) What train is announced?
(b) Is it arriving or departing?
(c) At which platform is it?

2 'Le train en provenance de Dijon arrivera à onze heures au quai numéro deux. Les passagers à destination de Mâcon sont priés de s'asseoir dans les cinq premiers wagons du train.'

(a) Where is the train coming from?
(b) What time will it arrive?
(c) At which platform?
(d) Where are the passengers for Mâcon asked to sit?

3 'Gare de Rouen. Un quart d'heure d'arrêt.'
How long will the train stop in Rouen?

4 'L'express en provenance de Lyon est en retard et arrivera en gare à dix heures vingt.'
At what time will the train arrive?

5 You have asked a porter for directions. He tells you . . .
'Le train pour Paris? Il faut aller au quai numéro quatre.'
Where do you have to go to catch your train?

6 You are at a railway station in France and hear the following announcement about your train . . .
'Le train pour Nice partira à seize heures trente, quai numéro huit.'

(a) When will your train leave?
(b) From what platform?

Tourist information

1 When enquiring about tourist facilities in a French town, you are told . . .
'Il y a une piscine, un complexe sportif et un vélodrome.'
What three facilities are mentioned?

2 After enquiring what they are, you are told . . .
'La piscine se trouve au jardin public. Le complexe sportif est en face de ce bâtiment et le vélodrome se trouve à deux kilomètres d'ici sur la route de Dijon.'
Where are they to be found?

3 You are looking for the youth hostel in a French town. You make enquiries at the tourist information office. You are told . . .
'L'auberge se trouve sur la route nationale trois, à cinq kilomètres d'ici.'
How far away is the youth hostel?

4 When you arrive at the youth hostel, a passer-by tells you . . .
'Le bureau d'acceuil se ferme entre dix heures et dix-huit heures.'
When will you be able to book in?

Weather

You are in France, listening to the weather forecast on the radio.

1 'Demain. Temps froid et nuageux dans la région de Grenoble.'
What will the weather be like tomorrow in the Grenoble district?

2 'Ce weekend le temps sera ensoleillé.'
What will the weather be like this weekend?

3 'Aujourd'hui il fait encore froid. Le ciel sera couvert toute la journée.'
What will the weather be like today?

4 'Des orages éclateront en fin de l'après-midi.'
What will the weather be like later in the afternoon?

5 'Le beau temps persistera avec des températures en hausse.'
What is going to happen to the weather?

10.3 Higher Level

'Candidates should be expected to demonstrate the skills listed under basic listening over a wider range of clearly defined topic areas. They should be able to identify the important points or themes of the material, including attitudes, emotions and ideas which are expressed; to draw conclusions from, and identify the relationship between, ideas within the material which they hear, and to understand a variety of registers, such as those used on radio and TV, in the home, in more formal situations . . .' (National Criteria)

1 Your French friend is describing her school and daily routine to you . . .
'Je suis élève au lycée de Poitiers. Je suis en seconde, section B. J'aime étudier les langues vivantes mais ma matière préférée c'est la biologie. Les cours au lycée commencent à huit heures. Je rentre à la maison à midi puis je reprends les cours à deux heures de l'après-midi jusqu'à cinq heures et demie. J'ai toujours beaucoup de devoirs le soir. Pendant la semaine je travaille jusqu'à onze heures. Le weekend je sors avec mes amis.'

(a) In which form is the speaker? (Give the English equivalent.)
(b) What does she like studying?
(c) What is her favourite subject?
(d) At what time do lessons start in the mornings?
(e) How long does she have for lunch?
(f) Where does she have lunch?
(g) At what time do the afternoon lessons begin?
(h) Until what time?
(i) Why can't she go out in the evenings during the week?
(j) What about the weekends?

2 Your French friend is telling you about his holidays . . .
'Pendant les grandes vacances je suis allé chez mes grands-parents au bord de la mer. J'y suis resté un mois. Royan, la capitale de la Côte de Beauté, est une des stations balnéaires les plus modernes de France. Elle a été reconstruite après les bombardements qui l'ont dévastée en 1945. Il y a une école de voile à Royan où j'ai passé la plupart de mon temps. J'y ai pratiqué aussi la planche à voile, sport très à la mode.'

(a) Where and with whom did the speaker spend his summer holidays?
(b) How long did he stay with them?
(c) Why is Royan one of the most modern holiday resorts?
(d) Where in Royan did the speaker spend most of his time?
(e) What else did he do?

3 You are staying with your French penfriend and he is discussing with another friend where they should take you . . .
Jean-Luc: Il faut profiter de la visite de John pour aller faire une promenade en bateau-mouche.
Pierre-Yves: D'accord. Nous avons mal aux pieds d'avoir tant marché.
Jean-Luc: Tu as l'horaire des bateaux-mouches?
Pierre-Yves: Oui. Sur le buffet. Alors, on peut prendre le bateau à trois heures. La promenade dure une heure et quart. Comme ça nous pourrons rentrer pour prendre le goûter à l'anglaise à cinq heures.

(a) What does Jean-Luc suggest doing?
(b) Why does Pierre-Yves think that this will be a good idea?
(c) Where is the time-table?
(d) How long will the trip last?
(e) Why is this a convenient time?

4 Your French friend is describing her family to you . . .
'Jai deux frères et une soeur. Mes deux frères sont mariés et j'ai deux petites nièces. Ma soeur a treize ans. Elle est de taille moyenne, et est assez mince. Elle porte des lunettes qu'elle n'aime pas du tout. Elle voudrait porter des lentilles cornéennes mais mes parents disent qu'elles coûtent trop cher. Mon père est fonctionnaire mais il va prendre la retraite bientôt. Il a marre de son travail. Ma mère est ménagère. Quant à moi, je voudrais être interprète. C'est un métier qui m'intéresse beaucoup. J'aimerais bien travailler pour la Communauté Economique Européenne. J'étudie deux langues–l'anglais et l'allemand–mais ma langue favorite, c'est l'anglais.'

(a) How many brothers and sisters does the speaker have?
(b) What young relatives besides her sister does she mention?
(c) How old is her sister?
(d) Give two details about her sister's physical appearance.
(e) What do her parents think are too dear?
(f) What job does her father do?
(g) What is he going to do soon?
(h) What job does her mother do?
(i) For whom would the speaker like to work?
(j) What is her favourite language?

5 Two French friends are discussing television programmes . . .
Françoise: Tu as vu le film à l'Antenne 2 hier soir?
Anne-Marie: Lequel? Celui de Hitchcock?
Françoise: Non. Celui de Jacques Deray, *La Piscine.*
Anne-Marie: Non, malheureusement. Mes parents insistent toujours sur leur choix d'émissions. Nous n'avons qu'un poste, alors, il faut regarder ce qu'ils veulent ou m'enfermer dans ma chambre pour écouter mes disques.
Françoise: Quel dommage! Moi, j'ai un poste portatif dans ma chambre.
Anne-Marie: Quelle veine!
(a) On what channel does Anne-Marie think the Hitchcock film was?
(b) Give in English the title of the Jacques Deray film.
(c) Why can't Anne-Marie always see the programmes that she wants?
(d) What does she sometimes do when not watching television?
(e) What does Françoise have in her bedroom?
(f) What does Anne-Marie think about this?

6 Two French friends are talking about their town and the changes that have taken place.
Guy: Notre ville a bien changé de visage pendant les années quatre-vingts. La construction du parking à plusieurs étages au centre-ville ainsi que le complexe sportif font preuve d'un manque d'intelligence de la part du conseil municipal!
Laurent: Mais toi, tu utilises le parking et le complexe sportif! Tu y joues au squash deux fois par semaine!
Guy: C'est vrai. Mais cela ne veut pas dire que je les accepte esthétiquement.
Laurent: Pour moi, les changements les plus remarquables de notre ville sont l'accroissement des crimes et le vandalisme.
Guy: Et l'accroissement du bruit et de la saleté des rues.'
Laurent: Tu te rappelles l'ancien cinéma qui a été remplacé par le supermarché?
Guy: Oui, quand j'étais petit, j'y allais toutes les semaines.
Laurent: Moi, aussi. A l'âge de dix ans je me passionnais pour les westerns mais aujourd'hui je préfère les films de science-fiction.
Guy: Tu sais qu'on passe *La Guerre des Etoiles* à la télé ce soir.
Laurent: A quelle heure, sur quelle chaîne?
Guy: A dix heures sur FR3.
(a) During what particular period of time does Guy say that the town has changed?
(b) What does he say is proof of the town council's lack of intelligence?
(c) Why does Laurent find Guy's answer surprising?
(d) How often does Guy play squash?
(e) What have been the most noticeable changes for Laurent concerning the town?
(f) What two additional changes does Guy then mention?
(g) What has the supermarket replaced?
(h) Why did Guy know this place well?
(i) What type of film does Laurent prefer today?
(j) Give in English the name of the film on television that evening. At what time and on what channel?

7 You are with your French friend when he meets another friend in town.
Denis: Salut, Marc. Que fais-tu en ville?
Marc: Salut. J'ai rendez-vous chez le dentiste. J'ai mal aux dents depuis deux jours et je n'en peux plus.
Denis: Le pauvre! Nous, John et moi, nous allons chez Antoine. Il vient d'acheter une moto, une Honda.
Marc: Chouette! Mais dis donc, je croyais qu'il manquait toujours d'argent.
Denis: C'est vrai, mais ses parents lui ont offert la moto pour son anniversaire.
Marc: Qu'il a de la chance! Mes parents disent que je dois gagner de l'argent avant d'acheter une moto. Il a son permis de conduire, Antoine?
Denis: Non, pas encore. Mais sa moto a moins de 50cm^3 donc il a le droit de la conduire sans permis.
Marc: Alors, mon vieux, je te quitte car je dois être chez le dentiste dans cinq minutes.
Denis: Il va te faire un plombage ou tu veux qu'il arrache la dent?
Marc: N'importe lequel pourvu que je n'aie plus mal aux dents! Au revoir, Marc. Au revoir, John.
(a) What is Marc doing in town?
(b) Where are John and Denis going?
(c) Why?
(d) Why does Marc find this surprising?
(e) What explanation does Denis have?
(f) Why does Marc think that Antoine is lucky?
(g) Does Antoine have a driving licence? Give a reason for your answer.
(h) Where does Marc have to be in five minutes?
(i) What alternatives face him?
(j) Which will he choose and why?

8 You are seeking information at the railway station about a train from Paris to Lyon. You are told . . .
'Il y a un rapide à 10h 30 et le TGV à midi. Si vous prenez le TGV vous arriverez à 14h 30. Le rapide arrivera à 14h 45. Mais le TGV coûte plus cher que le rapide.'

(a) Which train is the more suitable if you want to get to Lyon as quickly as possible?
(b) Which would you choose if you were looking for the cheapest train available?

9 You are entering a restaurant in France. The waiter says to you . . .
'Bonsoir madame, monsieur. Une table pour deux? Vous préférez une table à la terrasse? En voici une tout près de la porte. Vous voulez commander tout de suite? . . . Deux steaks à point? Bien monsieur.'

(a) Where exactly is your table?
(b) How does the waiter suggest your steaks should be cooked?

10 You hear the following announcement over the campsite loud-speaker . . .
'Bal costumé et feux d'artifice ce soir à 21 heures, près de la piscine. S'il fait mauvais temps le bal aura lieu dans la salle de jeux.'

What is going to take place this evening? (Choose the most appropriate answer.)

(a) A midnight swim.
(b) Fireworks.
(c) Games.
(d) A balloon race.

11 You are in the household department of a large shop in France. You hear the following announcement over the loudspeaker . . .
'Approchez-vous du rayon électro-ménager. Regardez bien les jolis petits gadgets à des prix ridicules. Les prix sont imbattables. Au revoir les longues heures dans la cuisine. Ces gadgets feront tout. Vous n'avez qu'à vous en servir pour retrouver une vie calme et heureuse.'

Give four reasons why you should buy the goods on offer.

12 You are on a guided tour of a French château. The guide is speaking . . .
'Le château de Colombes est situé à vingt kilomètres de Rouvray, dans la vallée de Neufchâtel. L'histoire de ce château remonte au treizième siècle. La tour octogonale et le colombier datent du quinzième siècle. Le parc et les jardins s'étendent sur trois hectares au bord de la rivière.
'Ils servent de cadre à une présentation permanente de sculptures modernes. Le château a été récemment restauré. Dans le grand salon, il y a une exposition d'art moderne et au colombier il y a une exposition de tapisseries d'Aubusson.'

(a) How far from Rouvray is the château?
(b) How far back does the château date?
(c) When was the dove-cote added on?
(d) What was also added at the same time?
(e) What are permanent features of the gardens?
(f) What has happened to the château recently?
(g) Where is the modern art exhibition?
(h) What is in the dove-cote?

13 Here is an extract from a French radio bulletin . . .
'Accident de chemin de fer en Haute-Savoie. Quinze personnes sont mortes, une vingtaine de blessés. L'accident s'est produit sur la ligne Gap/Briançon près du barrage de Serre-Ponçon. Il y a deux hypothèses pour expliquer le tragique accident: la fatigue de la part du mécanicien ou un animal sur la voie.'

(a) How many people have been killed in the accident?
(b) What kind of an accident was it?
(c) How many people have been injured?
(d) Give two details about the location of the accident.
(e) What two possible explanations for the accident are suggested?

14 Here is another extract from a radio bulletin . . .
'Une maladie contagieuse se propage dans la région de Villeneuve. Des centaines de gens sont déjà atteintes et l'on prévoit un grand accroissement de malades pendant le weekend. Il s'agit d'une maladie à virus non-identifié qui se transmet par contact direct avec les gouttelettes salivaires. On estime que la moitié de la population âgée de plus de cinq ans risque d'être atteinte. L'incubation dure en moyenne cinq jours mais la période de contagiosité commence deux à trois jours avant l'apparition d'une toux sèche et pénible. En l'absence de complications—les complications graves sont rares—la guérison se fait vers le dixième jour. Le traitement est, paraît-il, inutile hormis une petite prescription de confort contre la douleur et un sirop contre la toux.'

(a) What is happening in the area around Villeneuve?
(b) How many people have already been affected?
(c) What is predicted for the weekend?

(d) How is it transmitted?
(e) What prediction is made concerning the number of people likely to be affected?
(f) What lasts on average about five days?
(g) Are there likely to be serious complications?
(h) What happens about the tenth day?
(i) What appears to be ineffective?
(j) With what exceptions?

10.4 Specimen Examination Questions

There follow four specimen listening comprehension examination papers, two at Basic level and two at Higher level.

Attempt them in the same way as you have answered the questions so far.

BASIC LEVEL

Section A

1 You and your two friends are at the Tourist Office. The assistant gives you this information.
'L'Hôtel de la Gare est à deux cents mètres d'ici.'
Where is the Hotel de la Gare?

2 You arrive at the hotel and ask about accommodation. What exactly are you offered?
'Je peux vous donner une grande chambre au deuxième étage. Ça vous va?'

3 The following day, you want to do some shopping. You ask a passer-by the way to the market. His directions are:
'Pour aller au marché couvert? Eh bien, vous prenez la première rue à droite; vous continuez tout droit. C'est près de la poste.'

(i) you take the . . .
(ii) then you . . .
(iii) it's next to the . . .

4 At the market you are buying some fruit–you have asked for a pound of apples.
'Alors, voilà trois belles pommes. Ça fait huit francs cinquante.'

(i) How many apples does the assistant say there are?
(ii) How much do they cost?

5 You want to buy a present costing up to 30F.
'Dans ces prix-là, vous avez une poupée à 20F.'

(i) What does the assistant suggest?
(ii) How much does it cost?

6 You are in a supermarket and you hear the following announcement.
'Le magasin ferme dans cinq minutes.'

What information are you being given?

7 You telephone the home of a French friend. His mother answers you.
'Jacques vient de sortir avec des copains au cinéma. Il sera de retour à la maison après le film. Si tu veux rappeler vers onze heures, il sera certainement là.'

(i) Where is your friend?
(ii) Who is he with?
(iii) What does his mother suggest you do?

8 In your hotel you are ordering a meal.
'Je suis désolée, mais nous n'avons plus de rôti de porc mais je vous conseille fortement le plat du jour–le poulet provençal.'

(i) Why can't you have roast pork?
(ii) What does the waitress recommend?

9 At the reception desk you want to know at what time breakfast is served. What does the receptionist tell you?
'Le petit déjeuner est servi à partir de sept heures et demie.'

10 You also want to know if there is a library nearby.
'Il y a une bibliothèque, à trois km de l'hôtel . . . vous pouvez y aller à pied mais vous avez le car qui passe assez souvent devant l'hôtel.'

(i) How far away does the receptionist say it is?
(ii) What information does he give you about getting there?

11 You decide to spend your last evening at a concert. In the queue, you overhear a couple talking about the concert hall.

F: 'J'aime bien cette salle. Elle est chouette et on est bien assis.'
M: 'Oui, tu as raison. Mais regarde, il y a trois prix différents.'
F: 'On devrait aller au balcon. C'est pas trop cher et on entend mieux.'

(i) How many different ticket prices are there?
(ii) Which seats does the girl suggest?
(iii) What *two* reasons does she give?

12 After the concert, you'd like something to eat.
'Je regrette, mais le restaurant est fermé . . . mais si vous voulez prendre une consommation au bar . . . Il est ouvert jusqu'à 23 heures.'

(i) What is the problem about the restaurant?
(ii) What does the waiter suggest?
(iii) What further information does he give?

13 Your holiday is over, so you have to pay for your hotel bill. As well as the cost of the room, what exactly are the other two items on your bill?
'Bon, très bien, je vous fais la note tout de suite. Alors trois petits déjeuners . . . un coup de téléphone en Irlande du Nord et une chambre double pour une nuit . . . cela vous fait exactement 130F.'

What is the total cost?

14 You're going to Paris by plane. At Montséllier airport, there's a problem.
'Ah, je suis désolée mais vos bagages sont trop lourds. Ils pèsent 4 kg de plus que la limite autorisée et vous devez payer une taxe supplémentaire.'

(i) What seems to be wrong?
(ii) What do you have to do about it?

15 Finally, you arrive at Roscoff to get the boat to Cork. You hear this announcement. What is the problem?
'Nous informons les passagers que le départ du ferryboat en direction de Cork est retardé d'une heure. Merci.'

Section B

You will hear a young Frenchman talking about his stay in Belfast, where he shares a flat with two other people. Listen to the whole recording first; it will then be reread in sections, so you will hear each section twice.

'Je partage un appartement avec deux Irlandais. L'un est étudiant, l'autre est fonctionnaire. Chacun a sa chambre et le salon, la cuisine et la salle de bain sont en commun. Ma chambre n'est pas très grande mais elle est très claire et très agréable.

'L'appartement se trouve dans le quartier de l'université qui est certainement un des plus calmes de la ville . . . Je m'y plais bien et j'aime beaucoup cet appartement.

'En ce qui concerne les week-ends j'essaie le plus souvent possible de sortir de Belfast. J'ai pu ainsi visiter les environs de la ville et d'autres parties de l'Irlande comme le Donegal, le Connemara etc. Quand je ne pars pas . . . eh bien je fais du sport: tennis, squash, piscine . . . je joue aussi assez souvent au snooker. Enfin une chose est sure, c'est que je n'ai pas le temps de m'ennuyer.'

Section I

(a) What nationality are his flatmates?
(b) What are their occupations?
(c) What is his room like?

Section II

(a) Where exactly is his flat?
(b) What does he say about the area?

Section III

(a) What does he try to do at weekends?
(b) If he doesn't do this, what does he usually do instead?

(*Northern Ireland Schools Examination Council*)

HIGHER LEVEL

Section A

1 You are staying on a school exchange visit to France. Pupils from Northern Ireland are staying at the homes of French pupils. You overhear the parents of one of the French pupils, Catherine, talking about their guest—they seem to be worried about her. What two reasons are suggested?

M: 'Mais qu'est-ce qu'elle a, l'amie de Catherine?'
F: 'Je ne sais pas. Je commence à me faire du souci.'
M: 'Peut-être qu'elle regrette son pays.'
F: 'Je ne sais pas. Peut-être qu'elle a laissé son copain en Irlande?'

2 In order to plan what to do, you need to know what the weather will be like. So you listen to the weather forecast.
'Ce matin il pleuvra sur la majeure partie de la France. Ce temps continuera sur la partie ouest. Sur le bassin parisien et la partie est il y aura quelques éclaircies, dans l'après-midi.'

(a) What will the weather be like in the morning?
(b) And in the afternoon?

3 Unfortunately you've developed a heavy cold, and you've had to see the doctor. What TWO pieces of advice are you given?
'Alors un bon conseil si vous voulez vous rétablir rapidement . . . Tâchez de rester au lit pendant deux jours au moins et surtout ne prenez que des boissons chaudes.'

4 There's an item about a dock strike on the French news—Northern Ireland is also mentioned.
'Bonsoir. Voici les informations de 20h.
Sur Antenne 2.
A part la visite du Premier Ministre britannique en France, l'événement majeur c'est bien sûr la grève des dockers en France. Ils demandent en effet plus de sécurité dans leurs conditions de travail, et, pour faire aboutir leurs revendications, bloquent presque tous les ports français. C'est ainsi, par example, que des élèves en provenance d'Irlande du Nord et qui avaient passé 2 semaines en France pour un échange ne peuvent actuellement pas rentrer chez eux. Ils sont heureusement hébergés par des familles dans la région de Cherbourg. Nous espérons bien sûr que la situation va rapidement s'arranger pour eux.'

(a) Apart from the dockers' strike, what other item of news is mentioned?
(b) Why have the dockers gone on strike?
(c) How has the strike affected a group of Northern Irish pupils?
(d) What temporary solution has been found?

5 You've gone for an outing by car with the French family you've been staying with. You are involved in a minor road accident. The other driver is very angry.

'Mais enfin, ça ne va pas? Vous ne savez pas conduire peut-être. Vous ne savez pas qu'on s'arrête quand il y a un feu rouge? Vous avez votre permis de conduire dans une pochette surprise, à ce que je vois. Regardez tous ces dégâts—le pare-choc est tordu, mon phare est abimé.

'Qui va payer pour ces réparations? Ça va me coûter une vraie fortune. Il ne faut pas dormir quand on conduit, vous devriez le savoir. Et regardez—mon manteau est complètement déchiré. Il était tout neuf. Et j'ai du sang sur moi. Il faut m'emmener à l'hôpital: peut-être c'est grave, je ne sais pas. Allez chercher la police, c'est la seule solution maintenant.'

(a) What does she suggest that your friend's father has done wrong?
(b) Name one of the items on her car which she says has been damaged?
(c) What advice does she give your friend's father about driving?
(d) What other item has been damaged and in what way?
(e) Why does she want to be taken to hospital?
(f) What does she say is the only solution?

Section B

1 Read each part of the question carefully.
2 Listen to all of the French recording.
3 The recording will be played again in three parts.
4 Listen again to part one of the recording.
5 Answer the questions in English relating to part one.
6 Listen again to the recording. Check your answer.
7 Repeat stages 4, 5 and 6 for remaining parts of recording.

Jean-Pierre is a Frenchman who lives in Northern Ireland. He has returned home for a holiday and is being interviewed about his impressions of life in this country. Answer these questions.

Female voice
'Alors Jean-Pierre, vous venez de passer quelques mois en Irlande du Nord, parlez-nous de vos impressions du pays.'

Male voice
'Avant que je m'arrive en Irlande du nord, je me faisais beaucoup d'idées qui, finalement se sont révélées fausses. Je croyais que c'était un pays très froid et que les gens cherchaient uniquement à se battre contre la police et l'armée, car la télévision et la presse françaises ne rendaient compte que de l'actualité. Il est vrai aussi que ma première impression de Belfast quand je suis sorti de la gare n'a pas beaucoup aidé à changer mon point de vue. Je ne connaissais que très peu la langue, et l'état de la gare et des environs n'était pas très accueillant.

'Mais les personnes que j'ai recontrées m'ont montré un autre côté de la vie. Elles m'ont présenté beaucoup de leurs amis, et je suis allé dans beaucoup de pubs et je dois dire que j'ai recontré une ambiance que je n'avais jamais connue auparavant. Je crois qu'ici en Irlande, le sens des rapports–(très important)–demeure, à la différence de chez moi où beaucoup de gens restent chez eux le soir. Je suis allé dans différents endroits tels que Cookstown, Portrush, Newcastle, Enniskillen et j'y ai recontré la même hospitalité.

'Mais je dois avouer que j'ai eu quelques déceptions en Irlande. N'ayant pas de voiture, j'ai dû quelquefois prendre les transports en commun. La qualité de ces transports n'est pas très bonne. Le dimanche est un jour mort en Irlande du Nord car aucun divertissement n'est organisé. Beaucoup de gens restent chez eux au weekend. J'ai dû donc, souvent, rester seul, regarder la télévision, ou me promener dans les jardins publics. Mais malgré cela, je quitterai Belfast avec de très bonnes impressions.'

Female voice
'C'est bien intéressant Jean-Pierre, je vous remercie.'

Part A

1 What sort of country did Jean-Pierre think Ireland was?

2 What were his first impressions on arrival?

Part B

3 What quality does Jean-Pierre think people in Northern Ireland have, that is not so obvious in France?

4 What did he say about other towns in Northern Ireland?

Part C

5 Two things particularly disappointed him. What were these?

6 How did he spend Sundays when he was alone?

(*Northern Ireland Schools Examination Council*)

FOUNDATION/GENERAL LEVELS

Together with a friend, you decide to go on a package tour for a weekend to Paris to watch the France v. Scotland rugby match. You take the plane from Glasgow airport and after a two-hour flight you arrive just outside Paris, at the Charles de Gaulle airport. You've already made a hotel reservation through your travel agent. All you have to do is to find your way around Paris and enjoy yourselves.

1 You have touched down at Charles de Gaulle airport. As you enter the terminal buildings, you hear an announcement. Where do you have to go?
'Les voyageurs en provenance de Glasgow sont priés de se rendre an contrôle des passeports.'

2 The official at immigration control asks you a question as you come up to his desk. What does he want?
'Votre passeport, s'il vous plaît.'

3 Then he speaks to you again. What does he want to know this time?
'Combien de jours allez-vous rester en France?'

4 You go to the Customs check where the officer speaks to you. What is he asking you to do?
'Ouvrez la valise, s'il vous plaît.'

5 You want to get in to the centre of Paris, so you go to the information desk at the airport and ask. The girl replies. What ways are there of getting in to Paris?
'Eh bien, vous pouvez prendre un taxi, ou il y a le bus qui fait la navette aux Invalides.'

6 She asks you a question about the length of your stay. How many days does she mention?
'Vous allez rester deux jours au minimum?'

7 When you've told her, she advises you to buy something. What does she advise you to buy?
'Alors, je vous conseille d'acheter un billet spécial.'

8 She goes on to explain. What does this enable you to do? What does she say about the price? On what means of transport can you use it?
'C'est un billet qui vous permet de découvrir Paris pour un prix très modéré en bus ou en métro.'

9 Off you go. You get into Paris and find your hotel. You go to the reception, and speak to the girl on duty. She looks at her records. What is she offering you?
'Oui, voilà. Une chambre à deux lits, avec douche.'

10 Then she takes the key, and gives it to you. What number is the room? On what floor is it?
'C'est la chambre numéro deux cent dix, au deuxième étage.'

11 You're feeling hungry, and ask the receptionist if you can have a meal. However, there seems to be a problem. What is the problem? What does the receptionist suggest?
'Malheureusement le restaurant est fermé en ce moment... mais il y a un restaurant self-service tout près, Rue St Lazare.'

12 You go out to find the Rue St Lazare, but you can't find it. You ask a passer-by. Where do you have to go?
'Eh bien, vous allez au coin de la rue, vous tournez à gauche, et vous voilà. C'est très facile.'

13 After your meal, you go sightseeing, but it's tiring, so you stop for a drink. When you want to pay, you call the waiter. How much does he say that it is?
'Un crème et une bière, ça fait onze francs, monsieur.'

14 You're a long way from your hotel. You take a taxi. You get into a conversation with the taxi driver. What is he asking?
'Vous êtes anglais, non?'

15 You then go on to talk about the rugby match the following day. What does he say about rugby?
'Vous allez voir le match demain? Moi, je n'aime pas le rugby, je préfère le football. Pour moi, le rugby, c'est trop sauvage.'

16 Next morning, you wake up and switch on the radio to listen to some music. While you're getting dressed, you hear the weather forecast. What will the weather be like?
'Ce week-end, il fera encore froid. Le ciel sera plus nuageux, avec des risques de neige samedi soir.'

17 As you leave the hotel that morning, the receptionist speaks to you. What is she saying?
'Au revoir. Bonne journée. Amusez-vous bien!'

18 After the match, you meet a group of French teenagers and you start talking. One of them introduces himself and his friends. Where are they from?
'Nous sommes de Toulouse, dans le sud-ouest, près de la frontière espagnole.'

19 Eventually, he suggests that you join them. What two suggestions is he making?
'Vous voulez venir avec nous? On va manger dans un petit restaurant? Ou bien on va prendre quelque chose à boire?'

20 In the course of the conversation, one of the French boys says that he's been to Scotland. When did he visit Scotland? What did he and his friends do when they were there?
'L'année dernière je suis allé en Ecosse voir le match à Edimbourg. Nous avons passé quelques jours en Ecosse. On a visité le château d'Edimbourg, et on a écouté la musique folklorique.'

21 You wonder if you can meet the next day, and you begin to discuss what you can do. What do they suggest? Why is it not such a good idea?
'Oui, si vous voulez. Demain c'est dimanche. On peut prendre un bateau-mouche voir les monuments, mais c'est cher, ça.'

22 Then they come up with something completely different. What is it?
'Mais, le dimanche, il y a un marché très intéressant, c'est le marché aux oiseaux. C'est fantastique, ça.'

(*Scottish Examinations Board*)

GENERAL/CREDIT LEVELS

Together, with a friend, you are on a package tour for a weekend in Paris to watch the France v. Scotland rugby match.

1 After the match, you meet a group of French teenagers and you start talking. One of them introduces himself and his friends. Where are they from?
'Nous sommes de Toulouse, dans le sud-ouest, près de la frontière espagnole.'

2 Eventually, he suggests that you join them. What two suggestions is he making?
'Vous voulez venir avec nous? On va manger dans un petit restaurant? Ou bien on va prendre quelque chose à boire?'

3 In the course of the conversation, one of the French boys says that he's been to Scotland. When did he visit Scotland? What did he and his friends do when they were there?
'L'année dernière je suis allé en Ecosse voir le match à Edimbourg. Nous avons passé quelques jours en Ecosse. On a visité le château d'Edimbourg, et on a écouté la musique folklorique.'

4 You wonder if you can meet the next day, and you begin to discuss what you can do. What do they suggest? Why is it not such a good idea?
'Oui, si vous voulez. Demain c'est dimanche. On peut prendre un bateau-mouche voir les monuments, mais c'est cher, ça.'

5 Then they come up with something completely different. What is it?
'Mais, le dimanche, il y a un marché très intéressant, c'est le marché aux oiseaux. C'est fantastique, ça.'

6 You arrive back at the hotel and the receptionist has a message for you. What is the message?
'Votre agence de voyages vient de téléphoner. Il paraît qu'ils ont fait une erreur avec vos billets. Alors vous ne pourrez plus partir avec l'avion de 10 heures lundi matin. Vous devez prendre le vol qui part à midi. Votre car sera devant l'hôtel à neuf heures quarante-cinq pour vous emmener à l'aéroport.'

7 Next morning, two of the teenagers, a boy and a girl, come to fetch you in their father's car. They have decided to take you on a tour of Paris. Soon the car is forced to a halt in the traffic. What is causing the hold-up?
'Ah, il y a beaucoup de voitures aujourd'hui. Qu'est-ce qui se passe?'
'Il y a peut-être eu un accident? Tiens, Pierre, regarde si tu vois quelque chose.'
'D'accord. Ah, il y a une manifestation place de l'Eglise. C'est ça qui a causé l'embouteillage. Attendez, je vois des filles et des garçons qui distribuent des feuilles de papier.'

8 A girl approaches the car. What is she annoyed about?
'Aidez-nous à sauver nos arbres!'
'Pourquoi? Qu'est-ce qu'il y a?'
'Vous n'êtes pas au courant? Ils vont abattre les arbres de la place de l'Eglise. Bon, vous savez que ces arbres sont là depuis plus de cent ans. C'est un endroit tranquille pour les enfants. Les vieux y viennent jouer aux boules. Enfin, c'est le centre de la vie de ce quartier. Et vous savez pourquoi? C'est qu'ils vont construire un parking souterrain!'

9 Shortly afterwards you see a poster advertising a record win on the National Lottery. Your two friends talk about what they would do with a big win. What are their ideas? Are these ideas really so very different from each other?
'Tiens, quelle chance! Si moi je gagnais le gros lot . . .'
'Qu'est-ce que tu ferais?'
'Je ferais des voyages à des pays exotiques prendre le soleil toute la journée.'
'Parce que tu es paresseuse!'
'Tu as raison. Je voudrais vivre comme un millionnaire!'
'Moi au contraire, j'achèterais une maison de campagne pour mes parents . . . et une voiture sportive pour moi.'
'Capitaliste, toi aussi!'

10 You arrive at the Arc de Triomphe where you hear a guide addressing a group of French tourists. What information is he giving them?
'Nous voilà devant le célèbre Arc de Triomphe qui a été construit pour célébrer les victoires de Napoléon Bonaparte. Il se trouve au centre exact de la ville de Paris et au milieu d'une place qu'on appelait autrefois la place de l'Etoile, parce que les grands boulevards qui commencent ici donnent à la place la forme d'une étoile. Vous voyez ici la flamme éternelle qui brûle à la mémoire du soldat inconnu. C'est ici que chaque année, le 14 juillet, le Président de la République rend honneur aux soldats morts pour la Patrie.'

11 Your two friends start an argument with each other. What is the argument all about?
'Pour moi, je trouve ça affreux de faire des monuments pour célébrer la guerre.'
'Ce n'est pas pour célébrer la guerre, c'est pour honorer les morts. On ne doit pas oublier tout ce qu'ils ont fait pour la France.'
'Oui, mais c'est un monument à Napoléon et il a causé beaucoup de morts. On parle des victoires de Napoléon mais n'oublie pas que des milliers de soldats sont morts à cause de lui. Il n'y a pas de victoire. On perd toujours dans la guerre.'

(*Scottish Examinations Board*)

11 READING COMPREHENSION

11.1 Introduction

All GCSE examining groups include a reading comprehension test in their common-core objectives. At Basic Level 'Candidates should be expected, within a limited range of clearly defined topic areas, to demonstrate understanding of public notices and signs (e.g. menus, time-tables, advertisements) and the ability to extract relevant specific information from such texts as simple brochures, guides, letters and forms of imaginative writing considered to be within the experience of, and reflecting the interests of, sixteen-year-olds of average ability. Candidates should be required to demonstrate only comprehension, not to produce précis or summaries.' (National Criteria)

As the title (reading comprehension) states, these tests are designed to find out if a candidate is able to understand what he/she reads in French. The emphasis is on *reading* and *understanding*. Careful learning of key topic areas will help you greatly in this type of test. Here are some of the key words and phrases which you are expected to know at Basic Level to demonstrate your understanding of public signs and notices.

11.2 Notices and Signs

PUBLIC NOTICES (GENERAL)

APPUYEZ / APPUYER } press
CONCIERGE caretaker
DÉFENSE DE . . . it is forbidden to . . .
EN DÉRANGEMENT . . . out of order
À DROITE on the right
FERMÉ closed
À GAUCHE on the left
HORS SERVICE out of order
INTERDIT / INTERDICTION DE . . . } forbidden
LIBRE free
NE . . . PAS / NE PAS } don't . . .
OUVERT open
PRIÈRE DE . . . please
. . . PRIÉS DE . . . are requested to . . .
PRIVÉ private
POUSSEZ / POUSSER } push
SAUF . . . except . . .
S.V.P. (S'IL VOUS PLAÎT) please
SORTIE exit
TIREZ / TIRER } pull
TOUT DROIT straight on

NOTICES FOR ACCOMMODATION

ACCUEIL reception
S'ADDRESSER À LA RECEPTION ask at the reception desk
APPARTEMENTS flats
AUBERGE DE JEUNESSE youth hostel
CHAMBRES / CHAMBRES LIBRES / CHAMBRES À LOUER } rooms available
CHAMBRES MEUBLÉES furnished rooms
CHAMBRES TOUT CONFORT comfortable rooms
COMPLET full

DOUCHES showers
ÉTAGE floor/storey
GÎTE self-catering accommodation (in the country)
HÉBERGEMENT lodging
LOUER to rent
PETIT DÉJEUNER COMPRIS breakfast included
REZ-DE-CHAUSSÉE ground floor
TÉLÉPHONE DANS TOUTES LES CHAMBRES telephone in every room

NOTICES AT A BANK

BANQUE bank
BUREAU DE CHANGE foreign exchange office
CAISSE cash desk
CAISSE D'ÉPARGNE savings bank
CHANGEUR AUTOMATIQUE
CHANGEUR DE MONNAIE
CHANGEUR PIÈCES DE MONNAIE } coin-changing machines
DEVISES (ÉTRANGÈRES) foreign currency
GUICHET counter
Sce ÉTRANGER foreign counter

NOTICES AT CAMP SITES

ACCUEIL reception
BAC À LINGE sink for washing clothes
BAC À VAISSELLE sink for washing dishes
COMPLET full
DOUCHES showers
EAU POTABLE drinking water
EAU *NON* POTABLE water unsuitable for drinking
EMPLACEMENT pitch
LAVABOS wash basins
OBJETS TROUVÉS lost property
POUBELLES dustbins

NOTICES FOR EMERGENCIES

CROIX ROUGE Red Cross
DANGER DE MORT extreme danger
DANGER D'INCENDIE fire danger
POMPIERS
SAPEURS-POMPIERS } Fire Brigade
SECOURS help
ISSUE DE SECOURS
SORTIE DE SECOURS } emergency exit
SECOURS ROUTIERS FRANÇAIS motorway breakdown service
URGENCE emergency

NOTICES FOR PARKING

CAISSE AUTOMATIQUE automatic machine for paying
CÔTÉ DE STATIONNEMENT parking on this side
DÉFENSE DE STATIONNER no parking

DISQUE OBLIGATOIRE compulsory parking disc
DISTRIBUTEUR ticket machine
FAITES L'APPOINT put in the exact money
L'APPAREIL NE REND PAS LA MONNAIE the machine does not give change
GRATUIT free
HORODATEUR ticket machine
LIBRE free
NE PAS STATIONNER do not park
PARC AUTO
PARC DE STATIONNEMENT
PARKING } car park
PARKING SOUTERRAIN underground parking
PARCMÈTRE parking-meter
PARCOTRAIN car park for commuters
PAYANT you have to pay
RÉSERVÉ reserved

STATIONNEMENT ALTERNÉ SEMI-MENSUEL parking allowed on one side alternating bi-monthly
STATIONNEMENT AUTORISÉ parking allowed
STATIONNEMENT BILATÉRAL AUTORISÉ parking allowed on both sides
STATIONNEMENT INTERDIT no parking

STATIONNEMENT RÉGLEMENTÉ parking regulations in force
STATIONNEMENT TOLÉRÉ UNE ROUE SUR TROTTOIR parking allowed with one wheel on the pavement
VÉHICULES DE TOURISME SEULEMENT tourist vehicles only
ZONE BLEUE/DISQUE OBLIGATOIRE parking disc required in blue zone

ZONE D'ENLÈVEMENT DES VÉHICULES vehicles towed away in this zone

NOTICES AT A POST OFFICE

P et T
POSTES ET TELECOMMUNICATIONS } post office
BOÎTE AUX LETTRES letter box

AUTRES DESTINATIONS (letters) for other destinations
GROSSES LETTRES bulky letters
IMPRIMÉS printed matter
HEURES DES LEVÉES collection times
DERNIÈRE LEVÉE last collection
HEURES D'OUVERTURE opening times
TARIF RÉDUIT reduced rate
TIMBRES-POSTE postage stamps

INSTRUCTIONS IN A TELEPHONE KIOSK

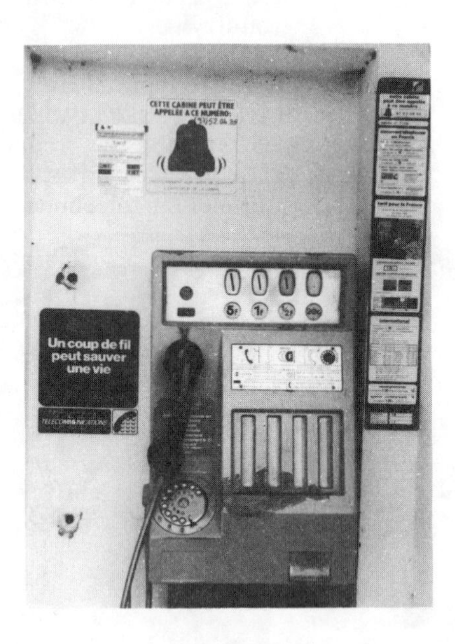

Consulter la carte de taxation ou l'annuaire. (*Please see taxation map or directory.*)

Décrocher le combiné.
(*Pick up the receiver.*)

Attendre la tonalité.
(*Wait for the dialling tone.*)

Appeler votre correspondant.
(*Make your call.*)

Au signal, introduire au moins le minimum indiqué sur la carte de taxation.
(*When you hear the signal, insert the minimum amount.*)

Introduire d'autres pièces si vous désirez poursuivre votre conversation. *Or*
Ajouter des pièces pour prolonger la communication.
(*Put in more coins if you want to continue your conversation.*)

Au raccrochage, les pièces visibles sont restituées. *Or*
Raccrocher à la fin de la conversation, les pièces restant apparentes vous seront restituées.
(*Visible coins are returned after hanging up.*)

NOTICES INSIDE PUBLIC BUILDINGS

ASCENSEUR lift
BUREAU D'ACCUEIL reception
CONCIERGE caretaker
DIRECTION manager's office
ENTRÉE entrance
ESCALIER stairs
ÉTAGE 1er first floor (etc.)
PRIVÉ private
RÉCEPTION reception
REZ-DE-CHAUSSÉE ground floor
SALLE room/hall
SANS ISSUE no exit
SONNETTE DE NUIT night bell
SOUS-SOL basement

SIGNS FOR PUBLIC CONVENIENCES

DAMES ladies
FEMMES ladies
HORS SERVICE out of use
LIBRE vacant
MESSIEURS gents
OCCUPÉ engaged
SANITAIRES toilets
TOILETTES toilets
WC PUBLICS public toilets

NOTICES AT A RAILWAY

ACCÈS AUX QUAIS to the platforms

AUTORAIL railcar for local travel
BANLIEUE suburban
BILLETS tickets

BILLETS DISTRIBUTION AUTOMATIQUE tickets from a ticket machine
BUREAU DES OBJETS TROUVÉS lost property office
CHARIOTS trolleys
COMPOSTER to date-stamp
COMPOSTEUR EN DÉRANGEMENT (utiliser un autre appareil pour valider votre billet) ticket stamping machine out of order, use another machine
CONSIGNE left luggage office
CONSIGNE AUTOMATIQUE luggage lockers
CORAIL air-conditioned inter-city trains
CORRESPONDANCES connections
COUCHETTES sleeping cars
GARE station
GARE MARITIME boat terminal
GRANDES LIGNES main line trains
GUICHET booking office
HORAIRES time-tables
IL EST INTERDIT DE TRAVERSER LES VOILES it is forbidden to cross the tracks
MÉTRO underground
PASSAGE SOUTERRAIN subway
POUR VALIDER VOTRE BILLET COMPOSTEZ-LE to validate your ticket, date-stamp it
QUAI platform
RAPIDES fast trains
RENSEIGNEMENTS information
RER (RÉSEAU EXPRESS RÉGIONAL) suburban rail network
SALLE D'ATTENTE waiting-room
SNCF (SOCIÉTÉ NATIONALE DES CHEMINS DE FER FRANÇAIS) the French railway network
SORTIE exit

TAC (TRAIN-AUTOS-COUCHETTES) car sleeper train
TAJ (TRAIN-AUTOS-JOURS) daytime motorail service
TEE (TRANS-EUROPE-EXPRESS)
TGV (TRAIN À GRANDE VITESSE) high speed train
TRAINS EN PROVENANCE DE trains arriving from . . .

NOTICES IN RESTAURANTS AND CAFÉS

ALIMENTATION food
BOISSONS drinks
BRASSERIE restaurant with bar
BUFFET snack bar, e.g. at a station
CASSE-CROÛTES snacks
CRÊPES pancakes

ENTRÉE entrance/first course
FRITES chips
FRUITS DE MER seafood
GLACES ice creams
GRILLADES grills

JAMBON ham
LIBRE-SERVICE self-service
MENU VACANCES special menu for holidaymakers
MOULES mussels
PLATS CUISINÉS cooked meals
PLATS À EMPORTER take-away food
PLAT DU JOUR today's speciality
POULET chicken
REPAS COMPLET complete meal
REPAS RAPIDES quick meals
REPAS À TOUTES HEURES meals at all hours
RELAIS ROUTIERS transport cafes which serve good cheap meals

SALON DE THÉ tea room
SAUCISSES sausages
SERVICE COMPRIS service charge included
STEAK FRITES steak and chips
VIN DU PAYS local wine

ROAD/STREET SIGNS

ACCÔTEMENT IMPRATICABLE/NON STABILISÉ soft verges
AIRE / AIRE DE REPOS lay-by
ATTENDEZ wait
ATTENTION ENFANTS watch out for children
AUTOROUTE motorway
BISON FUTÉ traffic information (available where there is a Red Indian sign)
CARS EN CORRESPONDANCE shuttle service buses connecting stations
CÉDEZ LE PASSAGE give way

CHAUSSÉE DÉFORMÉE uneven road surface
CÔTÉ DE STATIONNEMENT parking on this side
D (on yellow background) 'route départementale'/secondary road
DÉFENSE DE STATIONNER no parking
DÉVIATION OBLIGATOIRE compulsory diversion
ENTRÉE entrance
FIN DE ZONE BLEUE end of parking area requiring a blue disc
FIN DE CHANTIER end of roadworks
INTERDICTION DE TOURNER À DROITE no right turn
INTERDICTION DE TOURNER À GAUCHE no left turn
INTERDIT forbidden
ITINÉRAIRE BIS secondary route
ITINÉRAIRE CONSEILLÉ / ITINÉRAIRE RECOMMANDÉ alternative route
N / RN (on red background) 'route nationale' main road
PARKING GRATUIT free parking
PARKING SOUTERRAIN underground parking
PASSAGE INTERDIT no entry
PASSAGE PROTÉGÉ you have the right of way
PASSEZ pass
P PAYANT pay and display car park
PÉAGE toll
PÉRIPHÉRIQUE ring road
PIÉTONS pedestrians
PL (POID LOURDS) heavy/long vehicles
PRIORITÉ priority/right of way
PRIVÉ private

RALENTISSEZ slow down
RAPPEL reminder
ROCADE by-pass
ROULEZ AU PAS drive very slowly
ROULEZ LENTEMENT drive slowly
ROUTE BARRÉE road blocked
RUE PIÉTONNE pedestrian precinct
SENS INTERDIT no entry
SENS UNIQUE one way street
SERREZ À DROITE keep to the right
SECOURS ROUTIER roadside phones to summon assistance
SORTIE DE CAMIONS lorries emerging
SORTIE D'ÉCOLE schoolchildren emerging
SORTIE DE SECOURS emergency exit
STATIONNEMENT ALTERNÉ BI-MENSUEL parking on alternate sides of the road every half month
STATIONNEMENT BILATÉRAL AUTORISÉ parking allowed on both sides of the road
STATIONNEMENT TOLÉRÉ UNE ROUE SUR TROTTOIR parking allowed with one wheel on the pavement

STATIONNEMENT INTERDIT no parking
NE STATIONNEZ PAS no parking
NE PAS STATIONNER no parking
NI VITESSE NI BRUIT drive slowly, don't make any noise
TRAVERSEZ cross
NE TRAVERSEZ PAS don't cross
VÉHICULES LENTS slow vehicles
VOIE PIÉTONNE pedestrian zone
VOIE UNIQUE single lane

VOITURES LÉGÈRES SEULEMENT light vehicles only
ZONE BLEUE DISQUE OBLIGATOIRE blue parking discs required in this area
ZONE D'ENLÈVEMENT DES VÉHICULES illegally parked cars will be towed away in this area
ZONE PIÉTONNE pedestrian zone

NOTICES AT THE SEASIDE

BAIGNADE INTERDITE bathing forbidden
BAIGNADE NON SURVEILLÉE unsupervised bathing
BAINS INTERDITS bathing forbidden
BATEAUX À VOILES sailing boats
CANOTS À MOTEUR motor-boats
CHENAUX channels
EMBARCADÈRES landing stages
IL EST FORMELLEMENT INTERDIT DE SE BAIGNER bathing is strictly forbidden
JEUX DE BALLONS INTERDITS ball games forbidden
LOCATION DE BATEAUX boats for hire
LOCATION DE PLANCHES À VOILE sailboards for hire
LOCATION DE PARASOLS sun-umbrellas for hire
LOCATION DE VOILIERS sailing-boats for hire
PATAUGEOIRE paddling-pool
PISCINE CHAUFFÉE heated swimming-pool
PISCINE MUNICIPALE public swimming-pool
PLAGE beach
PLAGE PUBLIQUE } public beach
PLAGE EN RÉGIE MUNICIPALE } public beach

PLANCHES À VOILE sailboards

PORT DE PLAISANCE yachting harbour/marina
POSTE DE SECOURS first aid post
PROMENADE EN BARQUES } boat trips
SORTIES EN MER } boat trips
SOYONS PROPRES do not drop litter

VEDETTES } sight-seeing boat trips
BATEAUX MOUCHES } sight-seeing boat trips
VESTIAIRES changing cubicles
VIEUX PORT the old port

NOTICES AT PETROL/ SERVICE STATIONS

CAISSE pay desk
DERNIÈRE STATION AVANT L'AUTOROUTE last petrol station before motorway
EAU water
ESSENCE petrol
FAITES LE PLEIN fill up
FERMETURE HEBDOMADAIRE (e.g. DIMANCHE) weekly closing (e.g. Sunday)
GRAISSAGE lubrication

LAVAGE car wash
LIBRE SERVICE self service
LOCATION DE VOITURES car hire
ORDINAIRE 2 star petrol
PNEUS tyres
PNEUS TOUTES MARQUES all makes of tyres
PRIX AU LITRE price per litre
RÉGLAGES tuning
RÉPARATIONS repairs
SERVEZ-VOUS help yourself
SERVICE RAPIDE quick service
SUPER 4 star petrol
VÉRIFIER VOTRE NIVEAU D'HUILE oil check
VIDANGE oil change

NOTICES FOR SHOPPING

ALIMENTATION groceries
ARRIVAGES JOURNALIERS DE POISSONS FRAIS daily arrival of fresh fish
ASCENSEUR lift
BAGAGES luggage
BIJOUTERIE jewellery
BLANCHISSERIE laundry
BOULANGERIE baker's
BOUCHERIE butcher's
BRICOLAGE do-it-yourself
CADDIE / CHARIOT } trolley
PRENEZ VOTRE CADDIE ICI get your trolley here
CADEAUX presents
CAISSE till
CASSETTES cassettes
CHARCUTERIE delicatessen
CHAUSSURES shoes
COIFFEUR / COIFFURE } hairdresser
COMESTIBLES food
CONFISERIE confectioner's
COQUILLAGES / CRUSTACÉS } seafood/shellfish
CORDONNERIE shoemender's
CRÉMERIE creamery/dairy
DISQUES records
LA DOUZAINE dozen
DRAPS sheets
DROGUERIE drugstore
ÉLECTROMÉNAGER household appliances
ENTRÉE LIBRE free entry/come in and look around
ÉPICERIE grocery
ESCALIER stairs
ÉTAGE floor
FAÏENCE crockery
FAITES PESER have your goods weighed
FERMÉ closed
FERMETURE ANNUELLE annual holiday
FERMETURE HEBDOMADAIRE ... weekly closing ...
FOURRURE furs
FROMAGES cheeses
HALLES covered market
HORAIRES D'OUVERTURE opening times
HYPERMARCHÉ hypermarket
À L'INTÉRIEUR inside
JEUX games
JOUETS toys
JOUR(S) DE MARCHÉ market day(s)
JOURNAUX newspapers
kg kilogramme
LAVERIE AUTOMATIQUE launderette
LAYETTE babyclothes
LESSIVES detergents
LIBRAIRIE bookshop
LIBRE-SERVICE self-service
LINGE DE MAISON household linen
LA LIVRE pound
LIVRES books
MAISON DE LA PRESSE newsagent's
MARCHÉ market
MAROQUINERIE leather goods
MÉNAGE household (goods)
MODE FÉMININE ladies clothes
NE PAS TOUCHER À LA MARCHANDISE do not touch the goods
NE PAS SE SERVIR do not help yourself
NETTOYAGE À SEC dry-cleaning
ORFÈVRERIE gold/silverware
OUVERT open
OUVERT TOUS LES JOURS open every day
PANIERS baskets
PAPETERIE stationer's
PARFUMS perfumery
PÂTISSERIE cake shop
DU PAYS local
PHARMACIE chemist's
LA PIÈCE each
POISSONERIE fish shop
POUPÉES dolls
PRENDRE LA FILE ICI queue here
PRENEZ UN SAC take a bag
PRESSING dry cleaners
PRÊT-À-PORTER ready-to-wear
PRIMEURS early vegetables
PRIX CHOCS amazing prices
PRIX RÉDUITS reduced prices
PRODUITS ALIMENTAIRES food products
PROMOTION special offer
QUINCAILLERIE ironmonger's
RAYON shelf/department
RÉCLAME special offer
REZ-DE-CHAUSSÉE ground-floor
SERVEZ-VOUS help yourself
SOLDES sales
DERNIERS SOLDES end of sales
SORTIE exit
SORTIE OBLIGATOIRE only way out
SOUS-SOL basement
SUPERMARCHÉ supermarket
TABAC tobacconist's
TALONS ET CLÉS–MINUTE heel-bar/keys while you wait
TAPIS carpets
TRAITEUR delicatessen
USTENSILES DE CUISINE kitchenware
VAISSELLES crockery
VANNERIE basketwork
EN VENTE ICI on sale here
VERRERIE glassware
VÊTEMENTS clothes
VOLAILLE poultry

TOWN SIGNS

ABBAYE abbey
ARRÊT (AUTOBUS) bus stop
BASILIQUE basilica church

Bd (BOULEVARD) avenue
CENTRE COMMERCIAL shopping centre
CENTRE VILLE town centre

CHÂTEAU castle
CHEMIN way
ÉGLISE church
EXPO(SITION) exhibition
GARE station
GARE ROUTIÈRE bus station
GENDARMERIE NATIONALE local police HQ

HALLES covered market
HÔPITAL hospital

HÔTEL DE VILLE town hall
JARDIN D'ACCLIMATATION zoological gardens
MAIRIE town hall
MARCHÉ market
MÉTRO underground railway
MUSÉE museum
OFFICE DE TOURISME tourist office

P et T (POSTES ET TÉLÉCOMMUNICATIONS) post office
PALAIS DE JUSTICE law courts
Pl (PLACE) square
PLACE DU MARCHÉ market-place
PORT DE PLAISANCE yachting harbour
QUAI waterfront
REMPARTS ramparts
RESPECTEZ LES PELOUSES do not walk on the grass
ROND-POINT roundabout
Rte (ROUTE) route
ROUTE PITTORESQUE picturesque route
RUE street
SNCF railway
STADE stadium
SYNDICAT D'INITIATIVE tourist information office
TÉLÉPHERIQUE cable railway
VIEILLE VILLE old town
VIEUX PORT old port
VIEUX QUARTIER old district
VOIE PIÉTONNE pedestrian precinct
VOIE SANS ISSUE dead end
ZONE PIÉTONNE pedestrian precinct

TRAVEL SIGNS

AÉROGARE airport terminal
AIRE DE REPOS lay-by/rest area
AIRE DE SERVICE service area
ARRÊT stop

AUTOCARS DE TOURISME excursion coaches
BANLIEUE suburbs
BIFURCATION fork
BILLETS tickets
CARNET DE BILLETS book of tickets
CARS coaches
CORRESPONDANCE connection
CROIX intersection
DOUANE customs

ENTRÉE entrance
FACULTATIF request (stop)
FILE lane
INTERDIT AUX AUTOCARS no coaches
HORAIRES time-tables
PÉAGE toll
PISTE CYCLABLE cycle track
P 2 ROUES parking for bikes
RATP (régie autonome des transports parisiens) Paris transport system
RANDONNÉES excursions
SNCF French railway network
TAXIS TÊTE DE STATION head of the taxi queue
VOITURES DE LOCATION cars for hire
VÉLOS cycles
VOYAGEURS passengers

WEATHER SIGNS

averses showers
brumeux misty
bruines drizzle
ciel clair clear sky
couvert overcast
faibles weak/little wind
forts strong (winds)
fronts froids cold fronts
fronts chauds warm fronts
modérés moderate winds
neige snow
orages storms
pluies rain
peu nuageux little cloud
très nuageux very cloudy
tempête stormy
variable changeable
verglas icy

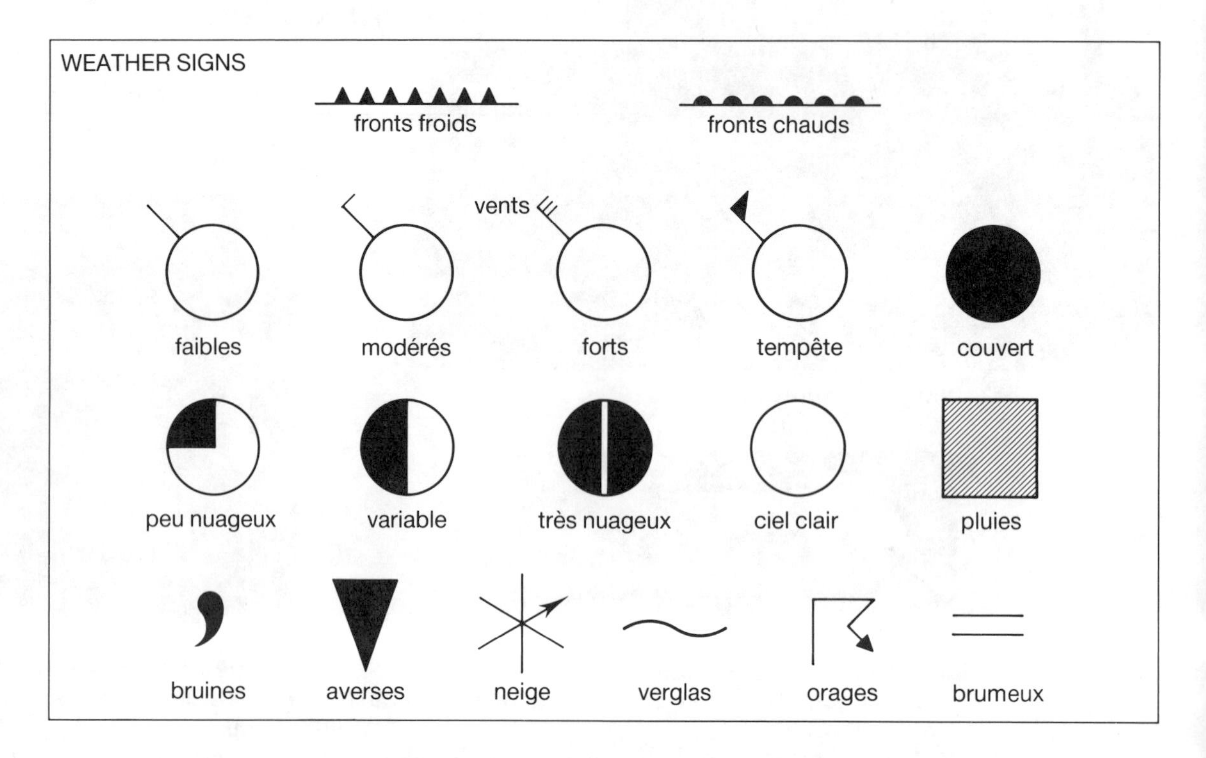

11.3 Test Yourself: Photos

1 What is being advertised here?
(a) Something for hire
(b) Something for rent
(c) Something for sale
(d) A warning

2 What will you be able to get here?
(a) A car for hire
(b) Unlimited credit
(c) Office premises for hire
(d) Banking facilities

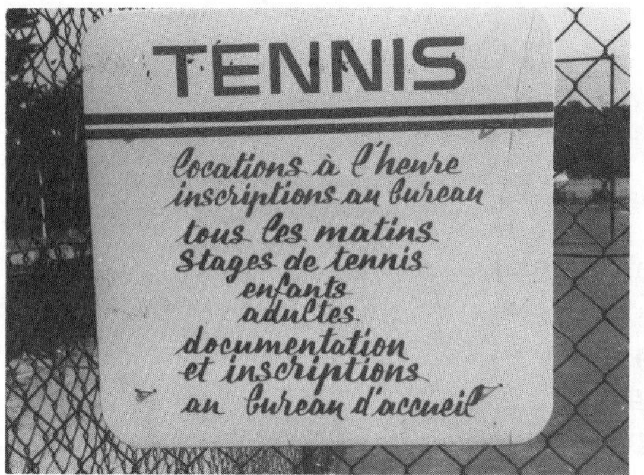

3 What takes place here every morning?
(a) Tennis coaching
(b) Tennis matches
(c) Tennis displays
(d) The courts are closed

4 What speciality is to be found at St Colomban?
(a) Lamb chops
(b) Oysters
(c) Bird-watching
(d) Supervised car-parks

11.4 Basic Level Comprehension

The Basic Level reading comprehension tests will be taken by all candidates. These tests will be short and will require relatively simple answers in English. The emphasis is on *reading* with understanding. You will be expected to understand a variety of short items, some perhaps only a word or two long. Here are some examples of the types of reading comprehension tests you might have to answer at Basic Level.

Public notices

1 You see the following notice on a beach in France. What are you told?

RÉGLEMENTATION DE LA PLAGE
Surveillance assurée du 15 juin au 15 septembre
de 10h à 18h

Signification des signaux
▶ Interdiction de se baigner
▷ Absence de danger
Poste de Secours → à 100m

2 You are at a campsite in France. What do the following notices tell you?
PISCINE EAU POTABLE ACCUEIL DOUCHES POUBELLES

3 You are at a railway station in France. What facilities are available?
SALLE D'ATTENTE CONSIGNE AUTOMATIQUE TÉLÉPHONE PUBLIC BUFFET CHARIOTS
What does the following sign tell you to do? GARDEZ VOTRE TICKET SUR VOUS

4 You are travelling by car in France. What does the following notice tell you?
DANGER RALENTIR RISQUE D'INONDATION SUR 100m

5 You are visiting France. What do each of the following notices tell you?
MÉTRO P et T FERMÉ SNCF SYNDICAT D'INITIATIVE OUVERT ALIMENTATION DOUANE BUREAU DE CHANGE TARIF RÉDUIT

6 You are in France on holiday with your family. Explain to them the different events which are taking place.
13 juillet Bal populaire 21h sur la place
14 juillet Fête Nationale
10.30h défilé et cérémonie devant le Monument des Morts
14 juillet Soirée Tricolore, dîner dansant au Casino
14 juillet Feu d'Artifice 22h sur la place

7 Some friends of yours are looking for a house to buy in France. They require a house about 2 kms from a railway station, with 3/4 bedrooms.
Which of the following would be suitable?
(a) Vend. maison, 4 pièces, cuisine, séjour, 2 chambres/sur lac/prox. gare 2kms.
Prix 250.000F
(b) Près gare/forêt/4 chambres, cuisine, séjour, salle de bains, grenier.
Prix 650.000F
(c) Prox. canal/maison rurale, cuisine, gd. séj., jard.
Prix 800.000F

8 LA LIBRAIRIE-BOUTIQUE
DU THEATRE NATIONAL
OPERA DE PARIS

(a) On what days of the week is the shop open?
(b) Where is the shop located exactly?
(c) On what other occasions is it open?
(d) On which floor?
(e) Name ten items which can be bought there.

TOUS LES JOURS DE 10 H A 17 H
(dans le hall d'accueil)

ET PENDANT LES ENTRACTES
(à la rotonde du 1er étage)

LA LIBRAIRIE-BOUTIQUE DU

VOUS PROPOSE

livres - disques - cassettes
photos des spectacles
posters

foulards - briquets
porte-clés - tee-shirts
sacs - agendas
etc...

AINSI QUE SON RAYON VIDÉO

LA TOSCA
(Puccini/Auvray/Ozawa)
ROMÉO ET JULIETTE
(Gounod/Lavaudant/Lombard)
LA BELLE HÉLÈNE
(Offenbach/Savary/Schnitzler)
GISELLE
(Ballet du Bolchoï)
ROMÉO ET JULIETTE
(Ballet du Bolchoï)

EN COLLABORATION AVEC

CINÉTHÈQUE

9 L'ASSOCIATION FAMILIALE RURALE

COURS DE COUTURE

L'Association Familiale projette de relancer les cours de couture la première semaine d'octobre.
Une réunion est prévue le 17 septembre 1988 à 20h 30, au Foyer-Club.
Les inscriptions se feront au cours de cette réunion.
Nous comptons sur votre présence.
L'Association Familiale

FAITES-LE SAVOIR AUTOUR DE VOUS

(a) What kind of a course is being advertised?
(b) When is it going to begin?
(c) When is the first meeting going to be held?
(d) Where?
(e) What will happen during the first meeting?

CHOISISSEZ VOTRE
STYLE DE VACANCIES EN
FRANCE
Séjours en hôtel, locations d'appartement, villages de vacances, résidences-clubs, location de roulottes, de bateaux, circuits.
Côte d'Azur
Languedoc-Roussillon
Côte Atlantique
Bretagne et Normandie
Auvergne-Cévennes
Alpes et Pyrénées
la Corse

10 (a) What is this an advert for?
(b) Name five of the types offered.
(c) Give the geographical locations of five of the areas specified, e.g. . . . north-west, . . . south-east, etc.

Camping

11 ARGENTAT-SUR-DORDOGNE
ler juin au 15 septembre
Ravitaillement sur place juillet et août.
Bar, restaurant, plats cuisinés, épicerie.
Abri, salle de jeux, piscine, terrain de jeux pour enfants, jeux pour adultes (terrain de boules, volley-ball). Pêche, canotage, voile sur le lac.
Site classé, château du XlVème siècle.
Propriété en bordure d'un lac.

(a) When is the campsite open?
(b) What is available in July and August?
(c) What facilities for games are there?
(d) What water-sports are offered?
(e) What is of historic interest there?

12 LE PRÉ DU CHÂTEAU DES GUERMANTES
2km N LA BAULE sur D92
20 mars au 30 septembre
50 caravanes; sanitaires chauffés au printemps; sauna; épicerie; glaces; gaz; plats cuisinés; machines à laver; table à repasser; barbecue; TV couleur; salon-bibliothèque; ping-pong; volley-ball.
Monument historique dans cadre fleuri; grand calme; grand comfort.
La Côte Bretagne; ses églises; ville d'art.
Réservation recommandée en juillet et en août.

(a) Where is the campsite located in relation to La Baule?
(b) What special facility is offered in spring?
(c) What provisions are made for buying food?
(d) What provisions are made for laundering clothes?
(e) What leisure activities are there for those who do not wish to play games?
(f) Give three reasons why people might choose this campsite?
(g) What three attractions are mentioned in the area?
(h) What advice is given to prospective visitors?

Exhibitions

13

EXPOSITION

MUSÉE DE PEINTURE ET DE SCULPTURE
PLACE DE VERDUN, CLERMONT-FERRAND
OUVERT DE 12h30 À 19h, FERMÉ MARDI
ET JOURS DE FÊTES LÉGALES
ENTRÉE GRATUITE

(a) Where is the exhibition being held?
(b) When is it open?
(c) On what days can't you go in?
(d) How much does it cost?

14

EXPOSITIONS

MUSÉE DAUPHINOIS, MUSÉE REGIONAL D'ART
ET DE TRADITIONS POPULAIRES.
30 RUE MAURICE-CIGNOUX, GRENOBLE.

PLUSIEURS EXPOSITIONS ÉVOQUENT EN
PERMANENCE LES DIVERS ASPECTS DE LA
VIE TRADITIONELLE EN DAUPHINÉ ET DANS
LES ALPES.
OUVERT DE 9h À 12h ET DE 14h À 16h
FERMÉ LE MARDI

(a) What kind of exhibitions are on display?
(b) When are the exhibitions closed?

Guides

15

BRÉTIGNOLLES

OFFICE DE TOURISME
37 rue La Vendée
Tel: (51) 96.45.53

Loisirs: piscine municipale; plages avec baignades sur le lac; location voiliers; planches à voile; canotage; pédalos; tennis; patinoire artificielle; centre équestre; école d'escalade; boulodrome; pétanque; golf miniature; tir aux pigeons; location bicyclettes et quadricycles; parcs de loisirs; casino; cinéma; bibliothèque municipale; musées; visites d'ateliers d'artisanat.

How much information can you give your family about leisure activities available in Bretignolles? List in English all the activities.

16

REMUZAT
LES LAVANDES

Chambres libres à partir du ler mai au ler octobre.
Peut recevoir des groupes de 25-30 personnes.
Site panoramique.
Nombreuses promenades et excursions.

(a) When are rooms available at Les Lavandes?
(b) What group arrangements can be made?
(c) What is there to see in the area?
(d) What is there to do?

17 Visite organisée de Lorient et de la région en autocar sous la conduite de guides du 12 juillet au 5 septembre. Départ à 14h 30 devant le Syndicat d'Initiative.

Pour les groupes venant avec leur autocar le Syndicat d'Initiative peut mettre toute l'année à leur disposition des guides et des hôtesses sur demande préalable pour un circuit de 30 kilomètres à Lorient.

Visite des plages en vedette (durée une heure), de Pâques au 5 septembre. Prix par personne 22 francs. Prix spéciaux pour groupes scolaires.

(a) Between which dates can you take a coach trip around Lorient and district?
(b) From where does the trip leave?
(c) What facility is offered for groups with their own coach?
(d) What must these groups do in advance of their arrival?
(e) What other excursion is available from Easter to the 5th of September?
(f) How long will each of these last?
(g) What is the cost per person?
(h) What is available for groups?

Letters

18

Poitiers, le 10 juin

Maryse Leclerc
4 place Vailland
Poitiers

Monsieur le Directeur
Bureau des Objets Trouvés
Gare d'Austerlitz
Paris

Monsieur,
Le 16 mai j'ai laissé mon sac à main sur un banc à la gare d'Austerlitz. C'est un sac en cuir rouge qui contient mon porte-monnaie et ma carte d'identité. Je vous serais reconnaissante de bien vouloir faire les recherches nécessaires et vous prie d'agréer mes sentiments les plus distingués.

Maryse Leclerc

(a) What has been lost?
(b) Where was it left?
(c) Give an accurate description of the article.
(d) What was inside?
(e) What does the writer ask them to do?

19

Paris, le 13 septembre

Paul Duval
34 rue de la Paix
Paris

Monsieur le Directeur
Bureau des Objets Trouvés
Arcachon

Monsieur,
Le 5 juillet j'ai perdu une montre sur la plage de votre ville. C'est une montre suisse. Je suis sûr que je l'ai perdue près du poste de secours. J'aimerais savoir si quelq'un vous a rapporté ma montre.

Je vous remercie d'avance et vous prie de croire à l'expression de mes sentiments distingués.

Paul Duval

(a) What has been lost?
(b) What make is it?
(c) Where was it lost?
(d) When was it lost?
(e) What does the writer wish to know?

Guides

20 LA CORSE
Corse, Île de Beauté. Des golfes, des criques, des montagnes, des villages perchés. Tout au fond de son golfe, le plus harmonieux de l'île, se trouve Ajaccio. Le vieil Ajaccio est ocre, la nouvelle ville, blanche. L'eau du golfe est bleue, le maquis des montagnes, vert sombre.

La maison natale de Napoléon se trouve à Ajaccio. Dans le port, une multitude de bateaux de plaisance voisinent avec ceux des pêcheurs ajacciens. Plus haut, l'Ajaccio moderne dresse ses immeubles blancs.

(a) What is the island of Corsica often described as?
(b) Where is Ajaccio located?
(c) What is the 'maquis' in this passage?
(d) How is Napoleon connected with Ajaccio?
(e) Describe the different boats to be found in the port.
(f) Give two details about the modern part of Ajaccio.

Letters

21 (a) Which school does Nathalie go to? Where is it situated?
(b) What form is she in? (Give the English equivalent.)
(c) How did she find a correspondent?
(d) Where has she been with a group of school-friends?
(e) What did she find strange? Why?
(f) What does she study at school?
(g) What does she ask her friend to send her?

Nancy, le 4 Juin

Chère amie,

Je m'appelle Nathalie et je vais au collège Hervé Bazin qui se trouve au centre-ville. Je suis en troisième. Mon professeur d'anglais m'a donné ton nom et ton adresse. Je suis très contente d'avoir une correspondante anglaise. Je suis déjà allée en Angleterre avec un groupe scolaire. Nous sommes allés à Eastbourne. Nous nous sommes bien amusés mais nous avons trouvé les repas bizarres. On nous a servi des légumes et de la viande en même temps et toujours avec la même sauce chaude!

A l'école j'étudie les maths, les sciences naturelles, le français, l'anglais, l'allemand, l'histoire et la géographie.

Et toi? J'espère que tu m'écriras bientôt. Peux-tu m'envoyer aussi une photo de toi?

En attendant de te lire,

Amicalement,

Nathalie

Menu à 65 F

Crudités
ou
Salade Russe

Poulet Rôti
ou
Jambon Grillé

Frites
ou
Salade

Glaces aux choix
ou
Tarte aux Cerises

Service Compris

Menus

22 **(a)** What is there to choose from for the first course?
(b) For the main course?
(c) What vegetables are there?
(d) What desserts are there?
(e) Is the service charge included?

Newspapers

23 UN LYCÉEN MEURT, LA GORGE TRANSPERCÉE PAR UN JAVELOT

Un élève du lycée d'enseignement technique Émile Zola à Aix-en-Provence a trouvé la mort vendredi sur le stade municipal: un javelot lui a transpercé la gorge.

Ce lycéen de 18 ans, qui s'entraînait sur le stade pour les épreuves de baccalauréat a reçu un javelot lancé par un autre lycéen. Au lieu de se piquer dans le sol, le javelot aurait rebondi sur l'herbe et atteint le malheureux jeune homme.

(a) When did the accident happen?
(b) Where did it happen?
(c) How was he killed?
(d) What was he doing at the time?
(e) Was anyone responsible for the accident? If so, who?

Weather Report

24 **LA MÉTÉO ANNONCE**

Lever du soleil à 5h 53

Coucher à 19h 52

SAMEDI: temps couvert et pluvieux en matinée avec vent de secteur sud assez fort l'après-midi, le temps faiblira un peu et le ciel sera variable avec alternances d'éclaircies et de passages nuageux accompagnés d'averses.
DIMANCHE: après des éclaircies matinales, le temps instable sera orageux avec des averses l'après-midi, vent sud-ouest modéré.

(a) What will happen at 19h 52?
(b) What is the weather forecast for Saturday morning?
(c) What will the wind be like in the afternoon?
(d) What will the weather be like generally in the afternoon?
(e) What is the weather forecast for Sunday morning?
(f) What will the weather be like in the afternoon?
(g) What will the wind be like in the afternoon?

Newspapers

25 TROIS PIÉTONS BLESSÉS HIER

Trois piétons ont été blessés dans trois accidents différents de la circulation au cours de la journée d'hier à Nice.
–Mme Rose Berthod, 62 ans, demeurant 3 avenue Félix-Faure a été renversée par une voiture vers 11h à la hauteur de la rue Arson.
–Mme Mathilde Nicolai, 31 ans, domiciliée 5 rue du Lycée, a également été renversée par une voiture vers 10h près du rond-point au centre-ville.
–M Jean-Jaques Marty, 77 ans, demeurant 8 boulevard Georges-Clemenceau, a été heurté par un véhicule vers 10h 30 sur la place Giardelli.

(a) When were the three pedestrians injured?
(b) Where did the three accidents take place. Give precise details.
(c) What happened to Mme Berthod?
(d) What happened to Mme Nicolai?
(e) What happened to M Marty?

Time-tables

26 Nom: Frédéric Dulac
Lycee: Edmond Rostand
Classe: seconde

HEURES	LUNDI	MARDI	MERCREDI	JEUDI	VENDREDI	SAMEDI
08.00	Maths	Anglais	Espagnol	Sciences	Maths	Français
09.00	Maths	Français	Géographie	naturelles	Maths	Anglais
10.00	Sciences	Latin	Histoire	Français	Perme	—
11.00	naturelles	Latin	Anglais	Géographie	Français	—
		DEJEUNER				
14.00	Français	Maths	—	Education	Travaux	—
15.00	Espagnol	Maths	—	Physique	Pratiques	—
16.00	Histoire	Anglais	—	Perme	Français	—

(a) What class is Frédéric Dulac in? (Give the English equivalent.)
(b) What does he have first lesson on a Wednesday?
(c) What does he have last lesson on a Tuesday?
(d) What does he have last lesson on a Thursday?
(e) How many lessons of French does he have each week?

11.5 Higher-Level Comprehension

For those candidates aiming for Grade D and above, additional assessment objectives will be necessary. One of these objectives is the Higher-Level Reading test. 'Candidates should be expected to demonstrate the skills listed under Basic reading over a wider range of clearly defined topic areas. To the range of types of text will be added magazines and newspapers likely to be read by a sixteen-year-old, and in addition to the types of comprehension expected under common-core assessment objectives, candidates should be expected to demonstrate the ability to identify the important points or themes within an extended piece of writing and to draw conclusions from, and see relations within, an extended text.' (National Criteria)

The advice given for Basic Level reading comprehension assessment tests also applies to the Higher Level tests. Careful reading and thorough revision of topic areas are essential. Do not try to translate sections of the passage(s) for comprehension into English. This will only waste time and produce a stilted, contrived answer. You should always attempt to answer *in your own words* while, at the same time, making sure that you answer the question fully. Imagine that you are explaining to someone, who does not understand French, what the passage is about.

Advertisements

1

ADHEREZ A LA F.U.A.J.!

La carte individuelle de la F.U.A.J. est internationale. Elle est valable du 1er janvier au 31 décembre.

Cependant, cette carte délivrée chaque année dès le 1er Octobre, est utilisable à compter de cette date et ce, jusqu'au 31 décembre de l'année suivante. Ainsi, un jeune qui adhère pour la première fois bénéficie d'une carte valable 15 mois au lieu de 12!

COMMENT?

Il suffit de présenter et de remettre les pièces suivantes:

– bulletin d'adhésion individuelle (rempli avec soin en caractères d'imprimerie)

– pièce d'identité (par correspondance: photocopie de la carte d'identité recto/verso)

– photo d'identité de face (par correspondance: indiquer nom et prénom au dos)

– autorisation des parents pour les MOINS de 18 ANS (ou signature du bulletin par ces derniers)

– règlement de la cotisation (voir tarifs en vigueur). Par correspondance: joindre un chèque postal (3 volets) ou bancaire établi à l'ordre de "AUBERGES DE JEUNESSE/FUAJ" sans autre indication.

Joindre 4F pour frais d'envoi.

OU?

PARIS/ILE-DE-FRANCE

PARIS
Association Interdépartementale des Auberges de Jeunesse/Ile-de-France
10, rue Notre Dame-de-Lorette
75009 PARIS
Métro: St-Georges
Tél. 1/285.55.40
(Lu/Ve 9-12.30 h. & 13.30-1830 h. Sa 10-16h)

Auberge de Jeunesse "Jules Ferry"
8, boulevard Jules Ferry
75011 PARIS
Métro: République
Tél. 1/357.55.60
(ts les jrs 8-21 h.)

CHOISY-LE-ROI
Auberge de Jeunesse
125 av. de Villeneuve St-Georges
94600 CHOISY-LE-ROI
Tél 1/890.92.30
(ts les jrs 10-22 h.)

RUEIL-MALMAISON
Auberge de Jeunesse
4, rue des Marguerites
92500 RUEIL-MALMAISON
Tél. 1/749.43.97
(ts les jrs 8-10 h. & 17-22 h.)

PROVINCE

REGION NORD
Auberge de Jeunesse
1, avenue Julien Destrée
59800 LILLE

REGION EST
Auberge de Jeunesse
9, rue de l'Auberge de Jeunesse
Montagne Verte
67200 STRASBOURG

REGION RHONE-ALPES
Association Départementale des Auberges de Jeunesse
5, Place Bellecour
69002 LYON

REGION CENTRE
Auberge de Jeunesse
23, Avenue Neigre
28000 CHARTRES

REGION SUD-OUEST
Auberge de Jeunesse
17, rue de la Jeunesse
B.P. 241
86006 POITIERS

REGION SUD
Auberge de Jeunesse
47, rue J. Vidal
Impasse du Dr Bonfils
13008 MARSEILLE

REGION QUEST
Auberge de Jeunesse
41, rue Schoelcher
Rives du Ter
56100 LORIENT

Auberge de Jeunesse
Rue de Kerbriant
Port de Plaisance du Moulin Blanc
29200 BREST

Egalement dans toutes les Auberges de Jeunesse marquées du sigle

(a) From when is the Youth Hostel membership card valid and to when?
(b) What three things do you have to present when applying for membership if you are over 18?
(c) What else do you have to present if you are under 18?
(d) How much do you have to send for postage?

panneaux touristiques

Vous allez rencontrer sur votre trajet des panneaux à fond brun.

Ils se présentent généralement sous la forme :

- *D'un symbole dessiné (pictogramme) précédant un texte message écrit.*

Vous avez quelques secondes pour deviner la signification du pictogramme précédant le texte.

- *De flèches précédant les textes qui se rapportent à des lieux que l'on peut découvrir de l'autoroute.*

 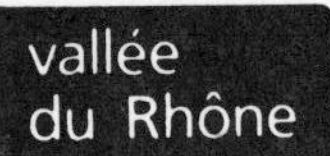

Les panneaux sont destinés :

- *A vous expliquer les régions traversées, les paysages aperçus, les particularités...*
- *A vous annoncer les principaux centres d'intérêt touristique, les grandes réalisations d'intérêt national, les centres d'information touristique.*

  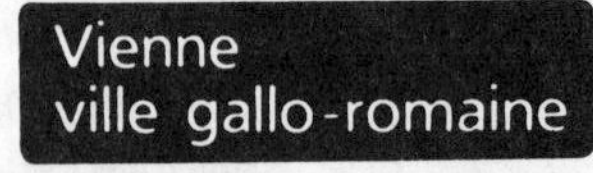

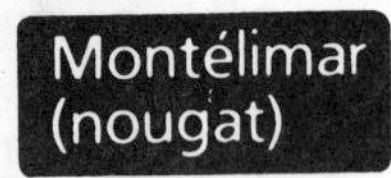

  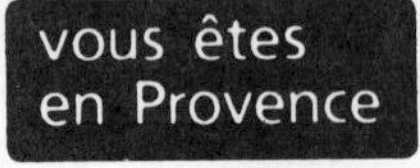

 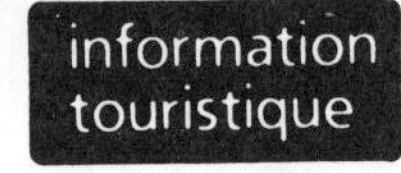

2 (a) What colour does it say that the signs are?
(b) How long will you have to read the signs?
(c) What kind of a town is Orange?
(d) What do the arrows indicate?
(e) What can be seen at Crussol?
(f) What three things do the signs explain to you?
(g) What other things do they tell you?
(h) What are you told about Vienne?
(i) Where is the region of Provence?
(j) What does the letter 'i' stand for?

3 (a) How many times a year does the Opera magazine appear?
(b) On which day of the month?
(c) Give the names of the two theatres at the Opera.
(d) Who is invited to contribute each month?
(e) What do they write about?

Brochures

4 *Les Services*
(a) What is provided every 10 to 15 km on a motorway?
(b) What is provided every 30 to 40 km?
(c) What do certain of these also have?
(d) What is provided in both of these places mentioned in (a) and (b)?

La Securité
(a) What are we told about the safety of motorways?
(b) Where can you stop in an emergency?
(c) What are you told to do in case of an emergency stop?

En cas de crevaison
(a) What are you told to do in case of a puncture?
(b) What is the time limit for repairing a puncture yourself?

Attention à la fatigue
(a) What risk do you run if you doze off for two seconds when travelling at 130 km/h when on a motorway?
(b) How can you avoid dozing off? (Give three details.)

Vérifiez vos pneus
(a) What can happen to a tyre which is under-pressurized?
(b) What advice is given to increase tyre safety?

TOUS LES MOIS
L'OPÉRA DE PARIS
ÉDITE SA PROPRE REVUE

Le premier du mois, dix fois par an, elle vous permet de suivre les activités de l'Opéra de Paris.

Des articles de fond vous présenteront les spectacles chorégraphiques et lyriques qui se dérouleront au Palais Garnier comme à la Salle Favart et dans tous les lieux où l'Opéra de Paris déploie ses activités.
Des analyses, des rencontres, des points de vue, des interviews : c'est toute la vie de l'Opéra de Paris que sa revue veut refléter. A travers ses spectacles, présentés par ceux qui les inventent, ceux qui les jouent, ou ceux qui, dans l'ombre, y contribuent. A travers son Histoire encore, aussi bien celle de l'École de Danse française qu'y perpétue le Ballet de l'Opéra et dont Pierre Lartigue raconte le feuilleton, que celle de l'architecture du Palais Garnier que, de promenade en promenade, de ses toits à ses caves, Jean-Loup Roubert et Pierre Flinois nous font découvrir. A travers ses anecdotes, ses figures, ses spectacles aussi, côté scène et côté salle, qu'évoque la chronique de Pierre-Jean Rémy et que conserve en images l'Album. Avec chaque mois un invité, écrivain ou personnalité du monde culturel, qui vient raconter son meilleur souvenir de l'Opéra de Paris. Et de page en page, de textes en photos, l'écho de ces voix qui font rêver, à en oublier le Fantôme.

l'autoroute pratique A10

les services

Sur l'autoroute, vous pouvez vous arrêter tous les 10 à 15 km sur des aires de repos (dotées de points d'eau et de sanitaires), et tous les 30 à 40 km sur des aires de service où vous trouverez des stations de pétroliers (avec boutiques), certaines étant équipées de cafétérias ou de restaurants.

Des téléphones publics, reliés au réseau général, sont installés sur les aires de service et de repos.

la sécurité

L'autoroute est 4 à 5 fois plus sûre que la route. A chacun de la rendre encore plus sûre, en appliquant quelques règles faciles à respecter.

Où s'arrêter ?
En cas de nécessité absolue, vous pouvez vous arrêter sur la bande d'arrêt d'urgence. Prenez le maximum de précautions car vous serez frôlé par les véhicules en circulation : stationnez-donc le plus à droite possible, faites fonctionner votre système clignotant «alarme» et n'hésitez pas à utiliser en plus le triangle de présignalisation.

En cas de crevaison
Choisissez autant que possible, un endroit où vous pourrez éloigner au maximum votre véhicule de la voie de circulation. (Si vous êtes arrêté contre une glissière latérale, roulez quelques dizaines de mètres au ralenti et vous trouverez une interruption de la glissière).
Si vous réparez vous-même, vous ne devez pas rester immobilisé sur la bande d'arrêt d'urgence plus d'une demi-heure.

Attention à la fatigue
La conduite sur autoroute tend à vous endormir. Deux secondes d'inattention à 130 km/h et vous parcourez 72 mètres incontrôlés. Evitez ce risque en cassant la monotonie de votre rythme de conduite en modifiant :
- votre vitesse
- la température intérieure de votre voiture.

N'hésitez pas à vous arrêter sur les parkings et les aires de repos.

Vérifiez vos pneus
Un pneu sous gonflé finit par éclater si vous roulez vite et longtemps. Car ce sont les flancs du pneu qui travaillent et la bande de roulement risque de se découper (même sur les pneus neufs).
Pour ne pas compromettre votre sécurité, faites gonfler vos pneumatiques 200 grammes au-dessus de la pression préconisée.

les téléphones utiles

- COFIROUTE (de Paris à Poitiers) : 505.14.13 – 77, av. R. Poincaré 75116 Paris
- ASF (de Poitiers à Bordeaux) : (49) 32.63.11 – échangeur 23 Niort Sud
- Centre de renseignement des autoroutes : 705.90.01
- CRICR* de l'Ile de France : 898.92.18
- CRICR* de Bordeaux : (56) 96.33.33
- Bureau de tourisme : (49) 75.67.30 – Aire des Ruralies (Niort)
  (46) 94.25.30 – Aire de St-Léger

* CRICR Centre Régional d'Information et de Coordination Routière

quel temps de parcours devez-vous prévoir ?

Temps approximatifs, calculés à une moyenne de 120 km/h sur autoroute.

PARIS-ORLEANS	1 heure	4 h 50
ORLEANS-TOURS	55 minutes	
TOURS-POITIERS	55 minutes	
POITIERS-NIORT	30 minutes	
NIORT-SAINTES	35 minutes	
SAINTES-BORDEAUX	55 minutes	

5 Située au carrefour de grandes vallées de communications, au pied de massifs majestueux et préstigieux qui ont pour nom le Vercors, la Chartreuse, Grenoble, capitale des Alpes françaises, fut de tout temps une étape pour les voyageurs. De l'époque romaine à l'épopée napoléonne, du règne des anciens dauphins à la naissance de l'alpinisme sportif, des premiers balbutiements des sports d'hiver jusqu'aux Jeux Olympiques d'hiver de 1968, Grenoble a toujours été une plaque tournante de tourisme. C'est d'ailleurs dans cette ville, où ont germé tant d'idées nouvelles, qu'est né le premier Syndicat d'Initiative. C'était en 1889. Un organisme de conception originale, conçu par des commerçants et des notables de la ville, dans le but de promouvoir la région grenobloise et sa couronne de montagnes, incontestablement une des plus belles régions de France, mais aussi de créer des infrastructures modernes, pour faciliter la circulation, le commerce et le tourisme.

(a) Give a geographical description of Grenoble.
(b) What has Grenoble always provided for travellers?
(c) What special event was held in Grenoble in 1968?
(d) What event took place in Grenoble in 1889?
(e) Who was responsible for this event?
(f) What was its aim?

Labels

6 You have bought a tin of beans in France and read the following instructions on the label . . .

HARICOTS
A consommer de préférence avant la date figurant sur le couvercle.
Mode d'emploi: réchauffer les légumes dans leur jus sans faire bouilir. Ajouter une noix de beurre. Persiller avant de servir.
Composition 90% haricots. Eau, sel.

(a) What information is given on the lid?
(b) What three things are you told to do to prepare these for eating?
(c) What information are you given about the contents?

Brochures

7 VACANCES À CHEVAL

Pour pratiquer l'équitation de randonnée, une manière particulièrement savoureuse de parcourir un paysage, il n'est pas nécessaire d'être un très grand cavalier. Pour faire la randonnée libre, vous pouvez partir à deux ou en groupe, sur des selles confortables, avec des chevaux bien adaptés, sur des circuits bien balisés. A l'étape: un bon lit et un bon dîner en auberge ou dans un gîte. Renseignez-vous au centre équestre de Bonne Famille.

(a) What kind of a holiday is being advertized?
(b) How much previous experience do you need?
(c) Will you be able to do this on your own?
(d) What three details are given about the activity?
(e) What will be waiting for you afterwards?
(f) From where can you get more information?

Letters

La Baule, le 10 mars

Monsieur le Gérant
Hotel Matignon
La Baule
France

Madame F.Smith
42 Acacia Avenue
Hornsea
London
Grande-Bretagne

Madame,

Nous accusons reception de votre lettre du 22 février.
Nous vous proposons deux chambres:une chambre à deux personnes avec douche et W.C. et une chambre à un lit avec salle de bain. Le prix des chambres est à 150F la double et à 120F la chambre individuelle, sans petit déjeuner. Le petit déjeuner est à 15F. Il y a un supplément pour la télévision de 12F par jour. Si vous voulez manger à l'hôtel, la pension complète est à 900F la semaine par personne et la demi-pension est à 600F la semaine. Vous pouvez garer votre voiture devant l'hôtel.

Notre hôtel se trouve dans une rue tranquille près du port de plaisance. Il n'y a pas de piscine à l'hôtel mais notre plage privée est à cent mètres de l'hôtel. La ville de la Baule est une station balnéaire qui se trouve sur la côte Atlantique. Près du port il y a un aquarium et un musée qui sont ouverts du ler juin au ler dimanche d'octobre. L'aquarium groupe les animaux marins les plus représentifs du bassin. Le musée présente les oiseaux, reptiles et poissons de la région.

Nous vous serions reconnaissants de nous envoyer une somme de 200F comme garantie aussitôt que possible.

Veuillez agréer madame, l'expression de mes sentiments distingués.

Denis Sagan

8 **(a)** How many rooms are being offered?
(b) Give details.
(c) Is breakfast included?
(d) What extras are available?
(e) Explain what 'pension complète' means.
(f) What are the arrangements for parking the car?
(g) Describe the location of the hotel.
(h) What facilities for swimming are there?
(i) What two places of interest are mentioned?
(j) What does the hotel manager ask at the end of the letter?

Newspapers

9 HOLD-UP POUR QUELQUES PIÈCES DE MONNAIE

Un bandit solitaire, visage découvert et armé d'un pistolet a commis un hold-up hier après-midi dans une agence bancaire de la rue Bonaparte.

Sous la menace de son arme, le gangster, sans doute un débutant, a voulu prendre le contenu de la caisse. Mais il a dû se contenter des pièces de monnaie que l'employée a consenti à lui remettre.

Le solitaire a cependant réussi à s'enfuir sans être inquiété avec son maigre butin.

(a) How many robbers were there?
(b) When did the robbery take place?
(c) Where exactly?
(d) What was the threat used?
(e) What was actually taken in the robbery?

10 TV 5
TV 5, la chaîne européenne francophone, diffuse une sélection des émissions de TF 1, A 2, FR 3, SSR (Suisse) et RTBF (Belgique) sur les réseaux câblés. Diffusé par un satellite de communication, TV 5 est capté par 2,5 millions de foyers qui possèdent des prises de câble. Il y a 3h 30 d'émissions quotidiennes de la chaîne, diffusées deux fois par jour. La rentabilité de TV 5 n'est pas quand même assurée à cause du léger rendement de la publicité. Les entreprises ne semblent pas se précipiter sur le sponsoring.

(a) What kind of TV channel is TV 5? (Give three details.)
(b) How many people can it reach?
(c) How many hours a day does it broadcast?
(d) Does the channel make a profit? Why/why not?
(e) What are TF 1, A 2, FR 3?

Magazine article

11 SUR LES DEUX RIVES DU RHÔNE, DES CUISINES RÉPUTÉES
L'influence de la cuisine lyonnaise a largement dépassé les limites de la cité et a fait école loin vers le sud, dans la vallée du Rhône. On trouve de très belles tables dans presque toutes les villes et dans les villages avoisinant le fleuve. Cependant certaines cuisines locales ont conservé leurs caractères propres. C'est le cas notamment pour:

LA RÉGION DES MONTS DU FOREZ, à l'ouest du Rhône. Les écrevisses et les truites du Lignon sont très réputés, la qualité des viandes est exceptionnelle, le gibier est important. Dans cette contrée, on dégustera avec un grand plaisir les pâtés en croûte, la rosette de fleurs, les terrines, les pâtés et l'on ne manquera pas d'apprécier le délicieux jambon du pays.

LE BAS-DAUPHINÉ. C'est un pays à la limite de deux grandes traditions: la cuisine lyonnaise et la cuisine provençale. Mais le Bas-Dauphiné est marqué pour quelques specialités locales telles le gratin du pays, les pommes de terre cuites au four dans le lait, la brioche aux oeufs que l'on trouve à Romans, le fromage de Saint-Marcellin, le boeuf braisé de Grignan, etc.

LE VIVARAIS. On y trouve les plus beaux fruits de France: cerises, pêches, prunes, pommes, poires, abricots. Mais la table y a aussi ses lettres de noblesse avec ses gibiers, ses poulets, ses dindes, ses écrivisses et ses célèbres cochonnailles.

(a) What gastronomic influence has Lyon had on the Rhône valley?
(b) Where is the Mont du Forez region to be found?
(c) Name two meat and two fish specialities in this region?
(d) What two regional types of cooking are to be found in the Bas-Dauphiné?
(e) Explain what 'gratin du pays' is.
(f) What are Saint-Marcellin and Grignan famous for?
(g) What is Le Vivarais famous for?
(h) Give five examples of this/these.
(i) What, gastronomically, is it also famous for?
(j) Give two examples.

12 ALLERGIES DE PRINTEMPS
Allergies de printemps: attention aux fleurs, aux arbres et surtout aux insectes.
Vous avez sûrement dans votre entourage quelqu'un qui devient irritable et rougeaud au premier vol d'hirondelles. Leurs maux n'ont rien à voir avec une grippe ou un coup de froid. Il s'agirait plutôt du bien connu 'rhume des foins'. Salves d'éternuement, obstruction nasale ou toux spasmodique constituent le lourd tribut payé par les allergiques au printemps. Le premier élément incriminie dans ces maladies: le pollen. Petits grains légers que le vent transporte à son gré pour féconder les fleurs. Certains arbres aussi provoquent des manifestations allergiques.
La floraison dure d'avril à octobre, si bien que les allergies peuvent débuter en mars et se poursuivre jusqu'à l'automne. Long, très long, pour une pollinose.

(a) What three things are responsible for spring allergies?
(b) What symptoms are mentioned?
(c) When exactly are they said to appear?
(d) What do they resemble?
(e) What is the English term for this allergy?
(f) What causes it? How?
(g) How long goes it last?

13 LE MUSÉE DE L'AIR

Être plus léger que l'air, voler comme un oiseau, c'est sans doute un des plus anciens rêves de l'homme. Au début de ce siècle lorsque les pionniers de l'aviation construisaient leurs engins volants, c'est toujours en s'inspirant du profil des ailes des oiseaux qu'ils les concevaient.

La France eut l'idée d'un musée pour conserver les modèles les plus intéressants. Meudon remplit dans un premier temps ce rôle mais l'endroit devient vite trop petit pour contenir les nombreuses pièces entreposées dans les hangars.

La création de l'aéroport de Roissy-Charles-de-Gaulle donna une solution au problème. Il fut décidé en 1973 d'y installer un musée digne du passé aéronautique de la France. Dans ce musée les avions sont présentés en situation dans un cadre clair et aéré. Avant d'être installés ils ont été soigneusement mis en état et repeints. Le musée comprend six halles. Chacun possède une salle de projection (films ou diaporamas), des panneaux muraux explicatifs (historiques ou techniques) et de belles collections de maquettes complètent la présentation des appareils. Une salle est consacrée aux sports aériens: on y trouve les différents modèles de l'aviation légère et de tourisme. Un hall est réservé à la conquête de l'espace. On peut y voir, entre autres, la capsule Soyouz et une pierre provenant de la lune, offerte par les Américains.

A l'extérieur sur les anciennes aires de stationnement sont présentés les appareils les plus volumineux que les hangars ne pouvaient recevoir, parmi lesquels la Caravelle et le Concorde. Une réplique de la fusée Ariane domine l'ensemble des installations.

(a) What is one of man's oldest dreams?
(b) What inspired the early aviation pioneers in their work?
(c) What place housed the first air museum in France?
(d) Why was another place sought afterwards?
(e) Where was this second museum established?
(f) What was done to the planes before they went on display?
(g) What three types of display were to be found in each hall?
(h) What can be seen in the hall devoted to aerial sports?
(i) What has been given by America for display?
(j) What replica dominates the exhibition?

14 AUTOROUTES

L'autoroute va vous permettre de maintenir, en toute sécurité, une moyenne regulière et élevée de voyager. Mais il faut rester cependant vigilant à chaque instant. Ne dépassez pas 130km/h (vitesse limite). N'oubliez pas que, par temps sec, après avoir freiné, vous parcourez encore 85 metres si vous roulez à 100km à l'heure et 120 metres si vous roulez a 120km/h.

Rappelez-vous aussi que vous ne pouvez pas stationner sur la bande d'arrêt d'urgence, sauf en cas d'urgence. Vous ne devez non plus changer de file pour doubler par la droite. Avant d'emprunter une bretelle de sortie, rabattez-vous suffisamment tôt sur la voie de droite et n'oubliez pas de signaler votre intention en mettant votre clignotant. Sur les autoroutes il y a deux types de péage: le péage ouvert (vous jetez une somme forfaitaire dans une corbeille spéciale) et le péage fermé (le tarif est indiqué sur une carte remise à l'entrée de l'autoroute. Ne pliez pas cette carte. Ne l'égarez pas).

En cas de panne, de crevaison ou d'accident, s'il vous est possible de déplacer la voiture, rangez-vous aussitôt sur la bande d'arrêt d'urgence, à droite de la chaussée, sinon signalez-vous par les feux de détresse, le triangle, etc. Empêchez enfants et animaux de sortir de la voiture. Utilisez le poste téléphonique le plus proche (le téléphone est gratuit. Il y a une poste tous les deux kilomètres). Vous serez en rapport avec les services de police qui se chargeront d'intervenir et de vous faire dépanner. Les tarifs de dépannage sont réglementés. Vous pouvez les procurer dans les gares de péage. Restez toujours prudent. N'oubliez pas de ralentir en cas de mauvais temps. Bonne route!

(a) What is the speed limit on motorways in France?
(b) In dry weather, what will happen if you apply the brakes when travelling at 100km/h?
(c) When *can* you stop on the hard shoulder of a motorway?
(d) What is 'une bretelle de sortie'?
(e) What two things must you do if you intend to use it?
(f) What two types of toll are there on French motorways? Describe each of these.
(g) If you break down on the motorway in France, what must you do? (Give three details.)
(h) How far apart are the emergency telephones?
(i) How much will it cost to use them?
(j) Which group of people is in charge of motorway breakdowns?

15 **(a)** How many TV channels are advertised?
(b) How many radio channels?
(c) On which TV channels are there news programmes?
(d) On which channels are there sports programmes?
(e) On which channel is there a computer programme?
(f) On which channels are there films?
(g) On which channel is there a soap opera?

(h) On which radio channel is there a programme about the Second World War?
(i) What kind of animal is the programme about on France-Culture at 23h
(j) Name three types of music to be heard on France-Musique.

Mardi 31 juillet

PREMIÈRE CHAINE: TF1

11 h 30 TF1 Vision plus.
11 h 55 Quarante ans déjà.
12 h Jeux olympiques. *Résumé.*
12 h 55 Consommer sans pépins.
13 h Journal.
13 h 30 Série: la conquête de l'Ouest.
14 h 20 Micro-puce. Magazine de l'informatique.
Le mur de R. Portiche, la ferme à Jean, de R. Prévot.
16 h 30 Croque-vacances:
Variétés, dessins animés, bricolage, feuilleton.
18 h 5 Série: Votre auto a cent ans.
La Rolls Royce, l'automobile des rois.
18 h 15 Contes à vivre debout.
Saint-Guilhem Story: l'ancienne étape de la rout de Saint-Jacques-de-Compostelle.
19 h 15 Emissions régionales.
19 h 35 Point: Prix vacances.
19 h 40 Jeux olympiques. Résumé.
20 h Journal.
20 h 35 Les Mardis de l'Information: la prison sans haine et sans crainte.
Magazine de la rédaction de TF1. (Rediffusion.)
Roger Gicquel et Alain Retsin ont franchi les hauts murs de la dernière centrale construite en France, celle de Saint-Maur, á quelques kilomètres de Châteauroux, une de ces prisons trois étoiles, béton et verre, où vivent quatre cents hommes condamnés à de lourdes peines (dont quatre-vingt-sept à perpétuité), des "dangereux" contrôlés par un double mur d'enceinte et un mirador. Les journalistes ont eu "carte blanche" pour filmer ce qu'ils voulaient et interroger qui ils voulaient à condition de respecter l'anonymat des détenus (d'où les cagoules). Quatre jours pour écouter,enregistrer un monde lourd où l'on ne parle pas à la légère. L'émission est passée en juin 1983.
21 h 50 Dialogue avec le sacré: la société des masques.
Réal, St. Kurc. Les chasseurs d'esprits maléfiques, les masques Wabele en pays senoufo.
Situé dans les savanes du Nord ivoirien, les Senambele ou Senoufos sont des agriculteurs qui partagent leur univers en deux mondes, celui des puissances inconnues et incontrôlées de la brousse et le monde des règles sociales du village et des champs. Chaque village possède un bois sacré — que l'on peut assimiler à un temple — où se déroulent les initiations, avec les différents objets liés au culte, dont les masques.
22 h 20 Journal.
22 h 35 Cinéma: le Troupeau.
Film turc de Y. Güney et Z. Okten (1978), avec M. Demirag, T. Akan, T. Kurtiz, L. Inanir, M. Niron (v.o. sous-titrée).
Une famille de bergers d'Anatolie, dominée par un patriarche tyranique, prend le train pour aller vendre un troupeau de moutons à Ankara. Une partie des bêtes meurt en route, la famille se désagrège. Ecrit en prison par Y. Güney, réalisé, sous son contrôle, par son ami le cinéaste Zeki Okten, ce film montre le choc violent et tragique de deux mondes (rural et urbain), la débâcle d'un ordre patriarcal; la condition féminine opprimée, les contradictions du développement industriel en Turquie, une grande oeuvre humaniste.

DEUXIÈME CHAIN: 2

8 h Journal météo.
8 h 5 Jeux olympiques.
10 h 30 Antiope.
12 h Journal (et à 12 h 45 et 18 h 40).
12 h 10 Série: Les globe-trotters.
12 h 30 Feuilleton: les Amours de la Belle Epoque.
13 h 35 Série: Chaparral.
14 h 30 Sports été: Jeux olympiques.
18 h Récré A 2.
18 h 50 Jeu: Des chiffres et des lettres.
19 h 15 Emissions régionales.
19 h 40 Le théâtre de Bouvard.
20 h Journal.
20 h 35 Cinéma: Anthracite.
Film français d'E. Niermans (1980), avec B. Cremer, J. Bóuise, J.-P. Dubois, J. Zucca, J.-P. Ragot, P. Bisciglia.
En 1952, dans un collège de jésuites, un surveillant s'élève contre l'éducation trop autoritaire. Son zèle évangélique, ses excès mystiques, ne lui valent que railleries, cruauté, abandon, de la part des élèves. Inspiré par les souvenirs d'adolescence du réalisateur, ce film est un peu forcé dans sa volonté de noirceur. On remarque le soin apporté à la mise en scène. Jérôme Zucca en garçon fragile et Jean-Pol Dobois, en "Anthracite".
22 h 5 Documentaire: Artistes contemporains.
Les sculpteurs Bernard Pagès et Toni Grand. Réal. P.-A. Boutang et Y. Michaud.
Troisème et dernière partie. Bernard Pagès, né en 1940 à Cahors,travaille aujourd'hui dans le haut pays niçois. Proche du groupe Suppprt-Surface, il a été peintre avant de devenir sculpteur, il est passé de la pierre aux tôles at aux branchages, puis des classements aux assemblages. Il se définit comme un "baroque européen". Toni Grand, né en 1935 près de Nîmes, travaille sur le bois et les branches, qu'il double depuis quelques années par des moulages.
23 h 5 Journal.
23 h 25 Bonsoir les clips.
23 h 45 Jeux Olympiques.

TROISIÈME CHAINE: FR 3

19 h 3 Jeu littéraire: Les mots en tête.
19 h 15 Emissions régionales.
19 h 40 André . . . Evelyne . . . Souvenirs, souvenirs.
Evelyne Dandry, bordelaise, basque de coeur, accompagnée des ballets et de la chorale d'Oldarra, nous fait découvrir son père — André Dassary — et les chants et danses de son enfance.
19 h 55 Dessin animé: l'Inspecteur Gadget.
20 h 5 Les jeux.'
20 h 35 Cinema: Lucky Luciano.
Film italien de F. Rosi (1973), avec G.M. Volonte, R. Steiger, Ed. O'Brien, C. Siragusa, V. Gardenia, C. Cioffi. (Rediffusion.)
Chef de la Mafia aux États-Unis, condamné à une lourde peine de prison, puis libéré au bout de neuf ans, pour avoir contribué à la réussite du débarquement allié en Sicile, expulsé à Naples, en 1946. Lucky Luciano a-t-il organisé le trafic international de la drogue? Film-enquête, film-puzzle, rassamblant des morceaux épars de chronologie, des faits vrais, des éléments de dossier; film politique qui n'a pu complètement déchiffrer une figure très complexe, mais établi, comme toujours chez Rosi, une réflexion sur le pouvoir, légal ou non.
22 h 20 Journal.
22 h 40 Histoire de l'art: la Vénus de Milo.
Deuxième émission d'une série consacrée à des oeuvres connues au point d'être mythiques, tableaux, sculptures, tapisseries.
22 h 55 Prélude à la nuit.
Sonate pour hautbois et piano, *de Francis Poulenc, par les lauréats de la Fondation Samson François, avec David Walter, hautbois, et Dominique My, piano.*

FRANCE-CULTURE

7 h Cinq regards sur la société d'aujourd'hui: l'ethique punk; pour un humanisme stellaire.
8 h Pages entomologiques de Jean-Henri Fabre.
9 h 5 Un métier comme art: le restaurateur de tableaux, René Vassalo.
10 h Histoire de la piraterie.
11 h Musique: Black and Blue, un disque, un livre.
12 h Panorama.
13 h 30 Feuilleton: "Aimé de son concierge".
14 h Les cultures face aux vertiges de la technique: Amazonie, le Grand parler et la Terre laide.
15 h 3 Embarquement immédiat: La Bulgarie.
15 h 30 Musique: les terrasses de l'été, en France et à Prague.
16 h 30 Promenades ethnologiques en France: Ramon dans les Pyrénées.
17 h 30 Entretiens—Arts plastiques: Mayo ou le bonheur par petites touches.
18 h La deuxième guerre mondiale: la remilitarisation de la Rhénanie le 7 mars 1936.
19 h 25 Lectures.
19 h 30 Itinéraires de la solitude féminine.
20 h Blaise Cendrars, poète intercontinental: le démon du voyage.
20 h 30 Dramatiques: "(Manque d') Aventures en Patagonie", par P. Keineg; avec P. Clévenot, B. Bloch, M. G. Pascal . . .'
22 h La criée aux contes autour du monde: Matteo Maximov, tzigane.
23 h Bestaire: le hérisson.
23 h 20 Musique limite.
23 h 40 Place des étoiles.

FRANCE-MUSIQUE (à Aix-en-Provence)

6 h Musique légère.
7 h 10 Actualité du disque compact.
9 h 5 Méditerranées: L'Antiquité revisitée; oeuvres de Stravinski, Debussy, Ravel.
12 h Concert; oeuvres de Xenakis, Ravel, Schumann, par l'Orchestre de la Méditerranée, dir. M. Tabachnik, sol. Z. Gal, soprano.
13 h 20 Jazz.
14 h Courier de Sud: Un hiver à Majorque.
17 h L'Imprévu (en direct des Deux Garçons) et à 19 h 5.
18 h Une heure avec . . . Ghyslaine Raphanel.
19 h 30 Jazz (au Festival de Juan-les-Pins).
20 h Musiques à danser: oeuvres de Debussy, Roussel, Scelsi, Boulez, Riley.
21 h 30 Concert (en direct du théâtre de l'Archevêché): oeuvres de Brahms, Strauss, Duparc, Satie, par Jessye Normam, accompagnée par Phillipp Moll, piano.
23 h 30 Les soirées de France-Musique: Jazz club (en direct du Hot Brass): les groupes Keops et Galigai.

Newspapers

16 LE TEMPS AUJOURD'HUI

(a) What is the weather going to be like in the Bouches-du-Rhône area?
(b) What is it going to be like in the Hautes-Alpes area?
(c) What is it going to be like in the Vaucluse area?
(d) What is it going to be like in the Var area?
(e) What is it going to be like in Corsica?
(f) What is it going to be like in the Alpes-Maritimes area?

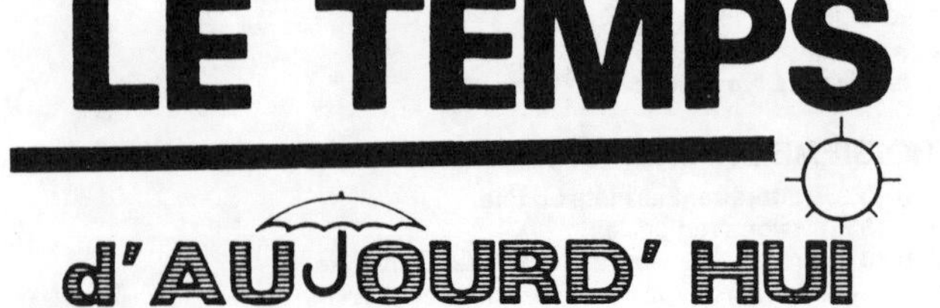

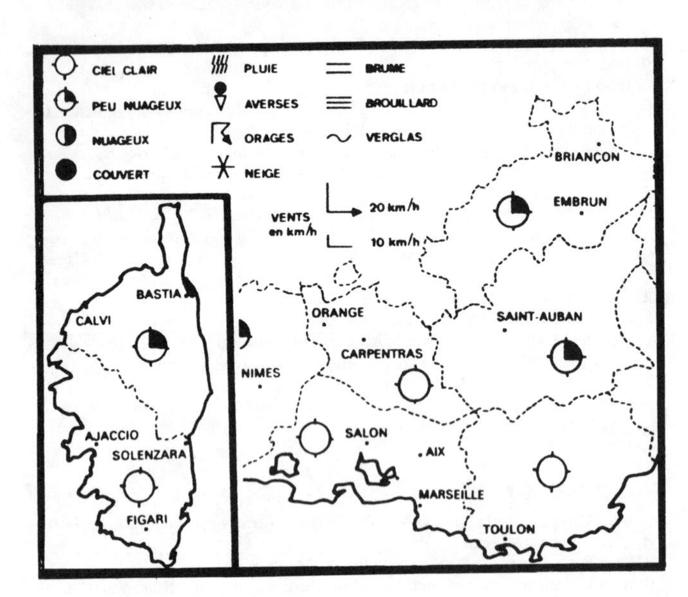

GARD, BOUCHES-DU-RHONE. — Beau temps localement brumeux avec quelques bancs de nuages bas près du littoral le matin, puis ensoleillé devenant passagèrement nuageux l'après-midi sur le relief, vent irrégulier faible avec brise côtière, mer belle, températures sans grand changement, minimales localement en faible hausse.

ALPES DE HAUTE-PROVENCE, HAUTES-ALPES. — Beau temps chaud avec une tendance orageuse sur les reliefs l'après-midi, températures minimales stationnaires, maximales en légère baisse, vent en vallée, brise de montagne.

VAUCLUSE. — Beau temps généralement ensoleillé, passagèrement nuageux l'après-midi, vent irrégulier faible, températures minimales 6 à 8 degrés, maximales 21 à 24 degrés.

VAR. — Beau temps malgré quelques passages nuageux, vent de secteur est modéré temporairement assez fort en début de journée, mer belle à peu agitée, températures maximales stationnaires ou en légère hausse.

CORSE. — Beau temps ensoleillé, brise côtière faible à modérée, mer calme à belle, températures sans changement.

ALPES-MARITIMES. — Beau temps ensoleillé et peu nuageux malgré quelques formations brumeuses, surtout le matin, régime de brise faible sur la côte, températures sans grand changement, minimales de l'ordre de 8 à 11 degrés, maximales 19 à 20 degrés sur la bande côtière, 23 à 24 dans l'intérieur, mer belle à peu agitée.

TEMPERATURES RELEVEES A 16 HEURES SOUS ABRI

Marignane 21 ; Bastia 21 ; Orange 26 ; Sète 17 ; Le Luc 27 ; Calvi 12 ; Perpignan 20 ; Embrun 24 ; Carcassonne 23 ; Salon 22 ; Nîmes 23 ; Cannes 18 ; Ajaccio 22 ; Toulon 19 ; Istres 21 ; Cap-Ferrat 16 ; Carpentras 25 ; Nice 17 ; Montpellier 18 ; Mont-Aigoual 15 ; Saint-Raphaël 19 ; Saint-Auban 23

12 WRITING

12.1 Introduction

Extract from the The National Criteria/French

Basic level writing: 'Candidates should be expected, within a limited range of clearly defined topic areas (mirroring those of the common-core assessment objectives for speaking), to carry out writing tasks which might include, for example, a simple letter in response to a letter in easily comprehensible French or to instructions in English, and short messages (post-cards, lists, notes) in response to instructions in English or easily comprehensible French.'

Candidates aiming at the award of Grade C and above will be required to take the Basic level Writing Test. To gain Grades A and B candidates will normally be required to take a test of writing at the Higher level.

Higher level writing: 'Candidates should be expected to write in continuous French, on a wider range of clearly defined topic areas, in response to a written stimulus in English or in easily comprehensible French, or in response to a visual stimulus.'

Letter writing does not form part of the compulsory common-core element of GCSE French, but it is a necessary element for those candidates aiming at the Higher level grades. The various types of letters which you may be asked to write in GCSE French will be either *formal* or *informal*.

THE INFORMAL LETTER

These are letters written to friends and relatives on a personal level. As in English, they differ in content and style from formal letters. The variety and authenticity of style, however, will be just as important as grammatical accuracy.

THE FORMAL LETTER

These are letters which you write to known or unknown officials, representatives, agents, etc. For example, you may be asked to write to a hotel to confirm a booking, or to a tourist information office requesting information, or to a lost property office, etc. All of the above letters would require you to write to someone in a formal capacity. There are special ways of writing these letters, especially for the beginnings and endings and you must know how to cope with these under examination conditions.

There are many things that you can do to practise letter writing even though you will not know, until you open your exam paper, exactly what you must include in your letter(s). Here are some of the things you must do in preparation for this part of the exam . . .

1 Learn your verb tenses carefully. The tenses which you are most likely to need for letter writing are: present, future, perfect, imperfect and conditional.

2 Learn the topic vocabularies carefully, e.g. holidays, accidents, daily routine, school, town, etc.

3 Learn how to set out and write both formal and informal letters.

12.2 Informal Letters

To a friend of your own age, you should begin the letter with . . .
e.g. to Pierre Cher Pierre, or Mon cher Pierre, or Cher ami,
e.g. to Anne-Marie Chère Anne-Marie, or Ma chère Anne-Marie, or Chère amie,

To a friend of your own age, you should end the letter with . . .
Amitiés,
or Amicalement, or A bientôt, or Bien à toi, or other phrases which you have been taught and know to be appropriate.

If you are writing to a friend of your own age, you should use the 'tu' form of the verb to address him/her.

If you are writing to an adult (e.g. parent/s of your friend), you should use the 'vous' form of the verb.

French people do not write their address in full at the top right-hand side of a letter when writing to a friend. They just put the date and the place . . . e.g.

Paris, le 3 octobre

They usually put their name and address on the back/top of the envelope after 'Expéd: (Expéditeur).'

USEFUL EXPRESSIONS FOR INFORMAL LETTERS

Thanking for letter received

Merci de ta gentille lettre qui m'a fait grand plaisir.
or Je te remercie de ta dernière lettre.
or J'ai été très heureux/heureuse d'avoir de tes nouvelles.
or J'ai été très content(e) de recevoir ta lettre.
or J'ai reçu ta lettre avec plaisir.

Apologies for a late reply

Je m'excuse de ne t'avoir pas écrit plus tôt mais . . .
or Excuse-moi de n'avoir pas écrit plus tôt mais . . .
or Je t'écris un peu en retard car . . .
or J'espère que tu m'excuseras de t'écrire avec un peu de retard.
or Je suis désolé(e) de te répondre avec un peu de retard.

General statements

Any combination of the following . . .

Je profite	d'un moment	libre	pour	t'écrire
	d'un instant			t'envoyer un petit mot
	d'une après-midi	de repos		
	d'un jour			te répondre

Expressing good wishes

Je te souhaite de bonnes vacances. (*for a good holiday*)
Je te souhaite un joyeux Noël. (*for Christmas*)
Je te souhaite un bon anniversaire. (*for a happy birthday*)
Je te souhaite bonne chance. (*for good luck*)
Je te souhaite 'bon voyage'. (*for a journey*)

Accepting invitations

Je te remercie de ta lettre qui m'a fait enormément plaisir.
J'aimerais bien venir passer une (deux, etc.) semaine(s) chez toi au mois de . . ./pendant les grandes vacances.
Je serai en vacances à partir du . . .
Je pourrai venir en avion/par le ferry/par le train . . .

Refusing an invitation

Je te remercie de ton invitation à faire un séjour chez toi pendant les grandes vacances.
Malheureusement je ne peux pas accepter.
Je suis desolé(e) d'être forcé de refuser.
J'ai déjà promis d'aller rendre visite à mes grands-parents, qui habitent au Canada . . .

Giving invitations

J'écris pour te demander si tu peux venir passer (e.g. une/deux semaines) . . . chez moi pendant les grandes vacances.
Nous pourrons venir te chercher à l'aéroport de . . ./à la gare de . . .

Expressing regret

Je suis désolé(e) de te dire que . . .

Expressing pleasure

Je suis ravi(e) de te dire que . . .

Endings

Mes parents t'envoient leur bon souvenir/leurs amitiés. (*Best wishes from your parents*)
Dis le bonjour de ma part à tes parents/toute la famille. (*Your best wishes to your correspondent's parents/family*)

Other endings . . .
Je vais te quitter car j'ai beaucoup de devoirs à faire.
or Je te quitte car j'ai beaucoup de travail à faire.

Before you actually end your letter, it is a good idea to use a 'winding-up' phrase, but *not* that awful expression 'I must go now'. This sounds even worse in French than it does in English! Here are some more useful 'winding-up' phrases . . .

Je te quitte en espérant te lire bientôt, *or* En attendant le plaisir de te lire, *or* Mes parents te disent un petit bonjour, *or* Ecris-moi vite, *or* Je te quitte, *or* Bonjour de ma part à ta famille, *or* A bientôt de te lire, etc.

Here are some examples of the type of letter you might be asked to write.

BASIC LEVEL

1 Write a letter in French (70–80 words) in answer to the following letter.

Toulouse, le 8 mai.

Cher ...
(Chère ...)

Merci bien de ta gentille lettre. Pour nous aussi, l'année scolaire va bientôt se terminer. J'attends avec impatience les vacances car je vais faire du camping en Suisse avec des copains. Et toi? que vas-tu faire pendant les grandes vacances? Où vas-tu? tu partiras seul(e) ou avec un groupe scolaire? J'espère que l'année prochaine tu pourras venir en France.

Amitiés,

.....

2 Write a letter (60–70 words) in French inviting your penfriend to come and spend the Easter holidays with you. Suggest possible dates, means of travel and various things that you hope to do during his/her stay.

3 You are writing your first letter to your French penfriend. Thank him/her for his/her letter and for the family photo. Describe your family and the town or village where you live. End your letter by saying that you are very pleased to have a French penfriend and that you will send a photo of your family in your next letter. Write about 75 words.

HIGHER LEVEL

1 The above letter may also be set at the Higher level but you will probably be asked to write about 150 or more words. You would also be expected to give much more detail, e.g. personal characteristics as well as a physical description of your family, greater detail about the area in which you live and why it is an interesting/uninteresting place, etc.

2 You are now writing your second letter to your French penfriend. Thank him/her for his/her letter. Say that you think French schoolchildren have a long school day but also longer holidays than you. Say that French schoolchildren are lucky not to have to wear school uniform. Describe your own school uniform and your school. Write out your own class time-table in French. Say which subjects you like/dislike and why. Describe what clubs and societies you have in school. Say how much homework you have each day/week. Finish your letter by saying that you are enclosing a photo of yourself and your family. Say that you are wearing your school uniform in the photo. End your letter by saying that you hope to hear from him/her soon. (Use about 180 words.)

12.3 Formal Letters

MINISTÈRE
DE L'ÉDUCATION NATIONALE

COMITÉ D'ACCUEIL
DES ÉLÈVES DES ÉCOLES PUBLIQUES
4, Rue des Irlandais, 4
PARIS-V

Tél: KELlermann 10.83
C. C. P. Paris 2259 84

GF/LL/8554

Paris, le 22 juin 1987

Monsieur Le Proviseur
Lycée, Émile Zola
24 Avenue des invalides
Annecy

Groupe no 6 5 0 5

Monsieur,

J'accuse réception de votre lettre du 15 juin. Je regrette de ne pouvoir donner notre accord sur la nouvelle composition de votre groupe.

Conformément aux conditions d'accès mentionnées dans le programme de Comité d'Accueil, pour 19 personnes de moins de 21 ans, 4 adultes seulement peuvent être reçus.

J'espère que vous pourrez modifier l'effectif de votre groupe en conséquence et dans l'attente de votre réponse, je vous prie d'agréer, Monsieur, l'expression de mes sentiments distingués.

Le Directeur

p.o. G. FRENAIS

Copie adressée au centre de CANNES

When writing formal letters in French, you must follow certain basic rules . . .

1 Write your own name and address at the top *left*-hand side of the page.

2 Write the name and address of the person to whom you are writing at the *right*-hand side of the page before you begin the letter.

NB The above instructions are the opposite of the instructions you will have learnt for setting out a formal letter in English. (You may find it easier to remember this rule if you also remember that the French drive on the opposite side of the road!)

3 Begin your formal letter *only* with the word *Monsieur* or *Madame* or *Mademoiselle* (this latter is not used as frequently as *Madame*). In any case, leave out Cher/Chère at the beginning of a formal letter.

4 Use the *vous* form throughout the letter to address the person to whom you are writing.

Example of a formal letter layout . . .

Paris, le 3 Octobre.

Guy Ferrière

4 Rue des Moines

Paris VII

Madame la Directrice

Lycée Goncourt

45 Boulevard Saint-Germain

Toulouse

Madame,

....

Veuillez agréer Madame, l'expression de mes sentiments distingués.*

Guy Ferrière

*This formal ending is used at the end of most formal letters. There are some variations also to be found, e.g. Je vous prie d'agréer, Monsieur/Madame l'expression de mes sentiments distingués.

Here are some useful expressions for formal letters . . .

On receipt of a letter

J'accuse réception de votre lettre.

Requesting information

Je voudrais savoir . . ., *or* Voulez-vous me dire . . ., *or* Voulez-vous m'envoyer . . ., *or*
Je vous serais (bien) reconnaissant si vous pouviez me fournir* . . .

HIGHER LEVEL

Applying for jobs

You have read an advert in the newspaper . . .
J'ai lu dans les petites annonces du (e.g. *Figaro*) du . . . (date) que vous cherchez . . . *or*
En réponse } à votre annonce dans le journal . . . du . . ., j'ai l'honneur
Comme suite } de poser ma candidature au poste de . . .

Possible jobs. . .
(une) jeune fille au pair (*au pair girl*)
(un) moniteur/(une) monitrice (*play group leader*)
(un(e)) pompiste (*petrol pump attendant*)
(un) garçon de café/une serveuse (*waiter/waitress*)
(un) vendeur/(une) vendeuse (*shop assistant*)
(un) plongeur/(une) plongeuse (*washer-up in restaurant*)
(un) gardien/(une) gardienne de plage (*beach life-guard*)
(un(e)) secrétaire (*secretary*)
(une(e)) babysitter (*babysitter*)

Ce poste m'intéresse beaucoup parce que . . . (You are very interested in the job . . .)
Je suis intéressé(e) par ce poste car . . . (reasons why)

J'adore les enfants.

J'aime travailler dans les restaurants/magasins/les garages/sur les plages, etc.

Je voudrais perfectionner ma connaissance de la langue française.
Je vous prie de bien vouloir trouver ci-joint mon c.v. (curriculum vitae) et une lettre de recommandation du censeur de mon collège (offering further information in support of your application . . .).

Endings . . .

Je me permets donc d'offrir mes services. *Or*
Je vous prie donc de prendre ma demande en considération. Veuillez agréer, Monsieur/Madame l'expression de mes sentiments distingués.

Expressing thanks

Je vous remercie beaucoup de . . .
Je vous suis très reconnaissant(e) . . .
Avec mes remercients anticipés . . . (at the end of a letter/in anticipation).

Expressing intention

J'ai l'intention de . . .
Je compte . . .

Booking accommodation

Je voudrais retenir une/deux (etc.) chambre(s) . . .
Il me faut une/deux (etc.) chambre(s).

In reply to an advert

J'ai lu dans le journal . . .
J'ai lu dans les petites annonces . . .
J'ai lu votre annonce dans le journal . . .

* fournir *to provide.*

Including material

Veuillez trouver ci-joint . . .
Je vous prie de bien vouloir trouver ci-joint . . .

Cancelling arrangements

Je regrette beaucoup de me trouver dans l'impossibilité de . . .
Je vous prie d'annuler ma réservation.

Complaining

J'ai le regret de vous informer que . . .
Je ne suis pas du tout satisfait(e) de . . .
J'ai à me plaindre de . . .
Cela ne répondrait pas du tout à ce qu j'attendais.
Le service était affreux.
J'espère que vous ne tarderez pas à me donner satisfaction.

Expressing regret

Je suis desolé(e) de vous dire que . . .

Expressing pleasure

Je suis ravi(e) de vous dire que . . .
Je suis très content(e) de vous dire que . . .

Hotels

1 Here is an advert for a hotel chain in France.

LE GUIDE DES HOTELS FRANCE–ACCUEIL VOUS EST OFFERT.
PROFITEZ-EN.
Hôtel France–Accueil
85 rue du Dessous-des-Berges
75013 Paris

En prime, une carte de France indique tous les hôtels de la chaîne: chaque hôtel a sa photo en couleur; classement par ordre alphabétique des localités: deux catégories de confort. Demandez le guide.

Write a letter to the above association asking for the guide to this hotel group. Say that you are especially interested in the Loire Valley region.

2 You are writing to the Hôtel Matignon in Arcachon. Explain that you and your parents would like to stay for one week. Say that you would like two rooms, a single room with shower and a double room with bath. Say that you would like to stay from the 20–27 July. Ask if there is a swimming pool at the hotel and ask if there is a garage.

3 You are writing to . . .

HOTEL SAINT-ROMAIN
5 et 7 rue Saint-Roch
75001 PARIS (Tuileries)

Say that you want to spend the Easter holidays in Paris. Say that you would like to stay from the 9–14 April. Say that you would like a single room with bath. Ask if the hotel has a restaurant. Ask them to send a list of what's on in Paris during April. Begin and end your letter in the usual formal way.

Tourist office

You are writing to the Syndicat d'Initiative at Auxerre. Say that you intend visiting Auxerre this summer and ask for brochures about the town.
Ask for some information about hotels which are comfortable but not too expensive.
Ask for information about the surrounding area and a list of local activities.
Ask if you will be able to hire bicycles in the town.

Lost property

On returning from your holiday in France, you discover that you have left your watch in the hotel where you were staying. Write to the hotel ('La Coquille' in Guincamp) to ask if they have found it. Give all the necessary details (e.g. make, type, when and where you left it, etc.)

Applying for jobs

Abbreviations:

env. envoyer
expér. expérience
indép. indépendant(e)
min. minimum
rech. recherche
se prés. se présenter
socx. sociaux

1 You read the following advert in the *Figaro* for 10 June . . .

Rech. SECRÉTAIRE/STÉNODACTYLO
pour Direction des Ventes,
expérimenté(e), initiative,
organisé(e), avantages socx.,
cantine.
Env. C.V., photo,
TRONCHET FRÈRES, 8 Boulevard Plessy,
AVALLON.

Write a letter in French to this firm applying for the job advertized. Give all the necessary details and ask for further information about the social advantages mentioned.

2 You read the following advert in the newspaper *Le Monde* for 24 March . . .

AIDA magasins prêt-à-porter
enfant et femme rech.
VENDEURS/VENDEUSES
bilangues anglais
se prés. 12 ave. Charles de Gaulle,
Boulogne.

Write a letter in French applying for this post. Give all the necessary details and say when you would be available (*disponible*) to begin work.

3 You read the following advert for a job in the newspaper *Ouest-France* on 18 April . . .

Rech. jeune fille au pair
pour Côte Atlantique
juillet/août
travaux ménagers
logée indép., nourrie
Mme Jourdan, 43 av. Foch,
LA ROCHELLE.

Write a letter in French applying for the post. Give all the necessary details.

4 You read the following advert in the *Figaro* for 6 May . . .

LA PIZZA-GRILL
246 rue du Bac, Paris
rech. plongeurs
juillet–septembre
aussi garçons/serveuses
parlant anglais
bon salaire.
Ecrire aujourd'hui

Write a letter in French applying for one of the above jobs giving reasons and stating when you would be available. Ask also about details of accommodation and free time.

5 A group of folk-dancers from Brittany is planning a visit to your town and region. You have been asked to organize the visit by writing to confirm the arrangements.
Read the letter given below . . .

Monsieur, J'accuse réception de votre lettre du 15 mars. Je suis heureux de vous annoncer que les préparatifs pour la visite de nos danseurs sont maintenant complets.

Nous comptons arriver en car le jeudi 16 avril vers six heures du soir. Nous attendons avec un grand plaisir d'être parmi vous et de faire la connaissance des familles qui nous recevront chez eux. Nous vous remercions vivement de tous les préparatifs que vous avez faits pour assurer notre confort ainsi que le succès de cette visite.

Avec nos amitiés les plus sincères,

Now write a reply in French to the above letter confirming the date of the visit and the time of the party's arrival. Give some details of your school and the surrounding area and outline the programme given below.

Thursday 16 April

6p.m.	arrival at school meeting with host families evening with host families at home

Friday 17 April

10a.m.	rehearsal at school
12.30p.m.	lunch at school
2p.m.	visit to nearby town
5.30p.m.	reception at town hall
7p.m.	folk dancing display at town hall

Saturday 18 April

10a.m.	visit to local sweet factory
lunch	at home of hosts
afternoon	rehearsal
5.30p.m.	tea at sports centre
7p.m.	dancing display at sports centre

Sunday 19 April

morning	and lunch at home of hosts
afternoon	excursion to beauty spot
tea	at beauty spot
7.30p.m.	disco at sports centre

Monday 20 April

10a.m.	departure from school

12.4 Cards

BASIC LEVEL

Here are some useful expressions for writing post-cards . . .

Je passe une semaine à . . . *I am spending a week at/in* . . . (name of town/village)

Me voici en vacances à . . . *Here I am on holiday at/in* . . . (name of town/village)

Il fait beau/très chaud, etc. *The weather is fine/very hot, etc.*

Je vais à la plage tous les jours. *I go to the beach every day.*

Je me baigne tous les jours. *I swim every day.*

J'ai visité . . . *I have visited* . . .

Je m'amuse beaucoup. *I'm enjoying myself very much.*

Je m'ennuie. *I'm bored.*

Je reste à l'hôtel car il pleut. *I stay in the hotel because it's raining.*

Je rentre . . . prochain(e). *I go home next* . . .

However, as in English, postcards can be written in an abbreviated form. Here are some such abbreviations . . .

Nous voici à . . . *Here we are at* . . . (name of town/village)
Nous voici en . . . *Here we are in* . . . (name of country)
Bien arrivé(e)(s). *Have arrived safely.*
Sommes arrivé(e)s . . . *We have arrived* . . .
Fait beau/chaud/froid. *The weather is fine/hot/cold.*
Beaucoup de monde. *There are a lot of people here.*
M'amuse beaucoup. *I'm enjoying myself very much.*
Fais ski/voile/planche à voile/etc. *Am skiing/sailing/wind-surfing/etc.*
Suis bronzé(e)/malade/etc. *I am sun-tanned/ill/etc.*
Bon hôtel *Good hotel*
Bon camping *Good campsite*
Hôtel bien/mal equipé *Hotel well/badly equipped*
Hôtel cher *Hotel expensive*
Ville chère *Town expensive*
Vues superbes *Superb views*
Excellente cuisine *Excellent food*
Mauvaise cuisine *Food awful*
Camping formidable *Camping/campsite great*

Ville formidable *Great town*
Grande piscine *Large swimming-pool*
Belles promenades *Fine walks*
Ai visité *Have visited*
Ai mal (e.g. aux pieds) *My feet hurt*
Vais . . . demain *Am going . . . tomorrow*
Rentre . . . *Returning . . .*

and to end with . . .
Bises or Amitiés *Love*

EXAMPLES

1 From a holiday resort.

Nous voici à Carnac. Bon hôtel au bord de la mer. Temps splendide. Me baigne tous les jours.

Bises . . .

2 In a mountain resort.

Bien arrivés à Chamonix. Faisons du ski tous les jours. Fait très froid. Marie est tombée et s'est cassé la jambe. Elle reste dans sa chambre.

Amitiés . . .

3 From a campsite.

Fais du camping depuis quelques jours. Pleut tout le temps. Je m'ennuie. Rentre Samedi.

Amitiés . . .

New Year's cards

French people send New Year's cards rather than Christmas cards. Here is an example . . .

Chers amis,

Permettez-moi au seuil de ce nouvel an de vous souhaiter un très joyeux Noël ainsi qu'une très bonne année. J'espère que cette carte vous trouvera tous en excellente forme.

Mes meilleurs souvenirs.

Carole.

Useful vocabulary for cards

Bon Anniversaire *Happy Birthday*
Bonne Année *Happy New Year*
Joyeux Noël *Happy Christmas*
Meilleurs Voeux *Best wishes*
Tous mes voeux de bonheur *My best wishes for your happiness*

QUESTIONS: POSTCARDS

1 Write a postcard to your penfriend in French telling him/her that you have arrived safely in Nice, the weather is very hot, the hotel good and the food excellent.

2 Write a postcard to your penfriend in French telling him/her that you are in Paris, that you have visited Notre Dame cathedral and the Eiffel Tower. Say that the weather is fine and that you will be going home on Saturday.

3 Write a postcard to your penfriend's parents in French saying that you have arrived home safely and that you had a good journey. Say that the weather is cold and that it is raining. Thank them for your visit.

4 Write a postcard to your penfriend in French saying that you are camping in Spain, that the campsite is excellent but that the food is awful. Tell him/her that there are a lot of people on the beach and that you are suntanned.

5 Write a postcard to your penfriend in French saying that you are on holiday in Rome. Tell him/her that the town is expensive, that you are staying in a good hotel with a big swimming-pool. Say that you are going to Milan tomorrow.

QUESTIONS: CARDS

1 Write a New Year's card in French to your penfriend sending your good wishes for the New Year and thanking him/her for a present.

2 Write a birthday card in French to your penfriend wishing him/her happy birthday and sending your best wishes.

HIGHER LEVEL

Announcements for Births, Weddings, Deaths are usually formal in French, e.g.

Births

LAURENT a la joie de vous faire part de la naissance de sa petite soeur
ELISABETH
de la part de M et Mme Denis BEAUDET

Engagements

M et Mme Lucien CHABANS
M et Mme Alexandre LECERF
sont heureux de vous annoncer les fiançailles
de leurs enfants
FLORENCE et ALAIN

Weddings

M et Mme Michel DUFAU
M et Mme Gaston CABROL
ont l'honneur de vous faire part du mariage de leurs enfants
CAROLINE et GILBERT
qui aura lieu en la chapelle Notre-Dame-de-Compassion, ce samedi 26 avril à 15 heures.

Deaths

Mme Henri FLEURIOT
et toute la famille
ont la douleur de vous faire part du décès de
M Henri FLEURIOT
survenue le 12 mai à Paris.
La cérémonie religieuse sera célébrée le mardi 17 mai à 8h 30 à la crypte de l'église Saint-Jean-Baptiste de Grenelle, sa paroisse.

Replies to such announcements can be more personal but are still relatively formal, e.g:

Reply to a birth announcement

... Je suis ravi d'apprendre la naissance de ... Je vous félicite et lui souhaite tout le bonheur possible.

Reply to an engagement announcement

... Je suis ravi d'apprendre que tu es maintenant fiancé(e) ...
Je vous souhaite, à tous les deux, tout le bonheur possible.

Reply to a wedding announcement

... J'ai été très heureux/heureuse de recevoir votre faire-part.
Je vous adresse toutes mes félicitations et tous mes voeux de bonheur.

Reply to a bereavement announcement

... J'ai été désolé(e) d'apprendre la mort de ...
Veuillez recevoir mes condoléances les plus sincères.

12.5 Notes/Lists/Forms

GENERAL ADVICE

The advice for writing Notes/Lists is similar to that for writing postcards. It is usually done in abbreviated form but it must be *comprehensible.*

Here is a shopping list for some essential medical supplies before going on holiday ...

mouchoirs en papier
crème antiseptique
sparadrap
bandage
quelque chose pour le rhume de foin

The list above contains the key-words but not the words for 'the'.

Similarly, an abbreviated form is used for writing notes. All you need to convey is the essential information.

e.g. You are alone in your penfriend's house when the telephone rings. You have to write a note for your penfriend's mother. The call is from a friend of hers (Janine) who can't come tomorrow because her father is ill. She will come on Friday instead.

The note you write might read as follows ...

Janine a téléphoné. Ne peut pas venir demain. Père malade. Viendra vendredi.

You may also be asked to write out in French for your penfriend a list of things that you will do when he comes to stay with you ... e.g:

Sunday	church
Monday	sports centre
Tuesday	shopping
Wednesday	swimming-pool
Thursday	trip
Friday	visit grandparents
Saturday	disco

Your notes in French would read as follows ...

dimanche	église
lundi	complexe sportif
mardi	achats
mercredi	piscine
jeudi	excursion
vendredi	visite/grands-parents
samedi	disco

Some examining groups may ask you to fill in a form in French. Here is an example . . .

You are applying for a French penfriend and have been asked to give the following details. Complete this form in French.

Collège ______________________

Adresse (du collège) ______________________

Votre nom ______________________

Prénom(s) ______________________

Date de naissance ______________________

Matières étudiées ______________________

Langues parlées ______________________

Intérêts ______________________

____

____

QUESTIONS: NOTES/LISTS

1 Put the following into French for your French friend . . .

Monday	dentist's
Tuesday	shopping
Wednesday	swimming-pool
Thursday	sports centre
Friday	disco
Saturday	party at Peter's
Sunday	beach

2 You are going out to meet your penfriend. You are alone in the house when the phone rings. It is your penfriend's grandmother. She leaves a message for your friend's mother. Write the following message in French . . .

CAN'T COME TOMORROW. HAVE TOOTHACHE. WILL COME ON SUNDAY.

3 You are alone at your penfriend's house. The phone rings. You take a message for your friend. Write it in French.
Say that his/her friend Laurent has phoned. Say that he would like to go to the cinema tomorrow. Say that he will phone in the morning.

4 Write a shopping list for your penfriend's mother in French . . .

salad meat eggs cheese yogurts orange juice ham crisps

12.6 Continuous Writing: Reports/Accounts

HIGHER LEVEL

At the Higher level, candidates may be required to write a report or account in French. This may take the form of a personal narrative, an accident, event, etc. which has happened to you. You may be asked to write this account in a letter or as a simple report in itself. Do check your examining group's syllabus to see which type of writing test you will have to do.

Try to think in French at all stages. Keep your account simple but *accurate*. Use those words and phrases which you know to be correct and which you have learned thoroughly beforehand. During the examination is not a time to experiment with new forms of writing. It is the time to show the examiner what you *know, understand* and *can do*.

Some continuous writing tests may be based on a series of pictures or on a written stimulus in English or French. Some specimen questions are given below. (Always check to see if there are any special instructions, e.g. tenses to use, number of words, etc.)

FURTHER QUESTIONS

1 Write an account in French (about 150 words) using the past tenses on the following topic.

You recently went on a school outing (e.g. biology or geography field trip) to the beach. The weather was fine when you set off and everybody was looking forward to the day but things did not turn out as everybody expected. Write an account of what happened to you.

2 Write an account (about 200 words) in French on the following topic.

You have been on an exchange visit to France. You are now going to write an account of your visit for the school magazine. Give as much detail as possible (e.g. Who did you go with? Where? What did you see/do?). Give an account also of the journey.

3 Write an account in French (about 180 words), using the past tenses, on the following topic.

You recently went on a day trip to a place of historic interest. Describe where you went, what you did and why you found the day particularly interesting/uninteresting.

4 Write an account in French (120 words) on the following topic.

Vous avez passé les vacances de Pâques en Suisse avec un groupe scolaire. Vous y êtes allés pour faire du ski. Racontez vos expériences.

5 Write an account in French (180 words) on the following topic.

Samedi dernier, vous avez fêté votre anniversaire avec des amis. Où êtes-vous allés? Qu'avez-vous fait? Comment avez-vous passé la journée/la soirée?

6 Write an account in French (150 words) on the following topic.

Votre famille vient de déménager. Décrivez le déménagement et la nouvelle maison. Vous êtes content(e) de déménager? Pourquoi/pourquoi pas?

7 You have gone on an exchange visit to France. You are asked to write an account in French of an incident which happened to you while you were in France. Base your account on the pictures below. Use about 180 words in French.

13 ANSWERS

13.1 Self-Test Unit

1 STRUCTURES AND GRAMMAR REVISION

Articles and nouns

les animaux
les cadeaux
les chevaux
les fils
les journaux
les yeux
les oiseaux
messieurs
mesdames
les timbres-poste

Adjectives

vieux/vieille
joli/jolie
grand/grande
blanc/blanche
cher/chère
premier/première
doux/douce
favori/favorite
beau/belle
nouveau/nouvelle

Adverbs

mal
heureusement
trop
vraiment
mieux
souvent

Pronouns

qui
dont
chacun(e)
n'importe qui
quelqu'un

Conjunctions

quand
parce que/car
donc
puisque
dès que/aussitôt que

Prepositions

parmi
devant
avant
à droite
à pied
jusqu'à
de l'autre côté
en vacances

Verbs

Present tense

1 Il finit
2 Nous mangeons
3 Vous appelez
4 Je viens
5 Elles vont
6 Tu jettes
7 Elle veut
8 Nous commençons
9 Ils sont
10 Elles ont
11 Vous faites
12 Il écrit
13 Tu sais
14 Vous dites
15 Nous nous couchons
16 Je reçois
17 Elles s'asseyent
18 Elle doit
19 Ils connaissent
20 Vous prenez

Future tense

1 Ils auront
2 Je pourrai
3 Elle s'assiéra
4 Vous viendrez
5 Tu voudras
6 Ils appelleront
7 Nous ferons
8 Il faudra
9 Tu seras
10 Elles recevront
11 Je courrai
12 Elle devra
13 Vous enverrez
14 Tu finiras
15 Il pleuvra
16 Elles répéteront
17 Je saurai
18 Nous apercevrons
19 Tu tiendras
20 Nous cueillerons

Imperfect tense

1 Nous finissions
2 Il était
3 Ils avaient
4 Vous alliez
5 Je faisais
6 Elles pouvaient
7 Elle envoyait
8 Il voulait
9 Je jetais
10 Vous disiez

Conditional tense

1 Je voudrais
2 Ils iraient
3 Nous serions
4 Tu pourrais
5 Vous demanderiez
6 Elle dirait
7 Elles auraient
8 Je viendrais
9 Il ferait
10 Vous enverriez

Perfect tense

1 Il a dû
2 Elle s'est assise
3 Vous avez mis
4 J'ai suivi
5 Tu es retourné(e)
6 Nous sommes descendu(e)s
7 Elles ont vu
8 Il a pris
9 Je suis devenu(e)
10 Nous avons vécu
11 Il s'est souvenu
12 Vous avez ouvert
13 Tu as connu
14 Ils ont reçu
15 Nous avons voulu
16 Je suis rentré(e)
17 Elles ont eu
18 Elle a craint
19 Vous avez été
20 Il a pu

Past historic tense

1 They put
2 I had to
3 We took
4 They had
5 She knew
6 They saw
7 They came
8 He was
9 He made/did
10 She drank

Imperative and present participle

1 knowing
2 being
3 having
4 Finish!
5 Be!

Negatives

Je n'aime pas les devoirs.
Je n'y vais jamais.
Personne n'est arrivé.
Elle n'a rien mangé.

2 FUNCTIONS

1 Au secours!
2 D'accord.
3 Cela ne fait rien.
4 Félicitations.
5 Allez tout droit.
6 C'est dommage.
7 Je m'intéresse beaucoup à. . .
8 Enchanté, monsieur/mademoiselle.
9 A bientôt.
10 Ce n'est pas possible.
11 Je suis désolé(e).
12 Bon anniversaire! Bonne année! Courage! Dors/dormez bien!
13 Je regrette mais je ne comprends pas.
14 Il est interdit de. . .

3 NOTIONS

Direction/distance

au loin
partout
à gauche
à droite
le nord
de l'autre côté
tout droit
là-bas

Place/position

ensemble
sous
tout près

Quality

roux
de cuir
en inox/d'acier inoxydable
de laine
de dentelle

Number/quantity

treize
trente-neuf
soixante-trois
quatre-vingt-quatre
cent un

une bouteille de
un pot de
une livre de
une boîte de
un paquet de

Emotions/feelings

avoir peur
ennuyer
déranger
s'amuser
heureux/heureuse
rire
triste
gronder

Time

enfin
avant
de temps en temps
une demi-heure
déjà
le lendemain matin
plus tard
bientôt
demain
longtemps

Dates/festivals

féliciter
Pâques
le Jour de l'An
l'anniversaire

4 VOCABULARY TOPIC AREAS

Café/hotel/restaurant

le petit déjeuner
la tasse
l'ascenseur
une chambre à un lit
la douche
l'assiette
la pension complète
la boisson
un invité
le déjeuner

Camping

le matérial de camping
la poubelle
un emplacement
le sac à dos
le bidon à eau
le sac de couchage
le camping gaz
le marteau
le piquet
le terrain de camping

Clothes

la ceinture
le blue-jean
la robe de nuit
la poche
la taille
la manche
les chaussettes
la chemise
le chandail/la veste
le veston/la veste

Countries/nationalities

la Belgique
la Grande-Bretagne
l'Écosse
la Suisse
le Pays de Galles
le Royaume-Uni
une Autrichienne
un Allemand
une Indienne
un Grec

Countryside

un rouge-gorge
un cygne
la grange
la fermière
un troupeau
le verger
le berger
la fourmi
les cailloux
le ruisseau

Daily routine

prendre une douche
se brosser les dents
attraper l'autobus
prendre le goûter
s'endormir

Education

la chimie
le Collège d'Enseignement Secondaire
l'informatique
le proviseur
apprendre
dessiner
l'emploi du temps
l'uniforme scolaire
étudier
être reçu/réussir à un examen

Food/drink

le petit pain
les chips
les raisins
le jus de fruit
la côtelette
un steak bien cuit
le veau
les choux de Bruxelles
le yaourt
le sel

Health/illness

un furoncle
la varicelle
être enrhumé
Ma tête me tourne
s'évanouir
le poste de secours
la grippe
se fouler/se faire une entorse
avoir mal au coeur
avoir de la fièvre

Human body

la cheville
la figure/le visage
le coeur
le dos
le poignet
la lèvre
la langue
l'épaule
le pouce
le menton

Accident/injury

Au secours!
un accident de la route
être piqué par
renverser
(se) casser
couper
un accident grave
un brancard
coincer
(se) blesser

Home/rooms

un immeuble
une armoire
le rez-de-chaussée
le/la concierge
le séjour/la salle de séjour
le/la locataire
louer
fermer à clé
l'étage
nettoyer
le robinet
le savon
le chevet
la couverture
le rayon
le couvert
l'aspirateur
l'électrophone
le magnétoscope
faire la vaisselle

Garden

l'allée
la plate-bande/le parterre
la serre
la brouette
la balançoire

Jobs/professions

le douanier
l'ingénieur
le comptable
la ménagère
le gérant
le routier
le coiffeur
l'avoué/le notaire
le personnel
le chômeur

Leisure

jouer aux cartes
le bricolage
le delta-plane/sport de l'aile libre
l'équitation
une boum
la spéléologie
le patinage
la planche à voile
les jeux vidéo
la natation

The media

la météo
le feuilleton
le sondage
le quotidien
la chaîne

Personal identification

les yeux verts
les cheveux roux
mince
de taille moyenne
les cheveux courts
laid(e)
les cheveux blonds

Family/friends

la petite-fille
le neveu
cadet/te
la tante
le/la meilleur(e) ami(e)

Pets

le lapin
la tortue
l'âne
l'épagneul
le cochon d'Inde
la souris

Seaside

la falaise
le transa(t)
la glace
le phare
le rocher
faire de la voile
le seau et la pelle
le parasol
faire du ski nautique
prendre des bains de soleil/se bronzer

Services

toucher un chèque
des chèques de voyage
le guichet
le portefeuille
l'appareil
la boîte aux lettres
mettre une lettre à la poste
le timbre-poste
composer le numéro
l'annuaire
le Syndicat d'Initiative/l'Office de Tourisme
une liste des randonnées

Shopping

la librairie
le consommateur
la bijouterie
le kiosque à journaux
la boucherie
le sous-sol
(C'est) combien?
la vitrine
la papeterie
peser

Town

le Syndicat d'Initiative
la gare routière
le bureau des objets trouvés
le passage clouté
le centre sportif
le quartier
le passage souterrain
les feux
la place
le rond-point

Travel

l'avion
l'arrêt d'autobus
l'aérogare
la galerie
le pneu
la plaque d'immatriculation
le quai
la valise
le billet d'aller et retour
le chariot

Weather

Il neige
des éclaircies
l'aube/le point du jour
l'arc-en-ciel
une averse
nuageux
la météo
au printemps
la chaleur
le clair de lune

13.2 The Oral Exam: Conversation

Family

Basic level

1 Il y en a (e.g., quatre)

2 J'ai (e.g. une soeur et un frère)

Higher level

1 e.g. Ma soeur Louise est l'aînée.

2 Mon frère Paul est le cadet.

3 e.g., Ils sont en chômage. (*out of work*).

4 Oui, j'ai une nièce et un neveux/Non, je n'en ai pas.

Family pets

Basic level

1 Oui, j'ai un chat/un chien, etc.

2 Il s'appelle . . .

3 Il est gros et noir, etc.

4 Il aime manger de la viande/Il aime boire du lait, etc.

Higher level

1 Parce qu'ils sont mignons et de toute façon mon épagneul ce n'est pas seulement un chien, c'est un ami.

2 Parce qu'on n'a pas besoin de les promener!

3 Parce que j'y suis allergique. Je crains toujours le poil de chat. Cela me fait éternuer sans arrêt.

Daily routine

Basic level

1 Je me lève à . . . (e.g. sept heures et demie)

2 J'ai fait mes devoirs/J'ai regardé la télévision.

3 Je suis allé en ville avec mes amis.

4 Je suis allé à l'église/J'ai rendu visite à mes grands-parents.

5 Je jouerai au tennis avec mes amis.

6 Je les fais dans ma chambre.

7 J'en ai beaucoup.

8 Je me couche à . . . (e.g. dix heures)

9 Oui mes parents me donnent de l'argent de poche.

10 J'achète des disques et des livres/Je l'économise (*to save*).

Higher level

1 Je me lève vers sept heures. C'est ma mère qui me réveille car j'ai horreur du réveille-matin. Ma mère m'apporte une tasse de thé—elle est très gentille. D'habitude je prends une douche

mais si je suis pressé je me lave et me brosse vite les dents. Je prépare mon uniforme scolaire la veille car je ne me débrouille pas très bien le matin! Je prends un petit déjeuner rapide, toujours préparé par ma mère. Puis vers huit heures je quitte la maison en courant car je suis toujours en retard pour l'école.

2 Oui je fais du babysitting.
. . . je livre les journaux.
. . . je travaille comme caissière au supermarché.
. . . je travaille comme pompiste à une station-service.
. . . je lave les carreaux. (*window-cleaning*)
. . . je suis garçon de café en ville.
. . . je suis serveuse dans un café.
. . . je suis employé(e) de magasin.

Education

Basic level

1 Oui, j'habite à . . . kilomètre(s) de l'école.
Non, j'habite tout près de l'école.

2 J'étudie . . . (le français, l'anglais, les maths, etc.)

3 Je préfère . . . (le français).

4 J'y arrive à . . . (huit heures et demie).

5 Je quitte l'école à . . . (quatre heures).

6 Je vais en classe le lundi, mardi, mercredi, jeudi et vendredi.

7 J'ai l'intention de quitter l'école cette année/dans deux ans.

8 Je l'apprends depuis . . . (cinq ans).

9 Il y en a . . . (trente).

10 Nous en avons . . . (cinq).

Higher level

1 Je voudrais continuer mes études à l'université de . . . J'espère devenir . . .

2 Alors, j'arrive à l'école vers neuf heures. Je suis toujours en retard car je trouve difficile de me lever de bonne heure. Mon professeur me gronde chaque jour mais sans résultat! Il y a un rassemblement des élèves dans la grande salle à neuf heures dix puis les cours commencent à neuf heures et demie. Après deux cours il y a la récréation pendant un quart d'heure, puis encore trois cours. L'après-midi il n'y a que trois cours et pas de récréation. Si l'on a une heure de perme (*free lesson*) on peut aller travailler à la bibliothèque. Moi, je préférerais rentrer à la maison mais ce n'est pas permis.

3 C'est un Collège d'Enseignement Secondaire. Il y a deux mille élèves et cent vingt professeurs. Nous avons beaucoup de salles de classe et des laboratoires de sciences ainsi que des ateliers et trois gymnases. Il y a deux cantines où on peut manger à midi mais beaucoup d'élèves préfèrent manger en ville dans des snacks. Nous avons quelques aires de jeux, des terrains de sports et cinq courts de tennis. Pour ceux qui ne sont pas sportifs, il y des clubs culturels ou on peut faire du dessin, de la sculpture ou jouer d'un instrument musical ou chanter.Il y a aussi des groupes qui aident les handicapés pendant leurs heures libres.

Food and drink

Basic level

1 J'ai mangé du pain grillé (*toast*).
. . . un oeuf à la coque (*boiled egg*).
. . . du bacon et un oeuf sur le plat (*fried egg*).
Je n'ai rien mangé pour le petit déjeuner.

2 J'ai bu du café (thé) au petit déjeuner aujourd'hui.

3 Je prends le petit déjeuner à . . . (e.g. huit heures)
Je prends le déjeuner à . . . (e.g. midi)
Je prends le goûter à . . . (e.g. quatre heures et demie)
Je prends le dîner (le souper) à . . . (e.g. huit heures)

4 J'aime . . . (e.g. les oranges)

5 Je préfère . . . (e.g. les haricots verts)

6 Oui, je rentre à la maison pour déjeuner.
Non, je déjeune à la cantine de l'école.
Non, je mange en ville au café.

7 Pour le petit déjeuner, j'ai mangé des croissants. A midi nous avons mangé de la viande, des légumes, de la salade, du fromage, et des fruits. Pour le souper, j'ai mangé une omelette, des pâtes, et un yaourt. J'aime bien les yaourts français.

8 C'est une sorte de gâteau chaud qu'on sert avec une sauce chaude et sucrée.

Higher level

1 J'achèterais des tranches de jambon (*slices of ham*), des pizzas, du pain, des pêches et de l'eau minérale.

2 J'achèterais des pommes de terre qui ne coûtent pas beaucoup puis je les mangerais avec des haricots blancs à la sauce tomate.

3 Oui, l'année dernière je me suis rendu compte que j'avais quelques kilos de trop et que mes amis se moquaient de moi. On m'a prescrit un régime sans danger pour ma santé. J'ai dû manger à des heures regulières et on m'a défendu de manger entre les repas. J'ai maigri de 5kg.

4 J'adore les pâtes (*pasta*) et surtout les nouilles (*noodles*), mais ça fait grossir (*put on weight*) donc je ne peux les manger qu'une fois par semaine.

Free time

Basic level

1 J'aime regarder la télé, écouter des disques, sortir avec mes amis, etc.

2 J'aime jouer au tennis.
J'aime monter à cheval.
J'aime jouer au football.
J'aime regarder la télévision.

3 Je préfère les livres d'aventures, (les romans, les romans policiers, la poésie, etc.)

4 Je préfère la musique pop (classique)

5 Je préfère les comédies, (les westerns, les films policiers, les films d'horreur).

6 J'y vais une fois par semaine, (mois).

7 Oui, je joue du piano, (du violon, de la guitare, de la flûte, etc.)

8 Je regarde la télévision ou j'écoute mes disques.

9 Je préfère le football, (le tennis, le squash, etc.)

10 On peut pratiquer le rugby, le hockey, le cricket et le tennis.

Higher level

1 Je suis amateur de théâtre. Je suis membre d'un groupe qui monte des pièces de théâtre trois fois par an. J'ai presque toujours un rôle dans les pièces mais j'aide aussi à faire les costumes et à peindre les décors. Dans une semaine nous allons jouer *La Cantatrice Chauve* d'Ionesco.

2 Je vais souvent au cinéma avec mes amis. J'aime toutes sortes de films—les westerns, les films d'espionnage, les films d'horreur et même les dessins animés. Ma mère est ouvreuse (*usherette*) donc je peux entrer dans le cinéma gratis. Mes amis, malheureusement, doivent payer leur place!

3 Oui je suis fana/fanatique de tennis. Je suis membre du club de tennis en ville et j'y joue chaque jour après les classes. J'aime bien regarder les matchs internationaux à la télé mais je préfère jouer le tennis moi-même.

4 Je préfère les émissions pour la jeunesse et les feuilletons mais je trouve qu'il y a trop de feuilletons américains à la télé. Je ne m'intéresse pas trop aux émissions politiques mais les documentaires m'intéressent s'ils sont au sujet des jeunes.

Holidays

Basic level

1 Oui, j'aime voyager. J'aime visiter les endroits intéressants.
Non, je n'aime pas voyager. Je préfère rester à la maison.

2 Je préfère passer les vacances au bord de la mer parce que j'aime faire de la planche à voile. (*wind-surfing*)
Je préfère passer les vacances à la campagne car je déteste la mer.

3 Oui, j'aime faire du camping car j'aime la vie de plein air.
Non, je n'aime pas faire du camping parce que je suis paresseux/paresseuse.

4 Je suis allé en France.
Je suis resté à la maison

5 Oui, l'année dernière nous sommes allés en Italie.
Non, mais j'espère le faire cette année. On fait des projets pour aller en France.

6 J'irai en France/Je resterai à la maison.

7 Je voudrais visiter les Etats-Unis

8 J'ai visité l'Espagne, l'Autriche et la France.

9 J'en ai . . . (e.g. douze)

Higher level

1 D'abord j'aurai un petit emploi pour gagner de l'argent. Je travaillerai comme . . . (e.g. caissière/pompiste/garçon de café, etc.) pour quatre semaines. Puis je partirai en vacances avec mes amis. Nous allons faire un tour de la France à vélo. Nous resterons dans des auberges de jeunesse.

2 Parce que nous pourrons organiser librement nos voyages et les auberges vous acceuillent dans une ambiance faite d'amitié. On a aussi l'occasion de rencontrer des jeunes de tous les pays.

3 Oui, j'y suis allé l'année dernière. J'ai bien profité de mes vacances car je suis resté chez mon correspondant à Grenoble. J'ai dû parler français tout le temps parce que les parents de Pierre-Yves ne parlent pas bien l'anglais. Nous avons fait des randonnées partout sur des chemins fleuris; nous avons escaladé les rochers et nous nous sommes baignés dans les eaux fraîches des sources. La France me manque beaucoup et j'espère y retourner l'année prochaine.

Home

Basic level

1 J'habite une maison individuelle. (*detached*)

2 Elle est grande et blanche. Il y a neuf pièces. Nous avons un grand jardin devant et derrière la maison.

3 Elle est petite. Les murs sont bleus et les rideaux sont blancs. J'ai un lit, une armoire, une table de toilette et une table de chevet.

Higher level

1 Je tapisserais les murs. (*to cover, e.g. with wallpaper*)
Je repeindrais le plafond. (*repaint the ceiling*)
J'accrocherais des tableaux aux murs. (*hang pictures*)
J'installerais mon magnétophone et le téléviseur.
Je choisirais un tapis blanc et des rideaux roses.

Garden

1 Je travaille dans le jardin pour gagner de l'argent de poche.
Je tonds le gazon. (*cut the grass*)
J'arrache les mauvaises herbes. (*to do the weeding*)
Je cultive des légumes. (*grow vegetables*)
(See **vocabulary topic areas** for extra vocabulary.)

Shopping

Basic level

1 Il y a une épicerie, une pharmacie et une boulangerie près de chez moi.

2 Les magasins se ferment à cinq heures et demie généralement en Grande Bretagne. Ils se ferment à sept heures en France et même à huit heures dans quelques régions.

3 Je préfère faire mes achats chez les petits commerçants parce que le service est toujours personnel.
Je préfère faire mes achats dans un hypermarché car ils ont toujours un grand choix de provisions.

4 On peut y acheter toutes sortes de choses—vêtements, meubles, provisions, livres, vaisselle et jouets.

Higher level

1 Il y a une grande surface à deux kilomètres de chez moi. On peut y acheter de tout. On y trouve une boucherie, une droguerie, une parfumerie, une pâtisserie. On peut y acheter des jouets, des aliments animaux (*petfood*), des installations-maison, des vins, des surgelés (*frozen food*), n'importe quoi!

2 Faire des achats dans une grande surface coûtent moins cher et on peut faire tous les achats au même endroit.
Mais la grande surface est souvent très éloignée de la maison et on y trouve un manque d'acceuil.

Time and date

Basic level

1 Je me lève à dix heures le samedi.

2 Je me lève à midi le dimanche.

3 Je me couche à onze heures le samedi.

4 Je quitte la maison à . . . (e.g. huit heures)

5 Je dois rentrer à la maison à . . . (e.g. cinq heures)

6 A dix heures.

7 A six heures du soir.

8 Le mercredi.

9 Je me lève de bonne heure. Je cherche mes cadeaux puis je les ouvre.

10 Je rends visite à mes grands-parents.

11 Mon anniversaire, c'est le . . . (e.g. le dix mars)

12 J'inviterai des amis à une boum chez moi. Mes parents vont sortir ce soir-là donc nous pourrons faire beaucoup de bruit!

Higher level

1 D'habitude je reste chez moi mais il y a beaucoup de choses à faire en ville et aux environs. Il y a un grand complexe sportif tout près de la maison où on peut jouer au badminton, nager, faire de l'escrime, jouer au pingpong, etc. A deux kilomètres de la ville il y a un musée folklorique, un centre d'équitation et un vieux château.

2 Je suis allé en France avec ma famille. Nous avons fait du camping dans le Midi. Il a fait très, très chaud et nous avons dû nous abriter du soleil pour éviter des coups de soleil. Nous avons rencontré des Français qui habitent Paris et ils nous ont invités à passer quelques jours à Paris chez eux l'année prochaine. Nous attendons avec impatience notre retour en France.

3 Je ferai un stage au centre de plein air de Brecon (*outdoors pursuits course*)
On peut y faire de la voile*, de la spéléo*, et aussi de l'escalade*/la varappe.*

Town and region

Basic level

1 Mon village est très joli. Il n'y a pas beaucoup de maisons mais il y a quelques fermes aux environs. Dans le village il y a une église, une épicerie et deux auberges.

2 Ma ville est grande. Il y a trente-cinq mille habitants. Il y a un grand centre commercial, un complexe sportif et un jardin public. On y trouve aussi une zone industrielle.

3 Je préfère la ville parce que j'aime aller au cinéma avec mes amis et j'aime faire les achats au centre commercial.
Je préfère habiter à la campagne parce que j'ai un cheval et je fais des promenades à cheval tous les jours.

4 Il y a le train et les autocars, mais presque tout le monde a une voiture.

5 Il y a un château qui date du seizième siècle. Il y a aussi un musée folklorique et des ateliers artisanaux (*craft workshops*).

* faire de la voile *sailing* faire de la spéléo *pot-holing* faire de l'escalade *climbing* faire de la varappe *rock-climbing*

Higher level

1 J'habite une région touristique. Les villages sont pittoresques, surtout les ports de pêche. La côte est très découpée et a l'aspect sauvage mais il y a des plages de sable dans la région qui attirent beaucoup d'estivants (*summer visitors*). Nous, les habitants, préférons l'hiver car il y a trop de monde au bord de la mer en été.

2 Il faut absolument voir la cathédrale. L'édifice actuel a été bâti au douzième siècle. On a reconstruit le clocher au quinzième siècle mais la statue du Christ est tout à fait moderne. Dans les petites chapelles il y a les tombeaux gothiques des princes qui habitaient cette région il y a longtemps.

3 Il y a tant de régions qu'il faut visiter; tout dépend de tes/vos goûts personnels. Moi, j'aime toutes les régions de la Grand-Bretagne. J'aime les montagnes de l'Ecosse et l'isolement qu'on y trouve. Si la neige y tombe abondamment en hiver, on peut faire du ski.
J'aime la région des lacs car on peut faire des randonnées à pied. En été le sud de l'Angleterre a un climat qui ressemble beaucoup au climat de la Bretagne. On peut passer des vacances agréables sans jamais quitter notre pays.

4 J'aime bien la Provence car on y trouve de tout–montagnes, vallées, plaines, littoral. Cette variété de paysages, cette diversité de vues ne cessent jamais à m'étonner. Tout le monde a entendu parler de la Côte d'Azur mais ce que j'aime beaucoup ce sont les champs de lavande de la Vaucluse, en été, et les arbres fruitiers en fleurs–abricotiers, amandiers, oliviers–au printemps.

Travel/transport

Basic level

1 Je prends un car de ramassage. (*school bus*)
J'y vais à pied. (*on foot*)

2 A un kilomètre seulement.

3 Non, je préfère le train. Je ne peux pas supporter de longs voyages en voiture.

4 On peut prendre l'avion, le ferry ou le hovercraft et bientôt ou pourra peut-être traverser par le Tunnel.

5 On peut le faire mais ça peut être dangereux.

Higher level

1 On me l'a appris à l'école mais je n'ai jamais eu l'occasion de la faire. On dit qu'il faut chercher le nom de la station en tête de ligne, puis si on doit changer de ligne on cherche Correspondances puis la tête de ligne encore une fois.

2 Parce que de tous les moyens de transport, c'est le plus rapide.

3 Parce que c'est plus pratique et parce qu'il n'y a qu'un seul tarif.

Weather

Basic level

1 En été il fait chaud.
En hiver il fait très froid. Il neige souvent.
En automne il fait beau.
Au printemps il fait froid. Il pleut souvent.

2 Il a fait très, très chaud. De temps en temps il y a eu des averses mais le soleil a brillé tous les jours.

Higher level

1 Non, pas du tout! De temps en temps il fait du brouillard en hiver mais il peut faire beau aussi. Il est vrai que le ciel est souvent couvert en hiver et au printemps mais en été et en automne il peut faire vraiment beau.

2 A la météo on dit qu'il va geler et qu'il faut faire attention sur les routes à cause du verglas. (*black ice*)

3 Je préfère un climat tempéré tel qu'on trouve en France, surtout son climat méditerranéen. J'adore le soleil mais pas le soleil des pays tropicaux.

4 Il a fait très chaud. Il y a eu une vague de chaleur dont les effets ont fait peur. Dans la région où nous étions il y a eu une sécheresse épouvantable. On manquait de l'eau dans les robinets. Les températures ont atteint des records jamais égalés. Il y a eu beaucoup d'incendies dont un mortel–un pompier–a été brûlé vif dans les Landes.

13.3 The Oral Exam: Role-Play

BASIC LEVEL

Seeking accommodation—campsite/hotel/youth hostel

1 Au terrain de camping

(a) Est-ce que vous avez une place libre pour une nuit, monsieur?
(b) Je suis seul et j'ai une tente.
(c) Où sont les lavabos et les WC, s'il vous plaît?
(d) Où est-ce que je pourrai acheter du pain demain matin, monsieur?

2 A l'auberge de jeunesse

(a) Est-ce que vous avez des lits, monsieur?
(b) Nous sommes trois, monsieur.
(c) Nous voudrions louer des sacs de couchage.
(d) Est-ce que le petit déjeuner est compris?

3 A l'hôtel

(a) Est-ce que vous avez des chambres libres pour cette nuit, monsieur?
(b) Je voudrais une chambre pour une personne, avec salle de bains.
(c) C'est combien la nuit? Le petit déjeuner est compris?

Asking for information/asking the way

1 Au bureau de renseignements

(a) Est-ce que les magasins sont ouverts tous les jours de la semaine?
(b) Qu'est-ce qu'il y a à voir en ville et aux environs?
(c) Je m'intéresse beaucoup aux châteaux. Est-ce qu'il y en a un près d'ici?
(d) Et pour y aller, monsieur?

2 Dans la rue

(a) Pardon, monsieur (madame), pouvez-vous m'aider s'il vous plaît?
(b) Pour aller à l'Hôtel Moderne, s'il vous plaît?
(c) Est-ce qu'il faut prendre l'autobus?

Meeting people/invitations

1 **(a)** Je suis heureux (heureuse) de faire votre connaissance, monsieur (madame).
(b) J'ai deux valises.
(c) Je voudrais une limonade, s'il vous plaît.
(d) Je n'ai pas grand'faim.
(e) Merci, monsieur (madame), je suis très fatigué.

2 **(a)** Merci pour l'invitation. Oui, je veux bien y aller.
(b) A quelle heure la boum commence-t-elle?
(c) Où est-ce qu'on se rencontre avant la boum?

Illness/injury

1 **(a)** Je ne vais pas très bien, j'ai mal aux dents.
(b) J'ai dû prendre de l'aspirine pendant la nuit.
(c) Voulez-vous téléphoner au dentiste, s'il vous plaît, monsieur (madame)?

2 **(a)** Bonjour, monsieur.
(b) J'ai mal à la tête.
(c) Je ne peux rien manger.
(d) Quand faut-il les prendre?
(e) Merci pour l'ordonnance et au revoir, monsieur.

Garage

A la station-service

1 **(a)** Voulez-vous faire le plein d'essence, monsieur?
(b) Ça fait combien, monsieur?
(c) Est-ce que vous vendez des cartes routières?
(d) Je voudrais une carte du Nord de la France, s'il vous plaît.

2 (a) La voiture est sur la route de Paris.
 (b) Elle est à trois kilomètres d'ici.
 (c) Elle est verte et noire.
 (d) C'est une Ford.
 (e) Je le regrette, mais je ne sais pas.

Travel

A la gare

1 (a) Un billet simple de seconde classe pour Paris, s'il vous plaît.
 (b) Je n'ai qu'un billet de 100 francs.
 (c) A quelle heure part le train?
 (d) Où se trouve la salle d'attente, s'il vous plaît?

2 (a) Est-ce que l'autobus va à Notre Dame?
 (b) Alors deux billets s'il vous plaît.
 (c) Nous sommes des étudiants.
 (d) Je n'ai pas de monnaie.
 (e) Je le regrette.

Restaurant/café

1 A la terrasse d'un café

(a) Je préfère m'asseoir à la terrasse.
(b) Est-ce que tu veux prendre des croissants?
(c) Garçon! Un café noir et un café-crème, s'il vous plaît.
(d) Oui. Depuis combien de temps habites-tu ici?

2 Au restaurant

(a) Avez-vous une table pour quatre personnes?
(b) Qu'est-ce vous voulez prendre?
(c) Trois steak-frites, et est-ce que vous avez une salade aussi?
(d) L'addition s'il vous plaît. Est-ce que le service est compris?

Cinema/theatre

1 (a) Nous pourrions aller au cinéma.
 (b) Passe-moi le journal, s'il te plaît. Il y a un bon film au cinéma Rex.
 (c) Il commence à vingt et une heures trente. Nous devons nous dépêcher.
 (d) As-tu assez d'argent?

2 (a) Je voudrais bien y aller.
 (b) Je voudrais voir un film français.
 (c) On y va ce soir?
 (d) A quelle heure commence-t-il?
 (e) D'accord. A sept heures et demie.

Post office/telephoning

1 (a) Je voudrais téléphoner à un ami.
 (b) Son numéro est Lisieux soixante-deux, zéro trois, vingt-quatre.
 (c) Quelle cabine, s'il vous plaît?
 (d) Merci monsieur (madame), ça coûte combien pour trois minutes?

2 (a) Je voudrais envoyer des cartes postales en Angleterre, s'il vous plaît.
 (b) C'est combien, une carte postale pour l'Angleterre?
 (c) Alors, cinq timbres à . . . francs, s'il vous plaît.

Shopping

1 (a) Je voudrais un demi-kilo de raisins, s'il vous plaît.
 (b) Est-ce que les petites pêches sont bonnes à manger?
 (c) Est-ce que les oranges sont plus chères que les pêches?

2 Chez le boulanger-pâtissier

(a) Deux gros pains, s'il vous plaît.
(b) Elles coûtent combien les tartes aux fraises?
(c) Elles sont chères, mais j'en prendrai une.
(d) Oui. Je n'ai pas mangé le petit déjeuner.

Bank/lost property

1 (a) Je voudrais toucher un chèque de voyage, s'il vous plaît.
(b) Voilà mon passeport, monsieur (madame). C'est un chèque de vingt livres.
(c) Oui, je signerai ici. Où se trouve la caisse?

2 (a) Mon père a perdu son portefeuille.
(b) Il l'a perdu cet après-midi devant l'Hôtel de Ville.
(c) Il y avait cinq cents francs, des photos et son permis de conduire.

HIGHER LEVEL

Garage

1 (a) Bonjour monsieur/madame/mademoiselle. Vingt-cinq litres de super s'il vous plaît.
(b) Voulez-vous vérifier l'huile, s'il vous plaît?
(c) Voulez-vous vérifier le niveau d'eau aussi?
(d) La roue de secours a une crevaison. Pouvez-vous la réparer aujourd'hui?
(e) Je vous dois combien?

2 (a) Notre voiture est en panne. Pouvez-vous envoyer quelqu'un?
(b) Nous sommes sur la route de Niort, à cinq kilomètres de Belleville.
(c) Nous n'avons pas eu d'accident.
(d) Nous ne pouvons pas démarrer.
(e) Pouvez-vous envoyer un camion de dépannage?

Seeking accommodation

Hotel

(a) Bonjour, mademoiselle, je m'appelle monsieur . . . j'ai réservé une chambre.
(b) Je l'ai réservée par téléphone il y a deux jours.
(c) C'est une chambre pour deux personnes avec douche.
(d) Puis-je payer par carte de crédit?
(e) La chambre se trouve à quel étage, s'il vous plaît?
(f) Merci, mademoiselle.

Camping

(a) Bonjour, monsieur.
(b) Je regrette mais je dois vous porter plainte au sujet du camping.
(c) Notre emplacement est trop près des poubelles.
(d) Les douches sont sales et il n'y a pas d'eau chaude.
(e) Il y a tant de bruit la nuit que je ne peux pas dormir.
(f) Nous partirons demain, monsieur.

Youth hostel

(a) Bonjour, monsieur.
(b) Avez-vous des places libres pour cette nuit?
(c) Nous sommes quatre, deux garçons et deux filles.
(d) Peut-on louer des sacs de couchage et des couvertures?
(e) Où est-ce que nous pouvons laisser nos vélos?
(f) Le repas du soir est à quelle heure s'il vous plaît? Y a-t-il un téléphone ici?

Illness/injury

1 (a) J'étais au coin de la rue quand l'accident est arrivé.
(b) Un cycliste a tourné à gauche sans regarder où il allait.
(c) Il a renversé une dame qui traversait la rue.
(d) Je m'appelle . . . je reste à l'hôtel . . .
(e) L'accident est arrivé il y a une demi-heure.

2 (a) Je me suis foulé le poignet.
(b) Il me fait très mal.
(c) Je jouais au tennis quand il est arrivé.
(d) Il me faut aller à l'hôpital?
(e) Je rentre chez moi la semaine prochaine.

Asking for information/directions

1 (a) Pardon, monsieur/madame.
(b) Nous n'avons presque plus d'essence. Y a-t-il une station-service près d'ici?
(c) Elle est ouverte toute la journée?
(d) Nous sommes à combien de kilomètres de Paris?
(e) Merci, monsieur/madame.

2 **(a)** Pardon, monsieur/madame.
(b) Je cherche la Rue St Honoré. C'est loin?
(c) Faut-il prendre le métro ou peut-on y aller à pied?
(d) Les taxis coûtent cher? Où puis-je en trouver un, s'il vous plaît?
(e) Merci, monsieur/madame.

Lost property

1 **(a)** Bonjour, mademoiselle/monsieur.
(b) J'ai perdu mon appareil (photographique).
(c) Je l'ai perdu hier soir sur la place du marché.
(d) C'est un Kodak.
(e) Je m'appelle . . . Je suis à l'hôtel . . .

Meeting people/invitations

1 **(a)** J'espère parler beaucoup de français pendant mon séjour.
(b) J'espère perfectionner ma connaissance de la langue française.
(c) Je suis très fatigué(e) après mon long voyage.
(d) J'ai rencontré dans le train des Français qui s'appellent Vermorel.
(e) Je voudrais me coucher. A quelle heure faut-il me lever demain?

2 **(a)** Je voudrais bien y aller.
(b) Je n'ai jamais vu un film français.
(c) On y va ce soir?
(d) La séance commence à quelle heure?
(e) C'est loin, le cinéma?

Restaurant/café

1 **(a)** Je préfère m'asseoir à la terrasse, à l'ombre.
(b) Merci, monsieur, ça va très bien.
(c) Je voudrais quelque chose à boire de bien frais.
(d) Je prendrai un citron pressé.
(e) J'ai trop chaud pour manger pour le moment.

2 **(a)** Garçon, s'il vous plaît!
(b) L'addition, s'il vous plaît.
(c) Je crois qu'il y a une erreur.
(d) Je n'ai pris qu'un café crème et un gâteau.
(e) Voulez-vous vérifier l'addition, s'il vous plaît?

Shopping

1 **(a)** Bonjour, mademoiselle/monsieur. Où est le rayon des disques s'il vous plaît?
(b) Je cherche des disques de musique pop.
(c) Quels disques figurent au { palmarès cette semaine? / hit parade }
(d) Quel est le chanteur/le groupe français le plus populaire?
(e) Puis-je écouter le disque?

2 **(a)** Bonjour, mademoiselle/monsieur. Où est le rayon des T-shirts, s'il vous plaît?
(b) Avez-vous des T-shirts en jaune?
(c) De la taille . . .
(d) Avez-vous des T-shirts moins chers?
(e) Merci, mademoiselle/monsieur. Où faut-il payer?

Telephoning

(a) Bonjour, mademoiselle/monsieur.
(b) Puis-je téléphoner à la Grande Bretagne d'ici?
(c) Je voudrais téléphoner en PVC.
(d) Je m'appelle . . . Le numéro de téléphone est . . .

Post office

(a) Bonjour, mademoiselle/monsieur.
(b) Je voudrais envoyer des lettres en Angleterre.
(c) C'est combien pour une lettre?
(d) C'est combien pour une carte postale?
(e) Alors, trois timbres pour les lettres et cinq timbres pour les cartes postales, s'il vous plaît.

At the tourist office

1 (a) Bonjour, mademoiselle/monsieur.
(b) Avez-vous une liste des hôtels dans cette ville?
(c) Pouvez-vous recommander un bon hôtel?
(d) Nous cherchons un hotel calme pas loin du centre-ville.
(e) Il se trouve à quelle distance d'ici?

2 (a) Bonjour, mademoiselle/monsieur.
(b) Avez-vous des renseignements sur la région?
(c) Y a-t-il des visites guidées?
(d) Le château est ouvert à quelle heure?
(e) On peut y aller a pied?

Travel

1 (a) J'ai deux valises.
(b) Je n'ai rien à déclarer sauf une bouteille de whisky.
(c) C'est un cadeau pour le père de mon correspondant.
(d) Ça coûte six livres sterling.
(e) Je vais rester trois semaines en France.

2 (a) Bonjour, mademoiselle. Où est la place soixante-huit, s'il vous plaît?
(b) L'avion va décoller à quelle heure?
(c) A quelle heure est-ce qu'on arrive à Londres?
(d) Où faut-il mettre mon sac?
(e) Merci, mademoiselle.

At the travel agent's

(a) Bonjour, mademoiselle/monsieur.
(b) Je voudrais visiter la vallée de la Loire.
(c) Je voudrais y aller en car.
(d) Avez-vous une liste des hôtels modestes et confortables?
(e) Je voudrais y rester cinq jours à peu près.

13.4 The Oral Exam: Oral Composition

ORAL COMPOSITION

Set questions on single pictures

1 The port

(a) Cette scène se passe dans un port.
(b) Il fait beau.
(c) Il est midi dix
(d) Il vend des bijoux, des ceintures et des sacs à main.
(e) J'en vois quatre.
(f) Il lit un journal.
(g) J'en vois cinq.
(h) Il décharge des bouteilles d'un camion.
(i) L'agence se trouve à côté de la pharmacie.
(j) Ils jouent au football.

2 Preparing for the holidays

(a) La voiture est devant la maison.
(b) Le chat est sur une valise sur la galerie de la voiture.
(c) Il y a un sac et une valise dans le coffre.
(d) Cette scène se passe en été.
(e) Il y a un garage à droite de la maison.
(f) Il y en a deux.
(g) Il tient une canne à pêche à la main droite.
(h) Elle prend une petite valise.
(i) Il est dans la voiture.
(j) La famille va au bord de la mer.

3 At the swimming pool

(a) Cette scène se passe à la piscine.
(b) Il fait beau.

(c) Elle est en train de prendre une photo.
(d) Elle se couche au soleil.
(e) Elles jouent avec un ballon.
(f) On nage dans une piscine.
(g) On porte un maillot (caleçon) de bain pour nager.
(h) Elle s'est couchée sur une serviette.
(i) Il va plonger dans l'eau.
(j) Oui, je sais nager./Non, je ne sais pas nager.

4 Snowscene

(a) Cette scène se passe en hiver.
(b) Il neige./Il fait froid.
(c) Les enfants font un bonhomme de neige.
(d) Ils jettent des boules de neige.
(e) Ils font de la luge.
(f) Elle porte une veste, une jupe, une écharpe, un bonnet et des bottes.
(g) Il est tombé dans l'eau à travers la glace.
(h) La forêt se trouve à gauche au loin.
(i) Il y a le mot 'danger'.
(j) Je jette des boules de neige à mes amis.

Other visual material

1 Il faut aller jusqu'au rond-point puis tourner à droite. Continuez tout droit jusqu'au rond-point prochain. Tournez à gauche. Continuez au rond-point. Tournez à droite et vous verrez l'église à votre gauche.

2 Il faut aller jusqu'au rond-point puis tourner à droite. Continuez tout droit jusqu'au rond-point prochain. Tournez à gauche. Continuez au rond-point prochain. Tournez à gauche encore une fois puis vous verrez l'église à votre droite.

3 Allez jusqu'au rond-point. Tournez à gauche. Continuez jusqu'au rond-point prochain. Tournez à droite. Continuez un peu et alors vous verrez l'église à votre gauche.

4 Allez tout droit jusqu'au rond-point. Tournez à droite. Continuez un peu puis vous verrez l'église à gauche.

(You will have noticed that the beginnings of the above instructions were the same in English but that there are different ways of giving these orders in French. Do remember that often there will be more than one way of giving a correct answer. Try to vary your oral work by using different expressions which you know to be CORRECT.)

5 Il y en a dix.
On peut prendre le bac.
Il y a des forêts sur l'Ile D'Oléron.
Non elle est plus petite que l'Ile D'Oléron.

6 On peut y voir le Grand Ballet argentin.
Le 20 et 21 juillet.
A Châteaudun et à Orléans.
Il y a un Parc Floral où on peut assister à un critérium des roses à massif et aussi à un critérium des dahlias.

7 Ils commencent à huit heures.
On en a trois.
C'est l'heure du déjeuner.
Le vendredi.

8 J'en connais quelques-uns.
Je suis allé . . . (e.g. à la Côte Atlantique)
Les Pyrénées se trouvent entre l'Espagne et la France.
C'est une sorte de caravane trainée par des chevaux ou par une automobile.
Elle se trouve à l'ouest de la France.

9 Oui, bien sûr.
On peut faire de la voile.
On peut assister au bal de l'Election de la Reine.
On peut assister au Festival d'Art Contemporain.
Le douze juin.

10 C'est une ville romaine.
On peut y acheter du nougat.
Il y a un château.
C'est un symbole dessiné.
A droite.

Photographs

1 C'est le jour du marché.
Il fait très beau.
On fait des commissions.
Cette scène se passe en été.
On voit des magasins.

2 Cette scène se passe en ville.
Il fait beau.
Elle demande la direction.
Il indique la direction.
On peut traverser sur le passage clouté.

3 On peut y faire des achats.
Non.
Il s'ouvre à neuf heures moins le quart.
Il se ferme le samedi soir à sept heures.
Il s'appelle le Coop.

4 Il s'appelle Les Dunes.
Trente-huit francs.
Douze francs.
Un franc dix.
Oui.

13.5 Listening Comprehension

BASIC LEVEL

A l'aéroport

1 **(a)** The English Channel.
(b) Two thousand feet.
(c) At Heathrow.
(d) Cloudy.

2 **(a)** Two hundred and forty.
(b) Passengers are about to embark
(c) Gate number eleven.

3 **(a)** London.
(b) Go to gate number ten.
(c) Five past nine.

Au terrain de camping

1 An information announcement for the campers to say that the butcher calls at the campsite every Wednesday at half past nine.

2 You are asked if you want one in French, English or German.

3 Whether you have a tent or caravan.

4 At the far end of the field.

5 Over there, near to the swimming-pool.

A la douane

You are being asked for your passport/if you have anything to declare.

Au bureau des objets trouvés

Where you lost it/what make it is.

A la banque

Go to the counter where there is the sign 'change'.

Directions

1 Take the first street on the right.

2 Go straight on.

3 On the third floor.

4 Five minutes on foot.
Go down the street then turn left.

Les visites

1 **(a)** Wednesdays.
(b) Two o'clock in the afternoon.
(c) One and a half hours.
(d) At the entrance to the museum.

2 **(a)** Every day.
(b) Between two o'clock in the afternoon and eight o'clock.

3 The Arc de Triomphe was built to celebrate Napoleon's victories.

4 Sixty-nine metres.

A l'hôtel/en vacances

1 Your room is on the third floor. It is room number 42.

2 There is no restaurant in the hotel, but there is a good restaurant opposite the hotel.

3 It will be cold and cloudy all day.

4 Goodbye. Have a nice walk.

5 He doesn't know how to get there as he is a stranger himself.

6 Where did you lose it/what was inside?

7 Your travel agent.

8 There will be a delay at the airport tomorrow. The plane will leave at midday instead of ten o'clock.

Medical situations

1 **(a)** If it's urgent/what is wrong with you.
(b) In a quarter of an hour.

2 **(a)** No.
(b) A prescription.
(c) A chemist's at the corner of the street.

3 Three tablets a day.

4 Give you a filling.

Social situations

1 **(a)** In front of the cinema.
(b) At eight o'clock.

2 **(a)** Your age.
(b) Young people under eighteen years of age are not allowed in.

3 **(a)** Ice creams and sweets.
(b) In the entrance-hall.

4 **(a)** Tuesday morning at ten o'clock.
(b) At Heathrow airport.

5 **(a)** From Jean-Pierre.
(b) To tell Bruno to meet his friends at the café at nine o'clock.

A la gare

1 **(a)** The fast train from Lille.
(b) Arriving.
(c) Platform 5.

2 **(a)** Dijon.
(b) At eleven o'clock
(c) Two.
(d) In the first five coaches.

3 A quarter of an hour.

4 Twenty past ten.

5 Platform 4.

6 **(a)** Half past four in the afternoon.
(b) Platform 8.

Tourist information

1 A swimming-pool/sports centre/cycle-racing track.

2 The swimming-pool is in the local park/the sports centre is opposite this building/the cycle-racing track is 2 kilometres away on the Dijon road.

3 Five kilometres.

4 Before ten o'clock in the morning and after six o'clock in the evening.

Weather

1 Cold and cloudy.

2 Sunny.

3 Cold and cloudy.

4 There will be storms.

5 The fine weather will continue and it will get warmer.

HIGHER LEVEL

1 **(a)** Fifth form.
(b) Modern languages.
(c) Biology.
(d) Eight o'clock.
(e) Two hours.
(f) At home.
(g) Two o'clock.
(h) Half past five.
(i) She has too much homework.
(j) She goes out with her friends.

2 **(a)** At Royan at his grandparents' house.
(b) A month.
(c) It was rebuilt after being destroyed during the Second World War.
(d) At the sailing school.
(e) He went wind-surfing.

3. **(a)** Go for a boat trip.
(b) Because their feet hurt after walking about so much.
(c) On the sideboard.
(d) An hour and a quarter.
(e) Because they will be back in time for tea.

4 **(a)** Two brothers and one sister.
(b) She has two nieces.
(c) Thirteen.
(d) She is slim and of medium build.
(e) Contact lenses.
(f) He is a civil servant.
(g) Retire.
(h) She is a housewife.
(i) For the EEC.
(j) English.

5 **(a)** Channel 2.
(b) The swimming-pool.
(c) Her parents always choose the programmes they want to see.
(d) Listens to her records.
(e) A portable television.
(f) That she is very lucky

6 **(a)** In the eighties.
(b) Building a multi-storey car-park and sports centre in the middle of the town.
(c) Because he uses both the car-park and the sports centre.
(d) Twice a week.
(e) The increase in crimes and vandalism.
(f) The increase in noise and litter.
(g) The cinema.
(h) He used to go there every week when he was little.
(i) Science-fiction.
(j) Star Wars on channel three at ten o'clock.

7 **(a)** He is on his way to the dentist's.
(b) To Antoine's.
(c) He has just bought a motorbike.
(d) Because he is always short of money.
(e) His parents have bought it for his birthday.
(f) Because he has to earn money before being able to buy a motorbike.
(g) He doesn't need one since his bike is under 50ccs.
(h) At the dentist's.
(i) To have a filling or to have the tooth out.
(j) He doesn't mind so long as the tooth stops hurting.

8 **(a)** The TGV.
(b) The express train..

9 **(a)** Outside, near the door.
(b) Medium.

10 Fireworks.

11 The price is unbeatable/the gadget will do everything for you/no more long hours in the kitchen/ life will be easier and happier.

12 **(a)** 20 kilometres
(b) To the thirteenth century.
(c) In the fifteenth century.
(d) The octagonal tower.
(e) Modern sculpture.
(f) It has recently been restored.
(g) In the great drawing-room.
(h) An exhibition of Aubusson tapestries.

13 **(a)** Fifteen.
(b) Railway accident.
(c) About twenty.
(d) Between Gap and Briançon near the Serre-Ponçon dam.
(e) Tiredness on the driver's part or an animal on the line.

14 **(a)** A contagious illness is spreading.
(b) Hundreds.
(c) An increase in the number of people ill.
(d) Direct contact with drops of saliva.
(e) Half of the population over the age of five is likely to be affected.
(f) The incubation period.
(g) No.
(h) People begin to get better.
(i) Any treatment.
(j) Except for mild pain-killers and cough-syrup.

13.6 Listening Comprehension Specimen Questions

BASIC LEVEL

Section A

1 200 metres away.

2 A large room on the second floor.

3 (i) The first street on the right. (ii) Go straight on. (iii) Post Office.

4 (i) 3. (ii) 8F 50.

5 (i) A doll. (ii) 20F.

6 The shop will close in 5 minutes.

7 (i) At the cinema. (ii) With friends. (iii) Call back about 11 o'clock.

8 (i) There is none left. (ii) Provençal chicken.

9 From half past seven onwards.

10 (i) 3 kilometres away. (ii) You can walk there but there is also a bus which comes past the hotel.

11 (i) 3. (ii) The balcony. (iii) It isn't too expensive and you can hear well.

12 (i) It's closed. (ii) A drink in the bar. (iii) It's open till 11p.m.

13 (i) 3 breakfasts. (ii) A telephone call to Northern Ireland. (iii) 130 francs.

14 (i) The luggage is too heavy. (ii) Pay a supplement.

15 There is one hour delay.

Section B

Section 1

(a) Irish.
(b) One is a student. The other is a civil servant.
(c) It isn't very big but it is light and pleasant.

Section 2

(a) In the university district.
(b) It is a quiet area.

Section 3

(a) To go out of Belfast and visit other areas.
(b) He plays sport–tennis, squash, snooker or goes swimming.

HIGHER LEVEL

Section A

1 **(a)** She is missing her home.
(b) She is missing her boyfriend.

2 **(a)** It will be rainy everywhere.
(b) It will be rainy in the west, but in the Parisian basin and in the east there will be some bright intervals.

3 **(a)** Stay in bed for at least two days.
(b) Only have hot drinks.

4 **(a)** The British Prime Minister's visit to France.
(b) They want greater safety at work.
(c) There is a dock strike so the Irish pupils can't go home.
(d) They are staying with French families in the Cherbourg area.

5 **(a)** He didn't stop at the red traffic lights.
(b) Bumper/headlight.
(c) Not to fall asleep at the wheel/to stay alert.
(d) Her coat has been torn.
(e) She has blood on her.
(f) To get the police.

Section B

Part A

1 A cold country where the people only wanted to fight against the police and army.

2 That this was true. The station and surrounding area were not very attractive.

Part B

3 Friendliness.

4 They were just as hospitable.

Part C

5 The standard of public transport. Sundays.

6 Stay in and watch TV or go for a walk in the parks.

FOUNDATION AND GENERAL LEVELS

1 To passport control.

2 Your passport.

3 How long are you going to stay in France.

4 Open your suitcase.

5 Taxi or bus.

6 Two days minimum.

7 A special ticket.

8 Go around Paris at reduced prices on the bus or underground.

9 A double room with shower.

10 210 on the second floor.

11 The hotel restaurant is closed but there is a self-service restaurant in nearby St Lazare Street.

12 Go to the corner of the street and turn left.

13 11 francs.

14 If you are English.

15 He doesn't like rugby. He says that it is too rough.

16 It will be cold, cloudy with perhaps some snow on Saturday evening.

17 Have a good day. Enjoy yourself.

18 From Toulouse.

19 To go and have a meal in a restaurant or to have a drink with them.

20 He visited Scotland last year. They went to Edinburgh castle and listened to some folk music.

21 They suggest going on a river sight-seeing trip, but it's rather expensive.

22 They suggest going to the bird market.

GENERAL AND CREDIT LEVELS

(Questions **1-5** require the same answers as questions **18-22** of the Foundation and General levels.)

6 The time of your departure has been changed. Your flight will be at midday instead of 10 o'clock. The bus will pick you up from your hotel at 9.45 a.m. to take you to the airport.

7 There is a demonstration going on.

8 The authorities are going to cut down the trees in the church square and build an underground car park.

9 One of them would travel to exotic places in the sun. The other would buy a house in the country for his parents and a sports car for himself. They are both capitalist ideas.

10 He says that it was built to celebrate Napoleon's victories. It is in the very centre of Paris at a place which was formerly called the Place de l'Etoile because avenues radiate from there like a star. There is an eternal flame which burns in memory of an unknown soldier. Every year on the 14 July, the President of the Republic honours there those soldiers who have died for their country.

11 The argument is about the glorification of war. One friend thinks that it is dreadful to celebrate war. The other says that they are honouring the dead who should not be forgotten. The first friend replies that there are never any victories in war, only deaths.

13.7 Reading Comprehension

TEST YOURSELF: PHOTOS

1 **(c)**
2 **(d)**
3 **(a)**
4 **(b)**

BASIC LEVEL

Public notices

1 REGLEMENTATION DE LA PLAGE Beach control
Surveillance assurée ... Constant supervision between 10h and 18h from the 15 June to the 15th September.
Meaning of the signs
▶ NO BATHING
▷ SAFE BATHING

Poste de Secours ... First Aid post ... at 100 metres

2 PISCINE Swimming-pool
EAU POTABLE Drinking water
ACCUEIL Reception
DOUCHES Showers
POUBELLES Dustbins

3 SALLE D'ATTENTE Waiting-room
CONSIGNE AUTOMATIQUE Left-luggage lockers
TÉLÉPHONE PUBLIC Public Telephone
BUFFET (Station) buffet
CHARIOTS Trolleys
GARDEZ VOTRE TICKET SUR VOUS Keep your ticket

4 DANGER Danger
RALENTIR Slow down
RISQUE D'INONDATION SUR 100m Danger of flooding for 100 metres

5 MÉTRO Underground
P et T Post Office
FERMÉ closed
SNCF French railways
SYNDICAT D'INITIATIVE Tourist Information Office
OUVERT open
ALIMENTATION food (shop)
DOUANE Customs
BUREAU DE CHANGE foreign exchange office
TARIF RÉDUIT reduced rate

Advertisements

6 13 July Dance at 21h in the square.
14 July National Holiday
10.30h parade and ceremony in front of the war memorial.
14 July Tricolour celebration, dinner/dance at the Casino.
14 July Fireworks in the square.

7 **(b)**

8 **(a)** Every day.
(b) In the entrance hall.
(c) During the interval.
(d) On the first floor.
(e) Books, records, cassettes, photos of the shows, posters, scarves, cigarette lighters, key-rings, T-shirts, bags, diaries.

9 **(a)** Sewing classes.
(b) The first week in October.
(c) On the 17 September.
(d) At the Foyer-Club.
(e) People will be able to enrol.

10 **(a)** Different types of holidays in different regions of France.
(b) Hotels, flats, holiday villages, holiday camps, caravans, boats, tours.
(c) Côte D'Azur ... south
Languedoc-Roussillon ... south
Côte Atlantique ... west
Bretagne ... north west
Normandie ... north
Auvergne ... central
Cévennes ... below centre
Alpes ... east/south-east
Pyrénées ... south west
la Corse ... Corsica (Mediterranean island)

Camping

11 **(a)** From the first of June to the fifteenth of September.
(b) Supplies.
(c) There is a games room, a play area for children, bowls and volley-ball for the adults.
(d) Swimming, fishing, boating, sailing.
(e) There is a fourteenth-century castle.

12 **(a)** It is 2 kilometres north of La Baule.
(b) Heated sanitary block.
(c) There is a grocer's shop. Cooked meals can also be bought.
(d) Washing-machines are provided and ironing-boards.
(e) There is a colour TV and reading-room.
(f) It is quiet, comfortable and in attractive surroundings.
(g) The Brittany coastline, churches, artistically interesting town.
(h) Book in advance for July and August.

Exhibitions

13 **(a)** In the Place de Verdun, Clermont-Ferrand.
(b) From half past twelve to seven o'clock in the evening.
(c) On Tuesdays and bank holidays.
(d) It is free.

14 **(a)** Local traditions.
(b) On Tuesdays.

Guides

15 Swimming-pool; beaches; lake; sailing; wind-surfing; boating; pedalos; tennis; skating; horse-riding; climbing lessons; bowls; miniature golf; clay-pigeon shooting; cycling; leisure park; casino; cinema; library; museums; craft shops.

16 **(a)** From the first of May to the first of October.
(b) Groups of 25–30 people can be received.
(c) Marvellous views.
(d) There are walks and excursions.

17 **(a)** From the twelfth of July to the fifth of September.
(b) From in front of the Tourist Information Office.
(c) Guides can be provided.
(d) Book a guide, if required.
(e) Boat trips.
(f) One hour.
(g) 22 francs.
(h) Special rates for school parties.

Letters

18 **(a)** A handbag.
(b) On a seat at the Austerlitz station.
(c) It is a red leather bag.
(d) A purse and identity card.
(e) To check to see if it has been found.

19 **(a)** A watch.
(b) It is a Swiss watch.
(c) On the beach at Arcachon.
(d) On the fifth of July.
(e) If it has been found.

Guides

20 **(a)** The beautiful island.
(b) In a bay.
(c) Scrubland.
(d) He was born there.
(e) There are pleasure boats and fishing boats.
(f) The modern part of Ajaccio is on a hillside overlooking the port. There are white blocks of flats.

Letters

21 **(a)** She goes to the Hervé Bazin school in the centre of Nancy.
(b) She is in the fourth form.
(c) Her English teacher gave her the name and address.
(d) To Eastbourne.
(e) The meals, because the vegetables were always served with the meat and with the same gravy.
(f) Maths, natural science, French, English, German, history and geography.
(g) A photo of herself.

Menus

22 **(a)** Raw chopped vegetables or Russian salad.
(b) Roast chicken or grilled ham.
(c) Chips or salad.
(d) Ice cream or cherry tart.
(e) Yes.

Newspapers

23 **(a)** On Friday.
(b) At the Émile Zola technical school in Aix-en-Provence.
(c) A javelin pierced his throat.
(d) He was training for the baccalaureat exam.
(e) Another pupil was responsible for the accident.

Weather report

24 **(a)** Sunset.
(b) Cloudy and rainy.
(c) Fairly strong southerly wind.
(d) Bright intervals and showers.
(e) Bright intervals.
(f) Stormy showers.
(g) Moderate south-westerly.

Newspapers

25 **(a)** Yesterday.
(b) At the top of Arson street/near the roundabout in the town centre/in Giardelli square.
(c) She was knocked over by a car.
(d) She was also knocked over by a car.
(e) A vehicle ran into him.

Time-tables

26 **(a)** The fifth form.
(b) Spanish.
(c) English.
(d) He has a free period.
(e) 6.

HIGHER LEVEL

Advertisement

1 **(a)** From the first of January to the thirty-first of December.
(b) Completed application form/some form of identification, e.g. identity card or if applying by post, a photocopy of both sides of your identity card/a personal photo.
(c) Parental permission in writing.
(d) 4 francs.

2 **(a)** Brown.
(b) A few seconds.
(c) A Roman town.
(d) The places which are accessible from the motorway.
(e) A castle.
(f) The region you are travelling through, the countryside, the places of interest.
(g) The main centres of interest for tourists.
(h) It is a Gallo-Roman town.
(i) In the south of France.
(j) Tourist information.

3 **(a)** Ten times a year.
(b) On the first day of the month.
(c) The Palais Garnier and the Salle Favert.
(d) A writer or a well-known cultural figure.
(e) What they remember best about the Paris Opera.

Brochures

Les services

4 **(a)** Rest areas.
(b) Service areas.
(c) Petrol pumps/shops/cafeterias/restaurants.
(d) Public telephones.

La securité

(a) They are four to five times safer than ordinary roads.
(b) On the hard shoulder.
(c) Park as far to the right as possible. Switch on your hazard warning lights and use the hazard warning triangle.

En cas de crevaison

(a) Try to move your car out of the line of traffic.
(b) Half an hour.

Attention à la fatigue

(a) You will travel for 72 metres out of control.
(b) Break the monotony of driving by changing speed/alter the temperature inside the car/have frequent stops.

Vérifiez vos pneus

(a) It can burst if you travel too fast for too long.
(b) Inflate the tyre 200 gms over the given tyre pressure.

5 **(a)** It is situated at the meeting-point of valleys and at the foot of majestic mountains.
(b) A stopping-off point.
(c) The Winter Olympic Games.
(d) The opening of the first tourist information office.
(e) The local shopkeepers and important townspeople.
(f) To promote the region and to help local business and tourism.

Labels

6 **(a)** The 'eat by' date.
(b) To heat the contents in their own juice but not to boil/to add a knob of butter/to add parsley before serving.
(c) 90% beans plus salt and water.

Brochures

7 **(a)** Pony-trekking.
(b) Very little.
(c) No. In twos or in a group.
(d) You will be provided with a comfortable saddle, a suitable horse, a well-marked route.
(e) A good bed and a good meal.
(f) From the riding centre at Bonne Famille.

Letters

8 **(a)** Two.
(b) Double room with shower and w.c./single room with bath.
(c) No.
(d) Breakfast at 15 francs. TV at 12 francs.
(e) Full board.
(f) Cars can be parked in front of the hotel.
(g) It is in a quiet street near the marina.
(h) There is a private beach a hundred metres from the hotel.
(i) There is an aquarium and a museum.
(j) He asks for a 200F deposit.

Newspapers

9 **(a)** One.
(b) Yesterday afternoon.
(c) In a Branch bank in Bonaparte Street.
(d) A weapon.
(e) A few coins.

10 **(a)** It is a French-speaking European channel with a selection of programmes from French, Swiss and Belgian TV.
(b) 2.5 million homes.
(c) 3½ hours, twice a day.
(d) It does not make a profit because of the lack of advertising revenue.
(e) Three French TV channels.

Magazine article

11 **(a)** Good restaurants are to be found in towns and villages all along the Rhône valley.
(b) To the west of the Rhône.
(c) Meat: pâtés, terrines, ham.
Fish: crayfish, trout.
(d) Specialities of Lyon and Provence.
(e) It is a potato dish with grated cheese.
(f) Saint-Marcellin is famous for cheese and Grignan for braised beef.
(g) Le Vivarais is famous for fruit.
(h) Cherries, peaches, plums, apples, pears, apricots.
(i) It is also famous for game-fowl.
(j) Chickens and turkeys.

12 **(a)** Flowers, trees, insects.
(b) Irritability, red-faces, sneezing and coughing.
(c) With the arrival of the swallows.
(d) 'Flu or a cold.
(e) Hay-fever.
(f) Pollen grains carried by the wind.
(g) It can last from April to October.

13 **(a)** Being able to fly.
(b) The wings of birds,
(c) Meudon.
(d) It became too small to house all the exhibits.
(e) At Roissy-Charles-de-Gaulle airport.
(f) They were repaired and repainted.
(g) Films/slides; posters; models.
(h) Models of light aircraft.
(i) A piece of rock from the moon.
(j) A replica of the Ariane rocket.

14 **(a)** 130 km/h.
(b) You will cover 85 metres before coming to a halt.
(c) Only in an emergency.
(d) A slip-road.
(e) Keep over to the right well in advance of the exit and use your indicator lights.
(f) Open and closed tolls.
At an open toll you throw the money into a special basket as you pass.
At a closed toll you stop and pay the amount stated on your toll-card.
(g) Move the car on to the hard shoulder, use your hazard warning lights and warning triangles.
(h) Every two kilometres.
(i) It is free.
(j) The motorway police.

15 **(a)** Three.
(b) Two.
(c) On all three.
(d) Channels 1 and 2.
(e) On Channel 1.
(f) On all three channels.
(g) On Channel 2.
(h) On France-Culture.
(i) The hedgehog.
(j) Light/classical/jazz/dance music.

Newspapers

16 **(a)** Fine with isolated mist patches and some low cloud near the coast in the morning, then sunny becoming cloudy again in the afternoon on high ground. Little wind but some coastal breezes.
(b) Fine and warm with some storms over the higher areas in the afternoon. Some wind in the valleys, breezes in the mountains.
(c) Fine and sunny with some cloud in the afternoon, little wind.
(d) Fine but with some cloud. Moderate east wind, quite strong in the morning.
(e) Fine and sunny, some coastal breezes.
(f) Fine and sunny, little wind, not much cloud, some mist especially in the morning.

13.8 Higher Level: Letters

Specimen answers are not provided for informal letters since these will vary widely according to the personal circumstances of each individual writer. Learn the phrases/sentences from the example section carefully and then use them, where appropriate, in your own personal way.

Hotels

1 (your name
and address)

(your town/date)
Monsieur le Gérant
Hôtel France-Accueil
85 rue du Dessous-des-Berges
75013 Paris
France

Monsieur,
Je serais reconnaissant si vous pouviez m'envoyer votre guide des Hôtels France-Accueil. Je m'intéresse surtout aux hôtels dans la région de la Vallée de la Loire. Avec mes remerciements anticipés, je vous prie d'agréer, Monsieur, l'expression de mes sentiments distingués.

2 (your name
and address)

(your town/date)
Monsieur le Gérant
Hôtel Matignon
Arcachon
France

Monsieur,
Mes parents et moi comptons passer une semaine à Arcachon entre le 20–27 juillet. Nous cherchons deux chambres–une chambre à un lit avec douche et une chambre à deux lits avec salle de bain. Nous voudrions savoir s'il y a une piscine à votre hôtel et s'il y a un garage aussi. Veuillez agréer, Monsieur, l'expression de mes sentiments distingués.

3 (your name
and address)

(your town/date)
Monsieur le Gérant
Hôtel Saint-Romain
5 et 7 rue Saint-Roch
75001 Paris (Tuileries)
France

Monsieur,
Je compte passer les vacances de Pâques à Paris entre le 9–14 avril. Je cherche une chambre à un lit avec salle de bain. Y a-t-il un restaurant à l'hôtel? Voulez-vous m'envoyer aussi une liste des événements à venir à Paris au mois d'avril?
Veuillez agréer, Monsieur, l'expression de mes sentiments distingués.

1 Tourist office

(your name
and address)

(your town/date)
Monsieur le Directeur
Syndicat d'Initiative
Auxerre
France

Monsieur,
Je compte visiter Auxerre cet été. Voulez-vous m'envoyer des dépliants de la ville et aussi des rensignements sur les hôtels. Nous cherchons un hôtel confortable mais pas cher. Je serais bien reconnaissant si vous pouviez me fournir des renseigements sur la région et une liste des activités locales. Peut-on louer des vélos en ville?
Avec mes remerciements anticipés, je vous prie d'agréer, Monsieur, l'expression de mes sentiments distingués.

2 Lost property

(your name
and address)

(your town/date)
Monsieur le Gérant
Hôtel La Coquille
Guincamp
France

Monsieur,
En rentrant de la France, j'ai trouvé que j'avais laissé ma montre à votre hôtel. J'espère que vous l'avez trouvée dans la chambre 23. J'ai quitté votre hôtel le 5 septembre. C'est une montre suisse en argent. Si vous l'avez trouvée, je serais bien reconnaissant si vous pouviez me l'envoyer à l'adresse ci-dessus.

Avec mes remerciements anticipés, je vous prie d'agréer, Monsieur, l'expression de mes sentiments distingués.

Applying for jobs

(your name
and address)

(your town/date)
Tronchet Frères
8 Boulevard Plessy
Avallon

Messieurs,
En réponse à votre annonce dans *Le Figaro* du 10 juin, j'ai l'honneur de poser ma candidature au poste de secrétaire/sténodactylo. J'ai dix-huit ans et je travaille actuellement à temps partiel pour la direction des ventes d'une grande usine à Calais. J'y travaille depuis six mois mais je cherche un poste à plein temps. J'aime bien le travail de bureau et j'ai un brevet de sténodactylo. Pour références je vous prie de vous adresser à Monsieur P. Schumann, Agence Bruno, rue Henri Quatre, Calais. Je serais bien reconnaissant(e) si vous pouviez me fournir encore des renseignements et les avantages sociaux de ce poste.

Veuillez agréer, Monsieur, l'expression de mes sentiments distingués.

Folk dancers from Brittany

Answers to the first part of this letter will depend on the personal situation and style of the individual writer but given below are suggestions for the outline programme.

jeudi 16 avril	18.00h	arrivée à l'école
		accueil/familles/hôtes
		soirée en famille
vendredi 17 avril	10.00h	répétition générale à l'école
	12.30h	déjeuner à l'école
	14.00h	visite/ville
	17.30h	accueil/Hôtel de Ville
	19.00h	Fête folklorique/Hôtel de Ville
samedi 18 avril	10.00h	visite/usine de bonbons
		déjeuner en famille
l'après-midi		répétition générale
	17.30h	goûter/complexe sportif
	19.00h	Fête folklorique/complexe sportif
dimanche 19 avril		matin/déjeuner en famille
l'après-midi		excursion/endroit pittoresque
	19.30h	Disco/complexe sportif
lundi 20 avril	10.00h	départ de l'école

POSTCARDS

1 Bien arrivé à Nice.
Fait très chaud.
Bon hôtel. Excellente cuisine.

2 A Paris. Ai visité Notre-Dame/Tour Eiffel.
Fait beau. Rentre samedi.

3 Bien arrivé à la maison. Bon voyage.
Fait froid. Merci beaucoup de ma visite.

4 Fais camping en Espagne. Terrain excellent.
Beaucoup de monde à la plage.
Suis bronzé.

5 En vacances à Rome. Ville chère.
Bon hôtel avec grande piscine.
Vais Milan demain.

NEW YEAR'S CARD

1 Au seuil de ce nouvel an, je te souhaite une très bonne année.
Merci beaucoup de ton gentil cadeau.

BIRTHDAY CARD

2 Bon anniversaire.
Meilleurs voeux.

NOTES/LISTS

1

lundi	dentiste
mardi	achats
mercredi	piscine
jeudi	complexe sportif
vendredi	disco
samedi	boum chez Pierre
dimanche	plage

2 Mme . . . ne peut pas venir demain. A mal aux dents. Viendra dimanche.

3 Laurent a téléphoné. Voudrait aller au cinéma demain. Téléphonera demain matin.

4 salade/laitue
viande
oeufs
fromage
yaourts
jus d'orange
jambon
chips

14 FAUX AMIS

Check the following words carefully. They resemble English words but in fact have different meanings.

assister à	to be present at
les cabinets	lavatories
le car	coach
causer	to chat
la cave	cellar
la crêpe	pancake
le délit	crime, offence
se dresser	to rise up
la figure	face
la journée	day
la lecture	reading
la librairie	bookshop
la location	hiring, renting
le médecin	doctor
la ménagère	housewife
le Métro	underground railway (*not* a car)
la monnaie	(loose) change
passer	to spend (*time*)
le pensionnaire	boarder
le pétrole	crude oil
le photographe	photographer
la place	square
le plat	dish
le record	record (e.g. sports, *not* music)
rester	to stay
le robinet	tap
sensible	sensitive
travailler	to work
la veste	jacket
le water (-closet)	W.C., toilet

Note the following in reverse:

to assist	aider
cabinets (*furniture*)	les meubles (mpl) à tiroir
car	l'auto (f), la voiture
to cause (to be done)	faire (faire)
cave	la caverne
crepe	le crêpe
delight	les délices (fpl), le plaisir
to dress	s'habiller
figure	la taille (*body*), le chiffre (*number*)
journey	le voyage
lecture	une conférence
library	la bibliothèque
location	l'emplacement (m), la situation
medicine	le médicament
manager	le directeur, le gérant
Metro car	*la* Metro (NB all cars are feminine)
money	l'argent (m)
to pass	réussir à (*succeed*), croiser (*e.g. person in the street*)
pensioner	le (la) retraité(e)
petrol	l'essence (f)
photograph	la photographie
place	l'endroit (m)
plate	l'assiette (f)
record (*musical*)	le disque
to rest	se reposer
robin	le rouge-gorge
sensible	raisonnable, sensé
to travel	voyager
vest	le maillot
water	l'eau (f)

15 USEFUL IDIOMS

aussitôt dit, aussitôt fait no sooner said than done
casser la croûte to have a snack
C'est du gâteau It's a piece of cake.
courir à toutes jambes to run quickly (*person*)
courir à plat ventre to run quickly (*animal*)
crier à tue-tête to shout at the top of one's voice
donner un coup de main to give a helping hand
dormir comme une souche to sleep like a log
l'avoir échappé belle to have a lucky escape
faire l'école buissonière to play truant
faire la grasse matinée to sleep late
Au feu! Fire!
mouillé jusqu'aux os soaked to the skin
sain et sauf safe and sound
Au secours! Help!
un temps de chien foul weather
tourner le bouton to switch on
Tout est bien qui finit bien. All's well that ends well.
travailler d'arrache-pied to work very hard

16 COMMON PITFALLS

Listed below are some of the words most frequently misspelt or misunderstood by candidates.

agent	policeman
a**r**gent	money
le bois	wood
la boisson	drink
chev**a**ux	horses
chev**e**ux	hair
combien **de** or **d'**	how much, how many

Combien **de** pommes veux-tu?
How many apples do you want?

but Combien **des** pommes sont rouges?
How many of the apples are red?

habi**t**er	to live in
s'habi**ll**er	to get dressed
monter	to go up
mont**r**er	to show
payer	to pay (*for*)
plusie**u**rs	several
r**a**conter	to tell (*a story*)
r**en**cont**r**er	to meet
la veille	the day before/eve
la v**i**eille	the old woman

17 GLOSSARY

Adjective This is a word which describes a noun or pronoun. It gives information about colour, size, type, etc.
e.g. la **jolie** fille.

Adverb This is a word which describes a verb.
e.g. Il travaille **bien**.

Clause Part of a sentence which has a subject and finite verb.
e.g. If he comes, . . .

Conjugation A scheme showing which parts of a verb go together.
e.g. J'ai fini, tu as fini, il a fini, elle a fini, nous avons fini, vous avez fini, ils ont fini, elles ont fini.

Infinitive That part of the verb which means 'To . . .'
e.g. **aller** to go
avoir to have

Irregular verbs Those verbs which do not follow the set patterns.

Present participle This is part of a verb which is expressed by '-ing' in English when it means 'by', 'while', or 'on' doing something.
e.g. go*ing*, eat*ing*, look*ing*, etc.

Past participle This is part of the verb which is used with 'avoir' or 'être' to form the perfect tense.
e.g. J'ai **donné**,
Je suis **allé**, etc.

Prepositions These are words which are placed in front of nouns or pronouns.
e.g. at (home), on (the table), with (me), for (them), etc.

Pronouns Words used instead of nouns but referring to them.
e.g. 'Il', 'elle', 'nous', 'vous', etc.

(a) **Interrogative pronouns** These are pronouns which ask questions.
e.g. **qui**?
que?

(b) **Relative pronouns** These are pronouns which link parts of a sentence together.
e.g. L'enfant **qui** travaille.
L'enfant **que** vous voyez.
also **lequel**, etc.

Reflexive verbs These are verbs which refer to actions done to oneself.
e.g. **se laver** to wash oneself.

Superlative/comparative Expressions which mean 'most' (superlative) and 'more' (comparative).
e.g. Il est **plus intelligent** que son frère.
He is *more intelligent* than his brother.
Il est **le plus intelligent**.
He is *the most intelligent*.

Tenses
(a) **Present tense** Those parts of the verb which tell us about the present.
e.g. Je vais en ville.
I am going to town.

(b) **Future tense** Those parts of the verb which tell us about the future.
e.g. J'irai en ville, tu iras en ville etc.
I shall go to town, you will go to town.

(c) **Conditional tense** Those parts of the verb which imply a condition.
e.g. J'irais en ville. . .
I would go to town. . .

(d) Imperfect tense A tense which tells you what *was happening* in the past. It describes continuous or repeated actions in the past.
e.g. Il pleuvait.
It was raining.
Nous jouions au tennis tous les jours.
We used to play tennis every day.

(e) Perfect tense A tense which tells you what *has happened* in the past. It recounts completed events.
e.g. Samedi dernier nous sommes allés au cinéma.
Last Saturday we went to the cinema.

Glossary of GCSE Terms

Common-core–that part of the course/exam which all candidates must take.

Coursework–part of the course assessed by the teacher; for French this will usually mean oral testing.

Differentiation–setting tests for candidates of different ability in order to show what they know, understand and can do at their particular level.

Function(s)–what we do with language, e.g. give/seek information, socialize, etc.

National Criteria–the national requirements for the subject.

Notion(s)–concepts expressed in speech and writing, e.g. quantity, location, size, etc.

Role-play–an oral exercise/test in which the candidate and examiner assume the roles of, e.g., customer/shopkeeper, tourist/guide, etc.

18 VOCABULARY

French/English Vocabulary

A
à bientôt see you soon
à bord de on board
à côté de next to
à demain see you tomorrow
à droite on the right
à gauche on the left
à l'heure on time
à la mode in fashion
à peine scarcely
à peu près approximately
à pied on foot
à temps partiel part-time
à travers across
une **abeille** bee
abîmer to spoil
aboyer to bark
un **abri** shelter
abriter to shelter
absolument absolutely
accabler to overwhelm
accepter to accept
accompagner to accompany
d'**accord** all right/agreed
s'**accoutumer à** to become accustomed to
acceuil welcome/reception
acceuillir to welcome
achats: faire des achats to go shopping
acheter to buy
achever to finish
l'**acier** (m) steel
un **acteur**/une **actrice** actor/actress
les **actualités** (fpl) news (e.g. TV); current affairs
actuellement now, at this present time
l'**addition** (f) bill
s'**adresser à** apply to . . .
un **aéroglisseur** hovercraft
un **aéroport** airport
les **affaires** (fpl) business
une **affiche** notice
affreux awful
une **agence de voyages** travel agency
s'**agenouiller** to kneel
un **agent** policeman
s'**agir de** to be a question of . . .
un **agneau** lamb
agréable nice
aider to help
aigre bitter
une **aiguille** needle
l'**ail** (m) garlic
une **aile** wing
ailleurs elsewhere
aimable nice
aimer to like/love
aimer mieux to prefer
aîné elder
ainsi so, thus
alimentation (f) groceries
une **allée** path, drive
l'**Allemagne** Germany
allemand German
aller to go
aller chercher to fetch
aller bien to be/feel well
allumer to light
les **allumettes** (fpl) matches
alors then
l'**alpinisme** mountaineering
amarrer to moor
améliorer to improve
une **âme** soul
amener to bring
amer bitter
un(e) **ami**(e) friend
l'**amitié** (f) friendship
une **ampoule** light-bulb/blister
s'**amuser** to enjoy oneself
un **an**/une **année** year
ancien old/former
anglais English
l'**Angleterre** (f) England
animé busy (e.g., of a street)
un **anneau** ring
un **anniversaire** birthday
un **annuaire** telephone directory
annuler to cancel
apercevoir to notice
apparaître to appear
un **appareil** (**-photo**) camera
un **appartement** flat
appartenir à to belong to
appeler to call
s'**appeler** to be called
apporter to bring
apprendre to learn
s'**apprêter** to get ready
s'**approcher** to approach
(s')**appuyer** to lean
après after
l'**après-midi** afternoon
une **araignée** spider
un **arbitre** referee
un **arbre** tree
un **arc-en-ciel** rainbow
l'**argent** (m) money
une **armoire** cupboard
arracher to snatch, to tear out
un **arrêt d'autobus** bus-stop
(s')**arrêter** to stop
arrière behind, back (in football, etc.)
l'**arrivée** (f) arrival
l'**arrondissement** (m) district (of Paris)

un **ascenseur** lift
un **aspirateur** vacuum-cleaner
un **assassinat** murder
s'**asseoir** to sit down
assez enough
une **assiette** plate
assis sitting
assister to help
assister à to be present at
un **atelier** workshop
attaquer to attack
atteindre to reach
attendre to wait for
s'**attendre à** to expect
atterrir to land
attraper to catch
au bord de by the side of
au bout de at the end of
au début de at the beginning of
au fond de at the bottom/end of
au lieu de instead of
au mois de in the month of
au moyen de by means of
au revoir good-bye
au secours! help!
au sujet de about
au-dessous de beneath
au-dessus de above
l'**aube** (f) dawn
une **auberge** inn
une **auberge de jeunesse** youth hostel
aucun any
ne . . . **aucun** not . . . any
augmenter to increase
aujourd'hui today
auparavant before/previously
aussi also
aussitôt immediately
autant as much
un **autobus** bus
un **autocar** coach
l'**automne** (f) autumn
l'**automobiliste** motorist
une **autoroute** motorway
(faire de) l'**auto-stop** hitch-hiking
autour de around
autre other
autrefois previously
autrement otherwise
avaler to swallow
s'**avancer** to advance
avant before/forward (in football, etc.)
avare miser
avec with
l'**avenir** (m) future
une **averse** shower
avertir to warn
aveugle blind
un **avion** plane
un **avis** notice
changer d'**avis** to change one's mind
un **avocat** barrister
avoir envie de to want/feel like
avoir raison to be right
avoir sommeil to feel sleepy
avoir tort to be wrong
avouer to admit
ayant having

B

le **baccalauréat** school-leaving certificate
les **bagages** (mpl) luggage
la **bague** ring
la **baguette** long French loaf
se **baigner** to bathe
la **baignoire** bath
le **bain** bath (e.g. to take a bath)
bâiller to yawn
baisser to lower
se **balader** (fam.) to go for a walk
un **baladeur** walkman (head-phones/cassette)
balayer to sweep
balbutier to stammer
la **balle** ball/bullet
le **ballon** ball (e.g. football)
la **bande magnetique** tape (in a tape-recorder)
la **banlieue** suburbs
la **banque** bank
la **banquette** bench
le **baptême** baptism
la **baraque** hut
la **barbe** beard
la **barque** (small) boat
la **barrière** gate
bas low
la **basse-cour** farmyard
le **bassin** pond
la **bataille** battle
le **bateau** boat
le **bâtiment** building
la **batterie** battery/drums
battre to beat
se **battre** to fight
bavarder to chat, gossip
beaucoup a lot of
le **bébé** baby
bêcher to dig
belge Belgian
le **berceau** cradle
la **berge** (steep) bank of a river
le **berger** shepherd
la **besogne** job, task, work
besoin need
(faire) des **bêtises** to act the fool
le **béton** concrete
le **beurre** butter
la **bibliothèque** library
bientôt soon
la **bienvenue** welcome
la **bière** beer
la **bijouterie** jeweller's, jewellery
les **bijoux** (mpl) jewels
le **billet** note/ticket
le **bistrot** pub
bizarre strange
blanc white
le **blé** corn
(se) **blesser** to hurt/injure
la **blessure** wound
bleu blue
un **bleu** a bruise
le **bloc sanitaire** washrooms and toilets
le **blouson** jacket
boire to drink
le **bois** wood
la **boisson** drink

la **boîte** box/tin
boiter to limp
le **bol** bowl
bon marché cheap
le **bonbon** sweet
(faire) un **bond** to leap
bondir to leap
le **bonheur** happiness
le **bonhomme** chap, fellow
le **bonhomme de neige** snowman
bonjour hello
la **bonne** maid (*servant*)
bonne année happy new year
la **bonté** kindness
bonsoir good evening
le **bord** edge
la **botte** boot
la **bouche** mouth
boucher to block
le **boucher** butcher
la **boucherie** butcher's shop
le **bouchon** cork
la **boue** mud
bouger to move
la **bougie** candle
bouillir to boil
la **bouilloire** kettle
le **boulanger** baker
bouleverser to knock over, upset
bousculer to jostle
la **boum** party
le **bout** end
la **bouteille** bottle
la **boutique** shop
le **bouton** button
le **brancard** stretcher
le **bras** arm
(nager à) la **brasse** to swim breast-stroke
brave good, honest
bricoler to do odd jobs
briller to shine
la **brioche** cake
le **briquet** cigarette lighter
briser to break
se **bronzer** to sunbathe
brosser to brush
la **brouette** wheel-barrow
le **brouillard** fog
le **bruit** noise
la **bruine** drizzle
brûler to burn
la **brume** mist
brun brown
bruyamment noisily
le **buisson** bush
le **bureau** desk/office
le **but** aim/goal

C

la **cabine téléphonique** telephone kiosk
(se) **cacher** to hide
le **cachet** tablet
le **cadavre** corpse
le **cadeau** present
cadet(te) younger
le **cahier** exercise book
le **caillou** pebble
la **caisse** cash-desk/till
le **caleçon de bain** swimming-trunks
le/la **camarade** friend
le **cambrioleur** burglar
le **camion** lorry
la **campagne** countryside
le **canard** duck
le **carnet** notebook
carré squared
le **carrefour** crossroads
la **carte** map
le **carton** cupboard
casser to break
la **casserole** saucepan
le **cassis** blackcurrant
le **cauchemar** nightmare
causer to chat
la **ceinture** belt
célèbre famous
célibataire single, unmarried
cependant however
certainement certainly
cesser to stop
chacun(e) each
chahuter to make a din
la **chaise** chair
la **chaleur** heat
la **chambre** bedroom
le **champignon** mushroom
la **chance** luck
le **chandail** sweater
la **chanson** song
chanter to sing
le **chapeau** hat
chaque each
la **charcuterie** delicatessen
charger to load
le **chariot** trolley
chasser to hunt
le **château** castle
chaud hot
le **chauffage** heating
les **chausettes** socks
les **chaussures** shoes
chauve bald
chavirer to capsize
le **chemin** way, path
la **chemise** shirt (*man*)
le **chemisier** shirt (*woman*)
cher(chère) dear
chercher to look for
le **cheval** horse (pl. les **chevaux**)
le **chevet** bedside table
les **cheveux** hair
chez at the house of
le **chien** dog
le **chiffon** rag
le **chiffre** figure
la **chimie** chemistry
choisir to choose
le **choix** choice
le **chômage** unemployment
le **chômeur** unemployed person
la **chose** thing
le **chou** cabbage
le **chou-fleur** cauliflower
chouette! great!
la **chute d'eau** waterfall
chuchoter to whisper

ci-dessous (here) below
ci-dessus above (mentioned)
le **cidre** cider
le **ciel** sky
le **cierge** candle (in a church)
la **circulation** traffic
le **cirque** circus
le **citron** lemon
clair light
la **clarté** brightness
la **clé/clef** key
le **client** customer
le **clochard** tramp
la **cloche** bell
le **clou** nail
le **cochon** pig
le **coeur** heart
le **coiffeur** hairdresser
le **coin** corner
(être en) **colère** to be angry
le **colis** parcel
le **collant** pair of tights
le **collège** school
collectionner to collect
coller to stick
le **collier** necklace
la **colline** hill
combien how much
commander to order
comme as
le **commencement** beginning
commencer to begin
comment how
le **commerçant** shopkeeper
commettre to commit
le **commissariat de police** police station
(faire) des **commissions** to do the shopping
commode convenient
le **compartiment** compartment
complet full
composer un numéro to dial a number
composter to (date) stamp
comprendre to understand
compter to count
le **comptoir** counter
le **concierge** caretaker
le **conducteur** driver
conduire to drive
une **conférence** lecture
la **confiture** jam
le **congé** holiday, leave
connaître to know
un **conseil** a piece of advice
conseiller to advise
conserver to preserve
la **consigne** left luggage office
construire to build
continuellement continually
continuer to continue
contre against
le **contrôleur** ticket-collector
le **copain**/la **copine** chum/pal
la **corbeille** basket
le **corps** body
la **correspondance** connection
le **correspondant**/la **correspondante** penfriend
corriger to correct
la **côte** coast
le **côté** side
le **coteau** hillside
le **cou** neck
le **couchant** setting sun
la **couchette** berth, bunk
le **coude** elbow
coudre to sew
couler to flow
la **couleur** colour
un **coup d'oeil** glance
un **coup de pied** kick
un **coup de téléphone** a telephone call
coupable guilty
couper to cut
la **cour** yard
courageux/courageuse courageous
couramment fluently
le courrier post, mail
courir to run
le **cours** lesson, course
la **course** race
(faire) des **courses** to go shopping
court short
le **couteau** knife
le **couvert** place setting
le **couvercle** lid
la **couverture** blanket
couvrir to cover
cracher to spit
craindre to fear
la **cravate** tie
le **crayon** pencil
le **crépuscule** twilight
creuser to dig, hollow out
la **crevaison** puncture
crevé punctured
crever to burst
croire to think, believe
croiser to pass (e.g. someone in a street), to cross
la **croix** cross
la **cuiller** spoon
cueillir to pick, gather (e.g. fruit)
le **cuir** leather
(faire) **cuire** to cook
la **cuisine** kitchen
la **cuisinière** cooker
cultiver to grow
curieux curious
le **curé** priest

D

d'abord first of all
d'accord all right
d'ailleurs moreover
d'habitude usually
d'occasion second-hand
le/la **dactylo** typist
davantage moreover
débarrasser (la table) to clear (the table)
se **débarraser de** to get rid of
se **débattre** to struggle
de bonne heure early
de bonne humeur in a good mood
debout standing
se **débrouiller** to manage
le **début** the beginning

décharger to unload
déchirer to tear
décider to decide
décoller to take off (of an aircraft)
la **découverte** discovery
découvrir to discover, uncover
décrire to describe
décrocher to lift (e.g. telephone receiver), to unhook
déçu disappointed
dedans inside
défendre to forbid
défense de it is forbidden to . . .
les **dégâts** (mpl) damage
dehors outside
déjà already
le **déjeuner** lunch
déjeuner to have lunch
le **délit** crime, offence
demain tomorrow
démarrer to set off
déménager to move house
demeurer to live, remain
démodé out of date
la **denrée** commodity
la **dent** tooth
se **dépêcher** to hurry
dépenser to spend
un **dépliant** leaflet
déplier to unfold
déposer to put down
depuis since
déranger to disturb
dériver to drift
dernier/dernière last
à la **dérobée** stealthily
descendre to go down
se **déshabiller** to get undressed
désolé(e) sorry
dès que as soon as
dessiner to draw
les **dessins animés** cartoons
se **détendre** to relax
détruire to destroy
devant in front of
devenir to become
deviner to guess
les **devoirs** (mpl) homework
devoir to have to
Dieu God
digne worthy
le **directeur** headmaster
la **directrice** headmistress
se **diriger vers** to make one's way towards
discuter to discuss
disparaître to disappear
disponible available
se **disputer** to quarrel
le **disque** record
distinguer to distinguish, to make out
se **distraire** to amuse oneself
distrait absent-minded
une **dizaine** about ten
le **doigt** finger
le/la **domestique** servant
C'est **dommage**! It's a pity!
donc so
donner to give
donner sur to overlook
dormir to sleep
le **dortoir** dormitory
le **dos** back
la **Douane** the Customs
le **douanier** the customs officer
doubler to overtake
doucement gently
la **douche** shower
la **douleur** pain
se **douter de** to suspect
une **douzaine** a dozen
le **drap** sheet
le **drapeau** flag
se **dresser** to rise up
la **drogue** drugs
le **droit** law, right
à **droite** on the right
tout **droit** straight on
drôle funny
dur hard
durer to last

E

échanger to exchange
s'**échapper** to escape
une **échelle** ladder
les **échecs** chess
un **éclair** lightning
éclairer to lighten
une **éclaircie** bright interval
éclater de rire to burst out laughing
une **école** school
les **économies** (fpl) savings
l'Ecosse Scotland
s'**écouler** to pass (of time)
écouter to listen
écraser to crush, squash
écrire to write
effrayer to frighten
effroyable frightful
égal(e) equal
une **église** church
s'**égarer** to lose one's way
s'**élancer** to dash, rush forward
un **électrophone** record-player
un/e **élève** pupil
s'**éloigner** to move away
embêter to annoy
un **embouteillage** traffic jam
embrasser to kiss
une **émission** broadcast
emmener to take (a person)
(faire) des **emplettes** to go shopping
s'**emparer de** to get hold of
empêcher to prevent
emporter to carry, take away
s'**emporter** to lose one's temper
s'**empresser de** to hurry to . . .
emprunter to borrow
ému thrilled
enchanté delighted
encombré crowded, packed
s'**endormir** to fall asleep
un **endroit** place
énerver to get on someone's nerves
s'**enfuir** to flee
enlever to take off, away

ennuyer to annoy, bore
s'**ennuyer** to be bored
ennuyeux annoying, boring
enregistrer to record
être enrhumé to have a cold
l'**enseignement** (m) education, teaching
enseigner to teach
ensemble together
ensuite then, afterwards
entendre to hear
entendu/bien entendu of course
entourer to surround
entre between
l'entrée (f) entrance
entreprendre to undertake
entr'ouvert half-open
l'**entretien** (m) upkeep
envelopper to wrap
(avoir) **envie de** to feel inclined to
environ about
les **environs** (mpl) the surrounding area
envoyer to send
épatant amazing, splendid
une **épaule** shoulder
une **époque** period, time
épouser to marry
épouvantable dreadful
les **époux** married couple
éprouver to feel, experience
épuiser to exhaust
une **équipe** team
errer to wander
une **erreur** mistake
un **escalier** stairs
un **escargot** snail
l'**Espagne** Spain
espagnol Spanish
espérer to hope
une **espèce** kind, species
un **espion** spy
l'**espoir** (m) hope
essayer to try
l'**essence** (f) petrol
essoufflé out of breath
essuyer to wipe
l'**est** (m) east
l'**estomac** (m) stomach
un **étage** floor, storey
éteindre to extinguish, put out
s'**étendre** to lie, stretch out
une **étoile** star
s'**étonner** to be astonished
étouffer to stifle, suffocate
un **étranger** stranger
étroit narrow
s'**évanouir** to faint
s'**éveiller** to wake up
un **événement** event
éviter to avoid
exactement exactly
un **examen** exam
s'**excuser** to apologize
un **exemple** example
une **expérience** experiment
une **explication** explanation
expliquer to explain
une **exposition** exhibition
exprès on purpose

F

fabriquer to make
en **face de** opposite
se **fâcher** to get angry
la **façon** way, manner
facile easy
le **facteur** postman
faible weak
faillir to fail
la **faim** hunger
avoir **faim** to be hungry
la **falaise** cliff
falloir to be necessary
il **faut** it is necessary
il **faudra** it will be necessary
fatiguer to tire
la **faute** fault
le **fauteuil** armchair
faux/fausse false
féliciter to congratulate
félicitations congratulations
la **fente** slot
fermer to close
le **fermier** farmer
la **fermière** farmer's wife
la **fermeture éclair** zip
férié/un jour férié public holiday
fêter to celebrate
le **feu** fire
la **feuille** leaf
les **feux** traffic lights
les **feux d'artifice** fireworks
la **ficelle** string
la **fiche** form (official paper)
fier proud
la **fièvre** fever
(avoir) de la **fièvre** to have a temperature
la **figure** face
la **fin** end
finir to end
flâner to stroll, hang about
la **fleur** flower
le **fleuve** river
les **flots** (mpl) waves
le **foin** hay
la **fois** occasion, time
foncé dark (colour)
le **fonctionnaire** civil servant
le **fond** bottom, end
fondre en larmes to burst into tears
formidable terrific
fort strong
fou/folle mad
la **foule** crowd
se **fouler la cheville** to twist one's ankle
le **four** oven
la **fourchette** fork
le **fracas** din
frais/fraîche fresh
les **frais** (mpl) expenses, cost
la **fraise** strawberry
français(e) French
franchir to cross
frapper to strike
freiner to brake
les **freins** (mpl) brakes
le **frère** brother
frissoner to shudder

les **frites** (fpl) chips
(avoir) **froid** to be cold
le **fromage** cheese
froncer les sourcils to frown
frotter to rub
fumer to smoke
le **fusil** gun

G

gâcher to spoil, waste
gagner to win, earn
le(la) **gamin(e)** child, kid
le **gant** glove
garder to keep
la **gare** railway station
la **gare routière** bus station
gaspiller to waste
le **gâteau** cake
gâter to spoil, damage
gauche left
le **gazon** lawn, turf
geler to freeze
gémir to moan, groan
gêner to annoy, hinder
le(s) **genou(x)** knee(s)
les **gens** people
le **gérant** manager
le **gîte** lodging
glisser to slip, slide
gonfler to inflate
la **gorge** throat
le **gosse** kid
le **goût** taste
le **goûter** (afternoon) tea
goûter to taste
la **goutte** drop
la **grange** barn
gras fat
gratuit free
grave serious
le **grenier** loft
la **grève** strike
grimper to climb
la **grippe** 'flu
gris grey
gronder to scold
gros big, large
la **guêpe** wasp
ne . . . **guère** scarcely
guérir to cure
la **guerre** war
le **guichet** booking office

H

s'**habiller** to get dressed
les **habits** clothes
d'**habitude** usually
la **haie** hedge
les **haricots** (mpl) beans
la **hausse** rise, increase
hausser les épaules to shrug one's shoulders
haut high
hésiter to hesitate
l'**herbe** (f) grass
l'**heure** (f) time, hour
heureusement happily
heureux happy
heurter to bump (into), knock
hier yesterday
l'**hiver** (m) winter
hocher la tête to shake one's head
(avoir) **honte de** to be ashamed of
un **horaire** time-table
l'**hôtel de ville** town hall
une **hôtesse de l'air** air hostess
hors de outside of
l'**huile** (f) oil

I

ici here
une **idée** idea
un **immeuble** block of flats
un **imperméable** raincoat
imprimer to print
un **incendie** fire
un **inconnu** stranger
incroyable unbelievable
indiquer to point out
un **individu** individual
un **infirmier**/une **infirmière** nurse
un **ingénieur** engineer
innonder to flood
(s') **inquiéter** to worry
(s') **installer** to install (oneself)
un **instituteur**/une **institutrice** junior school teacher
interdit forbidden
un **intérêt** interest
un(e) **interne** boarder
interroger to question
interrompre to interrupt
introduire to introduce
un **intrus** intruder
ivre drunk

J

jadis formerly
jamais ever
ne . . . **jamais** never
la **jambe** leg
le **jambon** ham
le **jardin** garden
jaune yellow
la **jetée** pier
jeter to throw
le **jeton** counter, token
le **jeu** game
jeune young
la **jeunesse** youth
joindre to join
joli(e) pretty
jouer to play
le **jouet** toy
le **jour** day
le **journal** newspaper
la **journée** day
le **juge** judge
juger to judge
les **jumeaux**/les **jumelles** twins
les **jumelles** (also) binoculars
la **jupe** skirt
le **jus** juice
jusqu'à until

K

le **képi** peaked cap

la **kermesse** village fair
le **kiosque** kiosk
klaxonner to sound one's horn

L

là there
là-bas over there
le **lac** lake
lâcher to let go
laid(e) ugly
la **laine** wool
laisser to leave
le **lait** milk
la **laitue** lettuce
la **lame** blade/wave
lancer to throw
la **langue** tongue/language
le **lapin** rabbit
la **larme** tear
las tired
le **lavabo** wash-basin
(se) **laver** to wash
lécher to lick
la **leçon** lesson
le **lecteur** reader
léger light
les **légumes** (mpl) vegetables
le **lendemain** the next day
lent slow
lequel/laquelle/lesquels/lesquelles which/who
la **lessive** washing-powder/the washing
la **lettre** letter
la **levée** letter collection
lever to lift
se **lever** to get up
la **lèvre** lip
la **librairie** bookshop
libre free
la **licence** university degree
lier to tie, bind
le **lieu** place
le **lièvre** hare
la **ligne** line
le **linge** household linen
lire to read
le **lit** bed
le **littoral** coast(line)
la **livraison** delivery (of goods)
le **livre** book
la **livre** pound
livrer to deliver
le **locataire** tenant
la **location** hire
la **loge** (porter's) lodge/box (theatre)
la **loi** law
loin far
lointain(e) distant
le **loisir** leisure
Londres London
longtemps a long time
la **longueur** length
le (gros) **lot** the (first) prize (in a lottery)
la **loterie** lottery
louche shady, suspicious
louer to hire, rent
le **loup** wolf
lourd heavy
le **loyer** rent
la **lueur** glimmer, gleam
la **luge** toboggan
luire to shine, glow
la **lumière** light
lundi Monday
la **lune** moon
les **lunettes** (fpl) spectacles
la **lutte** struggle
lutter to wrestle
le **lycée** high school

M

la **mâchoire** jaw
le **maçon** mason
le **magasin** shop
le **magnétophone** tape-recorder
le **magnétoscope** video-recorder
maigre thin
la **maille** stitch
le **maillot de bain** swimming-costume
la **main** hand
maintenant now
le **maire** mayor
la **mairie** town hall
la **maison** house
le **maître** master
la **maîtresse** mistress
mal badly
le **mal**/les **maux** evil(s), hurt(s)
malade ill
la **maladie** illness
malgré in spite of
le **malheur** misfortune
malheureusement unfortunately
malheureux/malheureuse unhappy
la **malle** trunk, box
malpropre dirty
la **manche** sleeve
la **Manche** English Channel
le **mandat** (postal) postal order
le **manège** roundabout, merry-go-round
manger to eat
la **manière** manner
la **manifestation** demonstration
manquer to lack, miss
le **manteau** coat
la **maquette** (scale) model
le **maquillage** make-up
le **marché** market
mardi Tuesday
la **mare** pond
la **marée** tide
le **mari** husband
le/la **marié**(e) married person
le **marin** sailor
la **marmite** (stew)pan
la **marque** (trade)mark, brand
(avoir) **marre de** to be fed up with
le **marron** chestnut
le **marteau** hammer
le **mât** mast
le **matelas** mattress
le **matelot** sailor
la **matière** matter, subject
le **matin** morning
la **matinée** morning
la **matraque** truncheon

maussade sullen
mauvais bad, evil
le **mazout** (fuel) oil
le **mécanicien** mechanic
méchant unpleasant, naughty
le **médecin** doctor
le **médicament** medicine
la **méduse** jellyfish
méfier to mistrust
meilleur better, best
mêler to mix
même same
la **menace** threat
menacer to threaten
le **ménage** household, housekeeping
la **ménagère** housewife
le **mendiant** beggar
mener to lead
mentir to tell lies
le **menton** chin
le **menuisier** carpenter
la **mer** sea
merci thank you
mercredi Wednesday
la **messe** mass (church)
la **météo** weather forecast
le **métier** trade, profession
le **métro** underground railway
mettre to put
les **meubles** (mpl) furniture
le **meunier** miller
le **meurtre** murder
le **microsillon** LP record
midi midday
le **miel** honey
mien/mienne mine
la **miette** crumb
mieux better, best
mignon sweet, adorable
le **milieu** middle
mince thin
le **ministère** ministry
la **mode** fashion
les **moeurs** manners, customs
moi me
moindre least
moins less
le **mois** month
la **moitié** half
mon/ma/mes my
le **monde** world
monsieur/messieurs gentleman/gentlemen
la **montagne** mountain
monter to go up
la **montre** watch
montrer to show
se **moquer de** to make fun of
le **morceau** piece, bit
mordre to bite
mort dead
la **mort** death
le **mot** word
le **motard** motorway policeman
la **moto** motorbike
mou/molle soft
la **mouche** fly
le **mouchoir** handkerchief
la **mouette** seagull
mouillé wet
le **moulin** mill
mourir to die
le **moustique** mosquito
la **moutarde** mustard
le **mouton** sheep
mouvoir to move
le **moyen** means
moyen(ne) average
muet(te) dumb
le **mur** wall
le **musée** museum
la **musique** music
myope shortsighted

N

nager to swim
la **naissance** birth
naître to be born
la **nappe** tablecloth
la **natation** swimming
la **natte** pigtail
le **naufrage** shipwreck
le **navet** turnip
la **navette** shuttle
néanmoins nevertheless
négliger to neglect
le **négociant** merchant
la **neige** snow
neiger to snow
nettement clearly
nettoyer to clean
neuf brand new
le **neveu** nephew
le **nez** nose
la **niche** recess, (dog) kennel
le **nid** nest
la **nièce** niece
le **niveau** level
la **noce**/les **noces** wedding
Noël Christmas
noir(e) black
le **nom** name
le **nombre** number
le **nord** north
la **note** bill
notre/nos our
nouer to tie, knot
les **nouilles** (fpl) noodles
nourrir to feed
la **nourriture** food
nouveau/nouvelle new
(se) **noyer** to drown
le **nuage** cloud
nuire to harm
le **numéro** number

O

obéir to obey
un **objet** object
obligé(e) compelled
l'**obscurité** (f) darkness
les **obsèques** (fpl) funeral
une **occasion** opportunity
d'**occasion** second-hand
l'**occident** (m) west
occupé(e) busy
un **oeil** eye (NB pl. les **yeux**)

un **oeuf** egg
une **oeuvre** work
une **offre** offer
offrir to offer
un **oignon** onion
un **oiseau** bird
l'**ombrage** (m) shade
un **oncle** uncle
une **onde** wave
un **ongle** nail
opprimer to suppress, stifle
l'**or** (m) gold
un **orage** storm
une **ordonnance** prescription
une **oreille** ear
l'**orient** (m) east
un **os** bone
oser to dare
un **otage** hostage
ôter to take off
ou or
où where
oublier to forget
l'**ouest** west
un **ours** bear
ouvert(e) open
un **ouvre-boîte** tin-opener
un **ouvre-bouteille** bottle-opener
un **ouvrier** workman
ouvrir to open
OVNI (objet volant non identifié) unidentified flying object, UFO

P

pagayer to paddle (canoe)
la **paille** straw
le **pain** bread
paisible peaceful
la **paix** peace
le **palais** palace
le **palier** landing
le **palmarès** hit parade
le **panais** parsnip
le **panier** basket
(être) en **panne** to break down
le **pansement** dressing
le **pantalon** trousers
le **pape** pope
le **papier** paper
le **papillon** butterfly
le **paquebot** liner (ship)
Pâques Easter
le **paquet** packet
par through
paraître to appear
le **parapluie** umbrella
le **parasol** sunshade
parce que because
le **pardessus** overcoat
le **pare-brise** windscreen
pareil like, similar
paresseux/paresseuse lazy
parfait(e) perfect
parfois sometimes
le **parfum** perfume
le **parking** car-park
le **parlement** parliament
parler to speak
parmi amongst
la **parole** word
le(la) **parrain(e)** godfather, godmother
partager to share
le **parterre** flower bed/(*theatre*) pit
le **parti** party
particulier special, personal
la **partie** part
partir to leave
partout everywhere
parvenir to reach
le **passage à niveau** level crossing
le **passage clouté** pedestrian crossing
passer to go along, spend (time)
la **passerelle** footbridge
le **passe-temps** pastime
passionant(e) fascinating
patauger to paddle (in water)
la **pâte** pastry/pasta
la **patère** coatpeg
patienter to wait patiently
les **patins** (mpl) skates
le **patinage** skating
patiner to skate
le **patineur** skater
la **patinoire** skating rink
la **pâtisserie** cake shop
le **patron** boss
la **patrouille** patrol
la **patte** paw
la **paume** palm
la **paupière** eyelid
pauvre poor
payer to pay
le pays country
le **paysage** landscape
le **paysan** peasant
le **PDG (président-directeur général)** managing director
le **péage** toll
la **peau** skin
la **pêche** fishing/(also) peach
pêcher to fish
le **pêcheur** fisherman
le **peigne** comb
peindre to paint
la **peine** punishment/trouble
le **peintre** painter
la **peinture** painting
peler to peel
le **pèlerinage** pilgrimage
la **pelle** (child's) spade
le **peloton** main body, group
la **pelouse** lawn
pencher to lean
pendant during
le **pendentif** pendant
pendre to hang
la **pendule** clock
pénible painful
la **péniche** barge
la **pensée** thought
penser to think
la **pension** allowance/boarding-house, -school
le **pensionnat** boarding-school
la **pente** slope
Pentecôte Whitsun
pépier to cheep

le **pépin** pip
perdre to lose
le **père** father
perfectionner to improve, perfect
périmé out of date
périr to perish
permettre to allow
le **permis** licence
la **perruche** budgie
le **persil** parsley
le **personnage** character
persuader to persuade
la **perte** loss
peser to weigh
la **pétanque** game of bowls
petit(e) little (adj.)
peu little (adv.)
le **peuple** people
(avoir) **peur** to be frightened
peut-être perhaps
le **phare** lighthouse
la **pharmacie** chemist's
le **phoque** seal
la **photographie** photo
la **physique** physics
la **pièce** piece/coin/room/play
le **pied** foot
le **piège** trap
la **pierre** stone
le **piéton** pedestrian
le **pilote** pilot
la **pilule** pill
le **ping-pong** table-tennis
la **pique** spade(s) (cards)
le **pique-nique** picnic
pique-niquer to picnic
le piquet stake, tentpeg
la **piqûre** prick, sting, bite
pire worse (adj.)
pis worse (adv.)
la **piscine** swimming-pool
la **piste** track
la **pitié** pity
le **placard** cupboard
le **plafond** ceiling
la **plage** beach
la **plaie** wound
plaindre to pity
la **plainte** complaint
plaire to please
plaisanter to joke
le **plaisir** pleasure
la **planche** plank, board
le **plancher** floor
la **plâque** plate (number, name)
plat flat
le **plateau** tray
plein(e) full
pleurer to cry
pleuvoir to rain
plier to bend
la **pluie** rain
la **plupart** the majority
plus more
plusieurs several
plutôt rather, sooner
le **pneu** tyre
la **poche** pocket
la **poêle** fryingpan
le **poêle** stove
le **poids** weight
le **poignard** dagger
le **poignet** wrist
le **poil** hair (animal)
poinçonner to punch (ticket)
le **poing** fist
la **pointure** size (shoes)
la **poire** pear
les (petits) **pois** peas
le **poisson** fish
la **poitrine** chest
le **poivre** pepper
poli polite
le **polisson** naughty child
la **politique** politics
polluer to pollute
la **pomme** apple
la **pomme de terre** potato
la **pompe** pump
le **pompier** fireman
le **pompiste** petrol-pump attendant
le **pont** bridge
portatif portable
la **porte** door
le **porte-bagages** roof-rack (car)
le **portefeuille** wallet
porter to carry
le **portillon** gate
poser to put down
poser un question to ask a question
la **poste** post, mail
le **poste** post, station
le **pot** pot, jar
potable drinkable
la **poterie** pottery
la **poubelle** dustbin
le **pouce** thumb
la **poudre** powder
la **poule** hen
le **poulet** chicken
le **pouls** pulse
le **poumon** lung
pour for
le **pourboire** tip
le **pourcentage** percentage
pourpre purple
pourquoi why
pourtant yet, however
pousser to push
la **poussière** dust
pouvoir to be able
la **prairie** field
préalable beforehand
précieux precious
précipiter to plunge, hurry
précis precise
préférer to prefer
le **préfet** prefect
premier first
prendre to take
le **prénom** Christian name
préparer to prepare
près near
presque almost
la **presse** press
presser to press, squeeze

le **pressing** dry-cleaners
la **pression** pressure
la **prestation** benefit, allowance
le **prestidigitateur** conjurer
prêt ready
le **prêt-à-porter** ready-to-wear
prêter to lend
le **prêtre** priest
la **preuve** proof
prévenir to warn
la **prévision** forecast
prier to beg
la **prière** prayer
le **printemps** spring
la **priorité** priority
le **prix** price, cost
le **problème** problem
prochain(e) next
proche close by
produire to produce
le **produit** product
le **professeur** teacher
profiter to take advantage of
profond deep
la **profondeur** depth
la **proie** prey
le **projet** plan
la **promenade** walk
la **promesse** promise
promettre to promise
prononcer to pronounce
le **propos** purpose, intention
propre clean
le **propriétaire** proprietor
protéger to protect
le **proviseur** headmaster
la **prune** plum
publier to publish
puis then
puisque since
la **puissance** power
la **punaise** bug/drawing-pin
punir to punish
le **pupitre** desk

Q

le **quai** quay/platform (railway)
quand when
quant à as for
la **quantité** quantity
le **quart** quarter
le **quartier** district
quel/quelle what, which
quelque some
quelquefois sometimes
quelqu'un(e) someone
la **queue** queue, tail
qui who
le **quincaillier** ironmonger
une **quinzaine** fortnight
quitter to leave
quoi what
quotidien daily

R

le **rabais** reduction
raccommoder to mend
un **raccourci** shortcut
raccrocher to hang up
raconter to tell, relate
le **radis** radish
raide stiff, steep
le **raisin** grape
ralentir to slow up
ramasser to pick up
la **rame** oar
ramener to bring back
le **rang** row, line
ranger to put away
râper to grate
rappeler to call again, -back
rapporter to bring back
la **raquette** racket
(se) **raser** to shave
rater to fail
ravi delighted
le **rayon** department (shop), shelf, ray
le **récepteur** receiver
la **recette** recipe
recevoir to receive
le **réchaud** stove
réclamer to complain
la **récolte** harvest
recommander to recommend
la **récompense** reward
reconnaître to recognise
la **récréation** relaxation, playtime, break
reculer to move backwards
la **rédaction** essay (school)
redoubler to redouble, repeat
réduire to reduce
réel real
réfléchir to reflect
refuser to refuse
regarder to look at
(être) au **régime** to be on a diet
la **règle** rule, ruler
le **règne** reign
regretter to regret
la **reine** queen
relâcher to loosen, slacken
relever to lift up again
remarquer to notice
rembourser to repay
le **remède** remedy
remercier to thank
remettre to put back
remplacer to replace
remplir to fill
remuer to stir
le **renard** fox
rencontrer to meet
le **rendez-vous** appointment, arranged meeting
rendre to give back
les **renseignements** (mpl) information
la **rentrée** return (e.g. to school)
renverser to overturn
renvoyer to send back
réparer to repair
repasser to go over/to iron
le **repère** (land)mark
répéter to repeat
répondre to reply
la **réponse** reply
le **repos** rest

reposer to rest
le **réseau** network
résister to resist
résoudre to resolve
respirer to breathe
responsable responsible
ressembler to resemble
ressentir to feel
rester to stay
le **résultat** result
le **retard** delay
retarder to delay
retenir to hold back
retentir to resound
retirer to pull back
retourner to return
la **retraite** retreat, retirement
le **retraité** pensioner
retrouver to refind
réussir to succeed
le **rêve** dream
le **réveil** alarm (clock)
(se) **réveiller** to wake up
révéler to reveal
revenir to come back
rêver to dream
le **réverbère** lamp-post, street-lamp
le **revers** reverse
réviser to revise
revoir to see again
la **revue** revue, magazine
le **rez-de-chaussée** ground floor
le **rhume** cold
le **rhume de foin** hayfever
la **ride** wrinkle
le **rideau** curtain
rien nothing
rigoler to have a laugh
rincer to rinse
rire to laugh
la **ritournelle** jingle (e.g. TV advert)
le **rivage** shore
la **rive** (also) shore
la **rivière** river
le **riz** rice
la **robe** dress
le **robinet** tap
la **rocade** by-pass
la **roche** rock
le **rocher** rock
rôder to prowl
le **roi** king
le **roman** novel
rompre to break
le **rond-point** roundabout (traffic)
ronfler to snore
ronger to gnaw
ronronner to purr
rose pink
rôti roast
la **roue** wheel
rouge red
rougir to go red/to blush
rouler to roll (along)
roux, rousse red (of hair)
la **rue** street
le **ruisseau** stream

S

le **sable** sand
le **sac** bag
le **sac de couchage** sleeping-bag
le **sac à dos** haversack
le **sac à main** hand-bag
sage well-behaved, wise
saisir to seize
la **saison** season
le **salaire** salary, pay
sale dirty
le **salon** sitting-room
saluer to greet
salut! hello!
le **sang** blood
le **sanglot** sob
sans without
la **santé** health
santé! Good Health! Cheers!
satisfait satisfied
le **saucisson** sausage
sauf except
sauter to jump
sauvage wild
se **sauver** to run away
savoir to know
le **savon** soap
le **seau** bucket
la **séance** sitting, session, meeting
sec, sèche dry
secouer to shake
au **secours!** Help!
le **séjour** stay, living-room
le **sel** salt
selon according to
la **semaine** week
semblable similar
sembler to seem
le **sens** direction
le **sentier** path
le **sentiment** feeling
(se) **sentir** to feel
serrer to squeeze, shake (of hands)
la **serrure** lock
la **serveuse** waitress
la **serviette** briefcase/napkin/towel
seul(e) alone
seulement only
si if/yes (after a negative)
le **siècle** century
le **siège** seat
siffler to whistle
singulier curious, strange
le **singe** monkey
(avoir) **soif** to be thirsty
soigner to look after
le **soin** care
le **soir** evening
le **sol** ground
les **soldes** (mpl) sale(s)
le **soleil** sun
sombre dark, gloomy
(avoir) **sommeil** to be sleepy
le **sommet** summit
le **son** sound
sonner to ring
la **sonnerie** bell (electric)
la **sortie** exit

sortir to go out
le **sou** penny
le **souci** care, worry
la **soucoupe** saucer
soudain sudden(ly)
souffler to blow
souffrir to suffer
souhaiter to wish
soulager to relieve, alleviate
soulever to lift up
le **soulier** shoe
soupçonner to suspect
soupirer to sign
le **sourcil** eyebrow
sourd deaf
sourire to smile
la **souris** mouse
sous under
le **sous-sol** basement
sous-titré subtitled
souterrain underground
se **souvenir** to remember
souvent often
le **sparadrap** sticking-plaster
le **stade** stadium
le **stage** course, period of training
le **stationnement** parking
stationner to park
le **stylo** pen
le **succès** success
le **sucre** sugar
le **sud** south
suggérer to suggest
suivre to follow
le **sujet** subject
le **supermarché** supermarket
sur on
sûr sure
le **surlendemain** the day after next, two days later
sursauter to start, give a jump
surtout especially
surveiller to watch over
le **syndicat** trade union
le **syndicat d'initiative** tourist information office

T

le **tableau** picture
le **tableau noir** blackboard
le **tablier** apron
tâcher to try
la **taille** figure, size, waist
se **taire** to be quiet
le **talon** heel
tandis que whilst
tant so much
la **tante** aunt
le **tapis** carpet
taquiner to tease
tard late
le **tarif** rate, tariff
la **tartine** slice of bread (and butter)
le **tas** pile, heap
la **tasse** cup
le **taureau** bull
le **taux** rate
le **téléferique** cable-car
tellement so
le **témoin** witness
le **temps** time, weather
tendre to hold out
tenir to hold
la **tenue** dress, clothes
terminer to end
le **terrain** ground
la **terrasse** pavement (e.g., *café*)
la **terre** ground, earth
la **tête** head
têtu stubborn
le **thé** tea
la **théière** teapot
tiède luke-warm
le **timbre** stamp
le **tire-bouchon** corkscrew
tirer to pull, draw out
tirer sur to fire on
le **tiroir** drawer
le **tissu** material
le **titre** title
le **toit** roof
tomber to fall
la **tonalité** dialling-tone
tondre to shear, mow (lawn)
le **tonnerre** thunder
le **torchon** duster
(avoir) **tort** to be wrong
la **tortue** tortoise
tôt early
toujours always, still
(se) **tourmenter** to worry
le **tourne-disque** record-player
tousser to cough
tout all
tout à coup suddenly
tout à fait completely
tout d'abord first of all
tout de suite at once
tout droit straight on
tout le monde everybody
traduire to translate
en **train de** in the process of
le **trait** feature
le **traitement** treatment
le **trajet** journey
la **tranche** slice
le **travail** work
travailler to work
traverser to cross
la **traversée** crossing
trempé soaked
très very
le **trésor** treasure
tricher to cheat
tricoter to knit
le **trimestre** term
triste sad
se **tromper** to make a mistake
trop too much
le **trottoir** pavement
le **trou** hole
trouver to find
le **truc** knack, trick, whatsit
tuer to kill
le **tuyau** pipe, tube

U

unique only
une **usine** factory
utile useful
utiliser to use

V

les **vacances** (fpl) holidays
la **vache** cow
la **vague** wave
(faire) la **vaisselle** to do the washing-up
la **valeur** value, worth
la **valise** suitcase
la **vallée** valley
valoir to be worth
varié varied
le **veau** calf
la **vedette** star (e.g., *pop*)
la **veille** eve, day before
le **vélo** bicycle
le **vendeur**/la **vendeuse** shop-assistant
vendre to sell
venir to come
le **vent** wind
la **vente** sale
le **ventre** stomach
le **verger** orchard
le **verglas** black ice
vérifier to check
la **vérité** truth
le **verre** glass
le **verrou** bolt
vers towards
pleuvoir à **verse** to pour with rain
verser to pour
vert green
la veste/le **veston** jacket
les **vestiaires** (mpl) changing-rooms, cloakrooms
le **vestibule** hall (entrance)
les **vêtements** (mpl) clothes
le **veuf**/la **veuve** widower/widow
la **viande** meat
vide empty
la **vie** life
le **vieillard** old man
vieux/vieille old
vilain nasty, bad
la **ville** town
le **vin** wine
le **vinaigre** vinegar
le **virage** turn, bend, corner
le **visage** face
la **visite** visit
visiter to visit
vite quickly
la **vitesse** speed
la **vitrine** shop window
vivre to live
voici here is
la **voie** road, track
voilà there is
la **voile** sailing
voir to see
le **voisin** neighbour
la **voiture** car
la **voix** voice
le **vol** flight/theft
le **volant** steering-wheel
voler to fly/steal
le **volet** shutter
le **voleur** thief
volontiers willingly
vouloir to want, wish
le **voyage** journey
voyager to travel
le **voyageur** traveller
le **voyou** hooligan
vrai true
vraiment truly
la **vue** sight, view

W

le **wagon** carriage, coach (of a train)

Y

le **yaourt** yoghourt
les **yeux** eyes

Z

zéro nought
la **zone piétonne** pedestrian area

English/French Vocabulary

A
able: to be able pouvoir
about (=*approximately*) à peu près, environ, vers; (=*concerning*), à propos de, au sujet de;
about: to be about to être sur le point de
above en haut, au-dessus (de)
abroad à l'étranger
to **accept** accepter
across à travers
to **add** ajouter
afraid: to be afraid avoir peur
after après
again de nouveau, encore une fois
against contre
ago il y a
alarm-clock le réveil, le réveille-matin
all tout
all the same tout de même
to **allow** permettre
almost presque
alone seul(e)
along le long de
aloud à haute voix
already déjà
also aussi
although bien que, quoique
always toujours
among parmi
angry: to be angry être en colère
angry: to get angry se fâcher
to **annoy** agacer, ennuyer
another un(e) autre
to **answer** répondre
anxious: to be anxious s'inquiéter
to **appear** apparaître
to **approach** s'approcher (de)
area la région
to **argue** disputer
armchair le fauteuil
around autour de
arrival l'arrivée (f)
as comme
as far as jusqu'à
as much as autant
as soon as aussitôt que
ashamed: to be ashamed of avoir honte de
to **ask** demander
asleep endormi
asleep: to fall asleep s'endormir
astonished: to be astonished s'étonner
attraction l'attraction (f)
aunt la tante
to **avoid** éviter
away: to go away s'en aller, partir
awful affreux/affreuse

B
baby la bébé
back le dos
back: to come back revenir
back: to give back rendre
back: to go back retourner, rentrer
bad mauvais(e)
bad: too bad! tant pis!
badly mal
bag le sac
bank la banque
bank (*of river*) le bord, la rive
bar (e.g. *chocolate*) la tablette
to **bark** aboyer
barn la grange
basket le panier
bath: to have a bath, to bathe se baigner
bathroom la salle de bain(s)
beach la plage
beard: with a beard barbu
to **beat** battre
because parce que
because of à cause de
to **become** devenir
bed le lit
bed: to go to bed se coucher
bedroom la chambre (à coucher)
before (*place*) devant; (*time*) avant
beggar le mendiant
to **begin** commencer (à), se mettre à
behind derrière
to **believe** croire
bell: to ring the bell sonner
to **belong** appartenir
below en bas
beside à côté de
besides d'ailleurs
best (*adj.*) le meilleur; (*adv.*) le mieux
better (*adj.*) meilleur; (*adv.*) mieux
better: it is better (to) . . . il vaut ,mieux . . .
between entre
birthday l'anniversaire (m)
to **bite** mordre
blanket la couverture
to **book** (e.g. *room, tickets*) retenir
to **bore** ennuyer
bore: to be bored s'ennuyer
born né(e)
born: to be born naître
to **borrow** emprunter
boss le patron/la patronne
both tous les deux
to **bother** déranger
bottle la bouteille
bottom: at the bottom of au fond de
box la boîte
to **break** briser, (se) casser
breakfast le petit déjeuner
breath: out of breath essoufflé
to **bring** (*person*) amener; (*object*) apporter
to **brush** (se) brosser
building le bâtiment
bull le taureau
burglar le cambrioleur
to **burn** brûler
to **burst out laughing** éclater de rire
business les affaires (fpl), les devoirs (mpl)
bus stop l'arrêt (m) d'autobus
busy (e.g. *town*) animé (e.g. *person*) occupé
but mais
to **buy** acheter
by (*near*) près de; (*on the edge of*) au bord de

C
to **call** appeler
to be called s'appeler

camping: to go camping faire du camping
can (*to be able*) pouvoir
card la carte
careful: to be careful faire attention
carefully avec soin
caretaker le (la) concierge
carpet le tapis
cart la charrette
case (*briefcase*) la serviette; (*suitcase*) la valise
to **catch** attraper, prendre
century le siècle
Channel: the (English) Channel la Manche
to **chat** bavarder, causer
cheap bon marché
chemist le pharmacien
chimney la cheminée
to **choose** choisir
Christmas Noël
Christmas Eve la veille de Noël
church l'église (f)
cinema le cinéma
city la ville
clean propre
to **clean** nettoyer
clever habile, intelligent(e)
cliff la falaise
to **climb** grimper
clock (*in a house*) la pendule; (*on a public building*) l'horloge (f)
close (by) tout près
to **close** fermer
clothes les vêtements (mpl)
cloud le nuage
coach le car
coast la côte
coat le manteau
coin la pièce
cold: to be cold avoir froid
cold: it is cold il fait froid
cold: to catch cold s'enrhumer
cold: to have a cold être enrhumé
to **collect** collectionner
to **collide with** entrer en collision avec
colour la couleur
to **come** venir
to **come back** revenir
to **come down** descendre
to **come in** entrer
to **come out** sortir
to **come up** monter
comfortable confortable
compartment le compartiment
to **complain** se plaindre
complete complet, entier
comprehensive school le Collège d'Enseignement Secondaire
to **continue** continuer
to **cook** (faire) cuire
cool frais, fraîche
corner le coin
corridor le couloir
cost le prix
to **cough** tousser
to **count** compter
country le pays
countryside la campagne
of **course** bien entendu, évidemment, naturellement
to **cover** couvrir
covered with couvert de
criminal le criminel
to **cross** traverser
crossing (*by boat*) la traversée; (*pedestrian*) le passage clouté
crossroads le carrefour
crowd la foule
to **cry** crier; (*tears*) pleurer
cupboard l'armoire (f), le placard
to **cure** guérir
curtain le rideau
customer le (la) client(e)
Customs la Douane
customs officer le douanier

D

to **dance** danser
dangerous dangereux
to **dare** oser
dark noir, obscur, sombre
dawn l'aube (f)
day le jour, la journée
day: the day after le lendemain
day: the day before la veille
dead mort
dear cher, chère
death la mort
to **decide** décider
to **declare** déclarer
deep profond
delighted enchanté, ravi
to **depart** partir
to **describe** décrire
to **deserve** mériter
diary le journal, l'agenda (m)
to **die** mourir
difficult difficile
dirty sale
to **disappear** disparaître
disappointed déçu
disco(theque) la discothèque, le dancing
to **discover** découvrir
to **discuss** discuter
dishes: to wash the dishes faire la vaisselle
distance: in the distance au loin
district (*country*) la région; (*town*) le quartier
to **disturb** déranger
to **dive** plonger
doubtless sans doute
downstairs en bas
drawer le tiroir
dreadful affreux/affreuse
to **dream** rêver
dress la robe
dress: to get dressed s'habiller
to **drink** boire
to **drive** conduire
driving-licence le permis de conduire
to **drop** laisser tomber
to **drown** se noyer
dry sec, sèche
during pendant
dust la poussière

E

each chaque
each one chacun(e)
ear l'oreille (f)
early de bonne heure
to **earn (one's living)** gagner (sa vie)
easily facilement
Easter Pâques
easy facile
to **eat** manger
edge: at the edge of au bord de
empty vide
end la fin
end: at the end of au bout de
to **end** finir, terminer
to **enjoy oneself** s'amuser
enough assez
to **escape** s'échapper
especially surtout
even même
every chaque
everybody tout le monde
everyone tout le monde
everywhere partout
examination un examen
except sauf
to **exclaim** s'écrier, s'exclamer
exit la sortie
to **expect** attendre
expensive cher, chère; coûteux, coûteuse
to **explain** expliquer
extremely extrêmement
eye un œil (pl. les yeux)

F

face la figure, le visage
factory l'usine (f)
to **fall** tomber
false faux, fausse
famous célèbre
far loin
far: as far as jusqu'à
fast (*adj.*) rapide; (*adv.*) vite
to **fear** avoir peur (de), craindre
to **feel** sentir
ferry le ferry
to **fetch** aller chercher
few peu (de)
a **few** quelques
field le champ, la prairie, le pré
to **fill** remplir
to **fight** se battre
finally enfin
to **find** trouver
fine: it is fine il fait beau
finger le doigt
to **finish** finir, terminer
fire le feu; l'incendie (m)
fireman le pompier
fireworks les feux (mpl) d'artifice
first premier, première
at first d'abord
to **fish** pêcher
flat un appartement
to **flow** couler
flower la fleur
floor le plancher
floor (=*storey*) l'étage (m)
fluently couramment
to **fly** voler
foggy: it's foggy il fait du brouillard
to **fold** plier
to **follow** suivre
following day le lendemain
food la nourriture
on **foot** à pied
for (*conj.*) car; (*prep.*) pour; (=*during*) pendant; (=*since*) depuis
to **forbid** défendre
foreigner l'étranger (m)
to **forget** oublier
to **forgive** pardonner
formerly autrefois
fortnight une quinzaine, quinze jours
fortunately heureusement
free libre
to **freeze** geler
to **frighten** effrayer
in **front of** devant
fun: to make fun of se moquer de
funny drôle
furniture les meubles (mpl)

G

game le jeu, la partie, le match
gate la barrière (*farm*; la grille (*iron*); la porte (*garden*)
generally généralement
gently doucement
to **get** (=*look for*) chercher; (=*find*) trouver; (=*obtain*) obtenir
to **get up** se lever
gift le cadeau
to **give** donner
glad content, heureux
to **glance** jeter un coup d'œil
glass le verre
glasses (*spectacles*) les lunettes (fpl)
gloomy sombre
glove le gant
to **go** aller
to **go away** s'en aller
to **go down** descendre
to **go for a walk** se promener
to **go home** rentrer
to **go in** entrer
to **go on** continuer
to **go out** sortir
to **go to sleep** s'endormir
to **go up** monter
Good evening! Bonsoir!
Good morning! Bonjour!
Good night! Bonne nuit!
good: to have a good time s'amuser
to **gossip** bavarder
grass l'herbe (f)
great! formidable! sensationnel!
ground la terre, le terrain
ground floor le rez-de-chaussée
to **grow** cultiver (*plants*); grandir (*person*)
to **grumble** grogner
to **grumble at** gronder
to **guess** deviner
guest l'invité(e)
gun le fusil

H

hair les cheveux (mpl)
hairdresser le coiffeur, la coiffeuse
half demi
half of la moitié de
half an hour une demi-heure
hand la main
handkerchief le mouchoir
handsome beau
to **happen** arriver, se passer
happiness le bonheur
happy heureux
harbour le port
hard dur
hardly à peine, ne . . . guère
hat le chapeau
to **hate** détester
to **have to** devoir
headache un mal de tête
headache: to have a headache avoir mal à la tête
headlamp le phare
headmaster le directeur, le proviseur (*secondary school*)
health la santé
to **hear** entendre
to **hear about** entendre parler de
heart le cœur
heat la chaleur
heavy lourd
hedge la haie
Hello! Bonjour! Salut!
to **help** aider
here ici
here is voici
to **hesitate** hésiter
to **hide** (se) cacher
high haut
hill la colline
to **hit** frapper
to **hold** tenir
hole le trou
holidays les vacances (fpl)
homework les devoirs (mpl)
to **hope** espérer
host l'hôte (m)
hot chaud
housework; to do the housework faire le ménage
how comment, comme, que
how long? combien de temps?
how much combien?
however cependant
huge énorme
hundred cent
hungry: to be hungry avoir faim
to **hurry** se dépêcher
to **hurt** (se) blesser, (se) faire mal à
husband le mari
hut le cabanon, la cabane, la hutte

I

ice cream la glace
idea l'idée (f)
if si
ill malade
illness la maladie
to **imagine** (s') imaginer
immediately immédiatement
to **inform** avertir, prévenir
information les renseignements (mpl)
inhabitant un habitant
to **injure** (se) blesser
inn l'auberge (f)
inside dedans, à l'intérieur
instead of au lieu de
to **intend to** avoir l'intention de
interesting intéressant
to **interrupt** interrompre
to **introduce** (*person*) présenter
to **invite** inviter
island une île

J

jacket le veston, la veste
jewel le bijou (pl. bijoux)
job l'emploi (m), le métier
to **joke** plaisanter
journey le voyage
to **jump** sauter
just: to have just venir de . . .
just now tout à l'heure

K

to **keep** garder
key la clef (clé)
to **kill** tuer
kind (*adj.*) aimable; (*noun*) l'espèce (f) le genre, la sorte
king le roi
to **kiss** embrasser
kitchen la cuisine
knee le genou (pl. genoux)
to **kneel** s'agenouiller
knife le couteau
to **knock** frapper
to **knock down** renverser
to **know** (*person*) connaître; (*fact*) savoir

L

ladder l'échelle (f)
land la terre
language la langue
large grand
last dernier
last: at last enfin
to **last** durer
late tard, en retard
later plus tard
latter celui-ci, celle-ci
to **laugh** rire
to **laugh at** se moquer de
lawn la pelouse
lazy paresseux/paresseuse
to **learn** apprendre
at least (*minimum*) au moins; (*at all events*) du moins
to **leave** (*behind*) laisser, (+ *object*) quitter; (=*depart*) partir
left gauche (*as opposed to right*)
leg la jambe
to **lend** prêter
less moins
to **let** (=*allow*) laisser, permettre
library la bibliothèque
to **lie** mentir

to **lie down** se coucher
life la vie
lift l'ascenseur (m)
to **lift** lever, soulever
light (adj.), (*weight*) léger; (*colour*) clair
light (*noun*), la lumière
to **light** allumer
lighthouse le phare
to **like** aimer
like comme
line la ligne
to **listen to** écouter
little petit
to **live** demeurer, vivre
to **live in** habiter
living: to earn one's living gagner sa vie
lock la serrure
to **lock** fermer à clef
to **look** (*appear*) avoir l'air, paraître
to **look after** garder, soigner
to **look at** regarder
to **look for** chercher
to **look like** ressembler à
to **look up** lever la tête
lorry le camion
to **lose** perdre
to lose one's temper se mettre en colère
a lot of beaucoup
loud fort
low bas(se)
lucky: to be lucky avoir de la chance
luggage les bagages (mpl)
lunch: to have lunch déjeuner

M

mad fou, folle
magazine le magazine, la revue
main road la grande route
majority la plupart
to **make** faire
to **make for** se diriger vers
to **manage (to do)** réussir à
manager le directeur, le gérant
many beaucoup
many: so many tant
many: as many autant
map la carte
mark la note
market le marché
to **marry** épouser, se marier avec
marvellous merveilleux/merveilleuse
matter: what's the matter? qu'y a-t-il?
matter: what's the matter with you? qu'as-tu? qu'avez-vous?
may I? puis-je?
meal le repas
to **meet** rencontrer
midday (le) midi
middle: in the middle of au milieu de
midnight (le) minuit
to **miss** manquer
mistaken: to be mistaken se tromper
money l'argent (m)
month le mois
mood: in a good (bad) mood de bonne (mauvaise) humeur
moon la lune
moped le vélomoteur
more plus
morning le matin, la matinée
morning: the next morning le lendemain matin
most la plupart
motorway l'autoroute (f)
to **murmur** murmurer
museum le musée
music la musique
must devoir

N

name le nom
name: what is your name? comment t'appelles-tu? comment vous appelez-vous?
naturally naturellement
naughty méchant
near près de
nearby tout près
nearly presque
to **need** avoir besoin de
neighbour le (la) voisin(e)
neither . . . nor ni . . . ni . . . (ne)
never (ne) . . . jamais
new nouveau, nouvelle; neuf, neuve
newspaper le journal
next (*adj.*) prochain; (*adv.*) ensuite, puis
next day le lendemain
next to à côté de
nice aimable
night la nuit
nightfall la tombée de la nuit, la nuit tombante
nobody (ne) . . . personne
noise le bruit
no longer ne . . . plus
no more ne . . . plus
nothing (ne) . . . rien
not yet pas encore
note le billet
notebook la carnet
to **notice** remarquer
now maintenant
now: just now tout à l'heure
nurse un infirmier, une infirmière

O

to **obtain** obtenir
obviously évidemment
to **offer** offrir
office le bureau
often souvent
old vieux, vieille
older aîné
once une fois
once: at once immédiatement, tout de suite
only ne . . . que, seulement
to **open** ouvrir
opposite en face (de)
orchard le verger
to **order** commander
other autre
ought (*conditional tense of*) devoir
out: to go out sortir
outside dehors, à l'extérieur
over there là-bas
overcoat le pardessus
to **overtake** (e.g. *car*), doubler

to **owe** devoir
own propre
own: on one's own seul(e)
owner le (la) propriétaire

P

pain la douleur
parcel le colis, le paquet
to **park** stationner
particular (on) that particular day ce jour-là
party la boum (*young people's*); la soirée
passenger le passager, le voyageur
passer-by le passant
path le sentier, l'allée (f)
patient le client, le (la) malade
patiently patiemment
pavement le trottoir
to **pay for** payer
peace la paix
pebble le caillou (pl. cailloux)
pen le stylo
pencil le crayon
people les gens (mpl)
people: a lot of people beaucoup de monde
perhaps peut-être
to **permit** permettre
petrol l'essence (f)
to **phone** téléphoner
to **pick up** ramasser
picture le tableau
piece le morceau
pity: what a pity! quel dommage!
pity: it's a pity! c'est dommage!
to **pity** plaindre
place l'endroit (m)
plan le projet, le plan
plane l'avion (m)
plate l'assiette (f)
platform le quai
play une pièce (de théâtre)
to **play** jouer
pleasant agréable
to **please** plaire à
please s'il te (vous) plaît
pleasure le plaisir
plenty (of) beaucoup (de)
pocket la poche
point: to be on the point of être sur le point de
point: to point out indiquer
policeman l'agent, le policier
police station le poste de police
police superintendent le commissaire de police
polite poli
poor pauvre
to **post** mettre à la poste
postcard la carte postale
postman le facteur
post office le bureau de poste
pound (*money and weight*) la livre
to **prefer** préférer, aimer mieux
to **prepare** préparer
present un cadeau
presently tout à l'heure
to **pretend** faire semblant de
pretty joli
to **prevent** empêcher
price le prix
probably probablement
programme le programme, l'emission (f)
to **promise** promettre
proprietor le (la) propriétaire
proud fier, fière
provided that pourvu que
to **pull** tirer
to **punish** punir
pupil un(e) élève
purse le porte-monnaie
to **pursue** poursuivre
to **push** pousser
to **put (on)** mettre
to **put down** poser

Q

to **quarrel** se disputer
quay le quai
queen la reine
to **question** interroger
quick rapide
quickly vite
quiet tranquille
quiet: to be quiet se taire
quietly doucement, silencieusement
quite assez; (=*completely*) tout à fait

R

racquet la raquette
railway le chemin de fer
railway station la gare
rain la pluie
to **rain** pleuvoir
rain: it is raining il pleut
rain: it was raining il pleuvait
it rained il a plu
rarely rarement
rather assez, plutôt
to **reach** arriver à, gagner
to **read** lire
ready prêt
ready: to get ready s'apprêter, se préparer
to **realize** comprendre, se rendre compte
really vraiment
to **receive** recevoir
to **recognize** reconnaître
to **reflect** réfléchir
relative un parent
to **rely on** compter sur
to **remain** rester
to **remember** se rappeler, se souvenir de
to **rent** louer
to **repair** réparer
to **repeat** répéter
to **reply** répondre
to **resemble** ressembler à
the **rest** (*others*) les autres
to **rest** se reposer
to **return** retourner, revenir; (=*give back*) rendre
to **ride** (*horse, bicycle*), se promener (à cheval, à vélo)
right droit(e)
right: on the right à droite
right: to be right avoir raison
to **ring** sonner

to **rise** (e.g. *smoke*) monter
road (*in country*) la route; (*in town*) la rue
rock le rocher
rod (*fishing*) la canne (à pêche)
roof le toit
room la pièce, la salle; la chambre (*bedroom*); la place (*space*)
round: to go round faire le tour de
to **rush (forward)** s'élancer, se précipiter
to **rush** (=*hurry*) se dépêcher

S

sad triste
same même
same: all the same tout de même
sand le sable
to **save** sauver; (*money*) faire des économies
scarcely à peine, ne . . . guère
scarf (*long*) l'écharpe; (*head*) le foulard
school l'école (f)
to **scold** gronder
to **scratch** gratter
sea la mer
sea-sick: to be sea-sick avoir le mal de mer
to **search (for)** chercher
to **see** voir
to **seem** sembler, paraître, avoir l'air
to **seize** saisir
to **sell** vendre
to **send** envoyer
serious grave, sérieux
to **set off** se mettre en route
to **set out** partir
several plusieurs
shade l'ombre (f)
to **shake** secouer
shake: to shake hands serrer la main (à)
shake: to shake one's head hocher la tête
to **shave** se raser
sheet le drap
shelf le rayon
to **shine** briller
ship le navire, le paquebot
shock le choc
to **shoot** tirer
shop la boutique, le magasin
shopping: to do some shopping faire des achats (emplettes, courses, commissions)
short court
to **shout** crier
to **show** montrer
shower (*bathroom*) la douche; (*rain*) une averse
to **shut** fermer
to **shut up** se taire
sick malade, souffrant
side le côté
side: at/by the side of à côté de, au bord de
side: on the other side de l'autre côté
silly stupide
silver l'argent (m)
since (*reason*) puisque; (*time*) depuis
to **sing** chanter
to **sit down** s'asseoir
sitting assis
sky le ciel
to **sleep** dormir
sleep: to go to sleep s'endormir
to **slip** glisser
to **slow down** ralentir
slowly lentement
small petit(e)
to **smile** sourire
smoke la fumée
to **smoke** fumer
to **snatch** arracher
snow la neige
to **snow** neiger
so (=*therefore*) donc; (*extent*) si, tellement
soaked trempé(e)
somebody quelqu'un
something quelque chose
sometimes quelquefois
somewhere quelque part
soon bientôt
sorry! pardon!
sorry: to be sorry être désolé
sound le bruit, le son
South (of France) le Midi
to **speak** parler
spectacles les lunettes (fpl)
speed la vitesse
to **spend** (*money*) dépenser; (*time*) passer
in **spite of** malgré
to **spoil** gâter
in **spring** au printemps
stairs l'escalier (m)
stamp (*postage*) le timbre (-poste)
to **stand** se tenir (debout)
to **stand up** se lever
to **start** commencer, se mettre à
to **stay** rester, demeurer
to **steal** voler
stick le bâton
stick: (walking-) stick la canne
still encore, toujours
stone la pierre
to **stop** (s')arrêter
storey l'étage (m)
storm l'orage (m)
story l'histoire (f)
straight on tout droit
strange étrange
stranger un étranger, une étrangère; un inconnu, une inconnue
stream le ruisseau
street la rue
to **strike** (*hit*) frapper
strike: to go on strike se mettre en grève, faire (la) grève
strict sévère
strong fort
to **study** étudier
suburbs la banlieue
to **succeed** réussir à
success le succès
such tel(le)
sudden soudain
suddenly tout à coup
suitcase la valise
in **summer** en été
sun le soleil
supermarket le supermarché
surprised: to be surprised s'étonner
to **surround** entourer
sweet-shop la confiserie
to **swim** nager

T

to **take** (=*pick up*) prendre; (*person*) emmener
to **take away** emporter
to **take off** enlever, ôter; décoller (*plane*)
to **talk** parler
tall grand
tape-recorder le magnétophone
tea (*drink*) le thé; (*meal*) le goûter
to **teach** enseigner
teacher le professeur; l'instituteur (*junior school*)
team l'équipe (f)
to **tear** déchirer
to **telephone** téléphoner (à)
television la télévision
television set le téléviseur
to **tell** dire, raconter (*relate*)
temper: in a temper en colère
to **thank** remercier
then alors, donc, ensuite, puis
there (*pronoun*) y; (*adverb*) là
there is (are) il y a
therefore donc, ainsi
thief le voleur
thin maigre
to **think** croire, penser
thing la chose
thirsty: to be thirsty avoir soif
as **though** comme si
to **threaten** menacer
through par, à travers
to **throw** jeter
ticket le billet
ticket office le guichet
till (=*until*) jusqu'à
time (*by the clock*) le temps, l'heure; (=*occasion*) la fois
time: a long time longtemps
time-table (*school*) un emploi de temps; (*train*) l'horaire (m), l'indicateur (m)
tip le pourboire
tired fatigué(e)
today aujourd'hui
together ensemble
tomorrow demain
too trop (*much*); aussi (*also*)
top le haut, le sommet
tourist le (la) touriste
towards vers
traffic la circulation
to **travel** voyager
tree l'arbre (m)
trip une excursion
to **trouble** déranger
true vrai
truth la vérité
to **try** essayer
to **turn off (out)** éteindre
to **turn round** se retourner
to **turn towards** se tourner vers
twice deux fois
twin le jumeau, la jumelle

U

ugly laid
umbrella le parapluie
unbearable insupportable
under sous
to **understand** comprendre
to **undress** se déshabiller
unfortunately malheureusement
unhappy malheureux/malheureuse
unknown inconnu(e)
unwell souffrant(e), malade
until jusqu'à (ce que)
up: to come up monter
up: to get up se lever
upstairs en haut
to **use** employer, se servir de, utiliser
useful utile
useless inutile
as **usual** comme d'habitude
usually généralement, d'habitude
to **utter a cry** pousser un cri

V

in vain en vain
vegetable le légume
very bien, fort, très
very much beaucoup
to **visit** (*person*) faire (rendre) visite; (*country, town etc.*) visiter
visitor le visiteur
voice la voix

W

to wait attendre
waiter le garçon
waitress la serveuse
to **wake up** se réveiller
to **walk** marcher, se promener
a **walkman** (*head phones*), un baladeur
wall le mur
wallet le portefeuille
to **wander** errer
to **want** désirer, vouloir
war la guerre
warm: to be warm (*person*) avoir chaud; (*weather*) faire chaud
to **warm oneself** se réchauffer
to **wash** (se) laver
washing: to do the washing (*clothes*), faire la lessive
washing: to do the washing-up faire (laver) la vaisselle
wasp la guêpe
to **waste (time)** perdre (son temps)
watch la montre
to **watch** regarder
water l'eau (f)
wave (*sea*) la vague
to **wave** (*an object*) agiter; (*to someone*) faire signe à
way la façon, la manière
way (=*path*) le chemin
weak faible
wealthy riche
to **wear** porter
weary las(se)
weather le temps
week la semaine
to **weep** pleurer
well bien
well: to be well aller bien
well-known célèbre, bien connu
wet humide, mouillé

what (*adj.*) quel
what: what! comment!
when lorsque, quand
where où
whether si
while pendant que
whilst (*contrast*) tandis que
to **whisper** chuchoter, murmurer
to **whistle** siffler
whole entier, tout
why pourquoi
wide large
widow la veuve
widower le veuf
wife la femme
wild sauvage
to **win** gagner
windy: to be windy faire du vent
wine le vin
in **winter** en hiver
to **wipe** essuyer
wise prudent, sage
to **wish** désirer, vouloir
with avec
without sans
to **wonder** se demander
wonderful merveilleux
wood le bois
word le mot, la parole (*spoken*)
work le travail
to **work** travailler
workman–woman, un ouvrier; une ouvrière
world le monde
worried inquiet, inquiète
to **worry,** s'inquiéter
worse pire (*adj.*); pis (*adv.*)
worth: to be worth valoir
to **wound** blesser
to **write** écrire
wrong: to be wrong avoir tort, se tromper

Y

year l'an (m), l'année (f)
yesterday hier
yet (*still*) encore, déjà; (*however*) cependant
young jeune

INDEX

(RP=Role Play; VT=Vocabulary Topic)